Vocabulary Workshop

Level D

Jerome Shostak

Senior Series Consultant

Alex Cameron, Ph.D.
Department of English
University of Dayton
Dayton, Ohio

Series Consultants

Sylvia A. Rendón, Ph.D.
Coord., Secondary Language Arts
and Reading
Cypress-Fairbanks I.S.D.
Houston, Texas

Mel Farberman
Supervisor of Instruction
Brooklyn High Schools
New York City Board of Education
Brooklyn, New York

John Heath, Ph.D.
Department of Classics
Santa Clara University
Santa Clara, California

Sadlier-Oxford
A Division of William H. Sadlier, Inc.

Reviewers

The publisher wishes to thank for their comments and suggestions the following teachers and administrators, who read portions of the series prior to publication.

Anne S. Crane
Clinician, English Education
Georgia State University
Atlanta, GA

Arlene A. Oraby
Dept. Chair (Ret.), English 6–12
Briarcliff Public Schools
Briarcliff Manor, NY

Patricia M. Stack
English Teacher
South Park School District
South Park, PA

Susan W. Keogh
Curriculum Coordinator
Lake Highland Preparatory
Orlando, FL

Susan Cotter McDonough
English Department Chair
Wakefield High School
Wakefield, MA

Joy Vander Vliet
English Teacher
Council Rock High School
Newtown, PA

Mary Louise Ellena-Wygonik
English Teacher
Hampton High School
Allison Park, PA

Sr. M. Francis Regis Trojano
Sisters of St. Joseph (CSJ)
Educational Consultant
Boston, MA

Karen Christine Solheim
English Teacher
Jefferson High School
Jefferson, GA

Lisa Anne Pomi
Language Arts Chairperson
Woodside High School
Woodside, CA

Keith Yost
Director of Humanities
Tomball Ind. School District
Tomball, TX

Photo Credits

Corbis: 57; Mark Gibson: 27; Bettmann: 34, 64, 130, 170; Philip Gould: 41; Frank Hurley: 97; Reuters NewMedia Inc.: 123. *Getty*: 71, 104, 116, 163, 182. *Samarra Khaja*/ASPCA: 137. *The Kobal Collection*: 83. *Minden Pictures*/Thomas Mangelsen: 156. *TimePix*/Sal Dimarco Jr.: 90; Allan Tannenbaum: 149.

Printed in the United States of America.
ISBN: 0-8215-7609-7
3456789/06 05 04 03 02

PREFACE

For over five decades, Vocabulary Workshop has proven a highly successful tool for guiding systematic vocabulary growth. It has also been a valuable help to students preparing for the vocabulary-related parts of standardized tests. In this, the latest edition of the series, many new features have been added to make Vocabulary Workshop even more effective in increasing vocabulary and improving vocabulary skills.

The **Definitions** sections in the fifteen Units, for example, have been expanded to include synonyms and antonyms and for each taught word an illustrative sentence for each part of speech.

In the **Synonyms** and **Antonyms** sections, exercise items are now presented in the form of phrases, the better to familiarize you with the range of contexts and distinctions of usage for the Unit words.

New to this edition is **Vocabulary in Context**, an exercise that appears at the end of each Unit and in the Reviews. In this exercise, you will read an expository passage containing a selection of Unit words. In addition to furnishing you with further examples of how and in what contexts Unit words are used, this exercise will also provide you with practice with vocabulary questions in standardized-test formats.

In the five Reviews, you will find two important new features, in addition to Analogies, Two-Word Completions, and other exercises designed to help you prepare for standardized tests. One of these new features, **Building with Classical Roots**, will acquaint you with Latin and Greek roots from which many English words stem and will provide you with a strategy that may help you find the meaning of an unknown or unfamiliar word.

Another new feature, **Writer's Challenge**, is designed to do just that—challenge you to improve your writing skills by applying what you have learned about meanings and proper usage of selected Unit words.

Finally, another new feature has been introduced in the four Cumulative Reviews. **Enriching Your Vocabulary** is meant to broaden and enhance your knowledge and understanding of the relationships, history, and origins of the words that make up our rich and dynamic language.

In this Level of Vocabulary Workshop, you will study three hundred key words, and you will be introduced to hundreds of other words in the form of synonyms, antonyms, and other relatives. Mastery of these words will make you a better reader, a better writer and speaker, and better prepared for the vocabulary parts of standardized tests.

CONTENTS

PRONUNCIATION KEY

The pronunciation is indicated for every basic word introduced in this book. The symbols used for this purpose, as listed below, are similar to those appearing in most standard dictionaries of recent vintage. The author has consulted a large number of dictionaries for this purpose but has relied primarily on *Webster's Third New International Dictionary* and *The Random House Dictionary of the English Language (Unabridged)*.

There are, of course, many English words for which two (or more) pronunciations are commonly accepted. In virtually all cases where such words occur in this book, the author has sought to make things easier for the student by giving just one pronunciation. The only significant exception occurs when the pronunciation changes in accordance with a shift in the part of speech. Thus we would indicate that *project* in the verb form is pronounced prə jekt', and in the noun form, präj' ekt.

It is believed that these relatively simple pronunciation guides will be readily usable by the student. It should be emphasized, however, that the *best* way to learn the pronunciation of a word is to listen to and imitate an educated speaker.

Vowels	ā	lake	e	str*e*ss	ü	l*oo*t, n*ew*
	a	m*a*t	ī	kn*i*fe	ủ	f*oo*t, p*u*ll
	â	c*a*re	i	s*i*t	ə	r*u*g, brok*e*n
	ä	b*a*rk, b*o*ttle	ō	fl*o*w	ər	b*ir*d, bett*er*
	aủ	d*ou*bt	ô	*a*ll, c*o*rd		
	ē	b*ea*t, word*y*	oi	*oi*l		

Consonants	ch	*ch*ild, lec*t*ure	s	*c*ellar	wh	*wh*at
	g	*g*ive	sh	*sh*un	y	*y*earn
	j	*g*entle, bri*dg*e	th	*th*ank	z	i*s*
	ŋ	si*ng*	t̶h̶	*th*ose	zh	mea*s*ure

All other consonants are sounded as in the alphabet.

Stress	The accent mark *follows* the syllable receiving the major stress: en rich'

Abbreviations	*adj.*	adjective	*n.*	noun	*prep.*	preposition
	adv.	adverb	*part.*	participle	*v.*	verb
	int.	interjection	*pl.*	plural		

THE VOCABULARY OF VOCABULARY

There are some interesting and useful words that are employed to describe and identify words. The exercises that follow will help you to check and strengthen your knowledge of this "vocabulary of vocabulary."

Denotation and Connotation

The **denotation** of a word is its specific dictionary meaning. Here are a few examples:

Word	Denotation
scholarly	learned
grasping	overly eager for material gain
travel	make a journey

The **connotation** of a word is its **tone**—that is, the emotions or associations it normally arouses in people using, hearing, or reading it. Depending on what these feelings are, the connotation of a word may be *favorable* (*positive*) or *unfavorable* (*negative, pejorative*). A word that does not normally arouse strong feelings of any kind has a *neutral* connotation. Here are some examples of words with different connotations:

Word	Connotation
scholarly	favorable
grasping	unfavorable
travel	neutral

Exercises *In the space provided, label the connotation of each of the following words F for "favorable," U for "unfavorable," or N for "neutral."*

_____ **1.** conceited   _____ **3.** valiant   _____ **5.** shiftless

_____ **2.** parallel   _____ **4.** excerpt   _____ **6.** hero

Literal and Figurative Usage

When a word is used in a **literal** sense, it is being employed in its strict (or primary) dictionary meaning in a situation (or context) that "makes sense" from a purely logical or realistic point of view. For example:

There were logs *floating* in the river after the storm.

In this sentence, *floating* is employed literally. The logs are resting on the surface of the water.

Sometimes words are used in a symbolic or nonliteral way in situations that do not "make sense" from a purely logical or realistic point of view. We call this nonliteral application of a word a **figurative** or **metaphorical** usage. For example:

The famous actress *floated* into the room with all the grace and elegance of a prima ballerina.

In this sentence, *floated* is not being used in a literal sense. That is, the actress was not actually resting on water. Rather, the word is intended to convey graphically the smooth way in which the actress moved.

Exercises In the space provided, write **L** for "literal" or **F** for "figurative" next to each of the following sentences to show how the italicized expression is being used.

_____ **1.** I accidently put my fingers *in some very hot water* and burned them.

_____ **2.** When the dean suddenly summoned me to his office, I knew I was *in hot water*.

_____ **3.** A *ribbon* of moonlight suddenly broke through the clouds and illuminated the scene.

Synonyms

A **synonym** is a word that has *the same* or *almost the same* meaning as another word. Here are some examples:

go—depart   know—understand
listen—hear   hurry—rush
happy—glad   roomy—spacious

Exercises In each of the following groups, circle the word that is most nearly the **synonym** of the word in **boldface** type.

1. absurd	**2. alert**	**3. generosity**	**4. conserve**
a. sensible	a. clear	a. likelihood	a. refill
b. foolish	b. dull	b. charity	b. use up
c. loud	c. watchful	c. selfishness	c. save
d. quiet	d. distant	d. cleverness	d. throw away

Antonyms

An **antonym** is a word that means *the opposite* of or *almost the opposite* of another word. Here are some examples:

awake—asleep   quiet—noisy
hurry—dawdle   gloomy—cheerful
wet—dry   friend—foe

Exercises In each of the following groups, circle the word that is most nearly the **antonym** of the word in **boldface** type.

1. amateur	**2. blur**	**3. intelligent**	**4. ferocious**
a. veteran	a. dim	a. charming	a. juvenile
b. beginner	b. close	b. studious	b. mild
c. professional	c. open	c. stupid	c. angry
d. resident	d. clarify	d. lively	d. expensive

VOCABULARY STRATEGY: USING CONTEXT

How do you go about finding the meaning of an unknown or unfamiliar word that you come across in your reading? You might look the word up in a dictionary, of course, provided one is at hand. But there are two other useful strategies that you might employ to find the meaning of a word that you do not know at all or that is used in a way that you do not recognize. One strategy is to analyze the **structure** or parts of the word. (See pages 11 and 12 for more on this strategy.) The other strategy is to try to figure out the meaning of the word by reference to context.

When we speak of the **context** of a word, we mean the printed text of which that word is part. By studying the context, we may find **clues** that lead us to its meaning. We might find a clue in the immediate sentence or phrase in which the word appears (and sometimes in adjoining sentences or phrases, too); or we might find a clue in the topic or subject matter of the passage in which the word appears; or we might even find a clue in the physical features of a page itself. (Photographs, illustrations, charts, graphs, captions, and headings are some examples of such features.)

One way to use context as a strategy is to ask yourself what you know already about the topic or subject matter in question. By applying what you have learned before about deserts, for example, you would probably be able to figure out that the word *arid* in the phrase "the arid climate of the desert" means "dry."

The **Vocabulary in Context** exercises that appear in the Units and Reviews and the **Choosing the Right Meaning** exercises that appear in the Reviews and Cumulative Reviews both provide practice in using subject matter or topic to determine the meaning of given words.

When you do the various word-omission exercises in this book, look for **context clues** built into the sentence or passage to guide you to the correct answer. Three types of context clues appear in the exercises in this book.

A **restatement clue** consists of a *synonym* for, or a *definition* of, the missing word. For example:

Faithfully reading a weekly newsmagazine not only <u>broadens</u> my knowledge of current events and world or national affairs but also _____ my vocabulary.

a. decreases   b. fragments   (c. increases)   d. contains

In this sentence, *broadens* is a synonym of the missing word, *increases*, and acts as a restatement clue for it.

A **contrast clue** consists of an *antonym* for, or a phrase that means the *opposite* of, the missing word. For example:

"As you say, my view of the situation may be far too <u>rosy</u>," I admitted. "<u>On the other hand</u>, yours may be a bit (**optimistic,** (**bleak**))."

In this sentence, *rosy* is an antonym of the missing word, *bleak*. This is confirmed by the presence of the phrase *on the other hand*, which indicates that the answer must be the opposite of *rosy*.

An **inference clue** implies but does not directly state the meaning of the missing word or words. For example:

> "A treat for all ages," the review read, "this wonderful <u>novel</u> combines the _____ of a <u>scholar</u> with the <u>skill</u> and <u>artistry</u> of an expert _____.
>
> a. ignorance . . . painter   c. wealth . . . surgeon
> b. wisdom . . . beginner   (d. knowledge . . . storyteller)

In this sentence, there are several inference clues: (a) the word *scholar* suggests the word *knowledge* because a scholar by definition is someone who has acquired knowledge; (b) the words *novel*, *artistry*, and *skill* suggest the word *storyteller*. A *novel* tells a story, and someone who is an expert at telling a story necessarily uses both *artistry* and *skill*. Accordingly, all these words are inference clues because they suggest or imply, but do not directly state, the missing word or words.

Exercises   *Use context clues to choose the word or words that complete each of the following sentences or sets of sentences.*

1. I like visiting small towns and rural villages from time to time, but the big city is my _____ home.

a. permanent   c. original
b. former   d. temporary

2. The child's stubborn refusal to do what he was told (**infuriated, delighted**) his normally even-tempered parents.

3. The radio, the television set, and other forms of mass _____ with which we are all familiar today were entirely unknown at the _____ of the twentieth century.

a. hysteria . . . end   c. communication . . . beginning
b. employment . . . middle   d. transportation . . . turn

VOCABULARY STRATEGY: WORD STRUCTURE

One important way to build your vocabulary is to learn the meaning of word parts that make up many English words. These word parts consist of prefixes, suffixes, and **roots**, or **bases**. A useful strategy for determining the meaning of an unknown word is to "take apart" the word and think about the parts. For example, when you look at the word parts in the word *invisible,* you find the prefix *in-* ("not") + the root *-vis-* ("see") + the suffix *-ible* ("capable of"). From knowing the meanings of the parts of this word, you can figure out that *invisible* means "not capable of being seen."

Following is a list of common prefixes. Knowing the meaning of a prefix can help you determine the meaning of a word in which the prefix appears.

Prefix	Meaning	Sample Words
bi-	two	bicycle, biannual
com-, con-	together, with	compatriot, contact
de-, dis-	lower, opposite	devalue, disloyal
fore-, pre-	before, ahead of time	forewarn, preplan
il-, im-, in-, ir, non-, un-	not	illegal, impossible, inactive, irregular, nonsense, unable
in-, im-	in, into	inhale, import
mid-	middle	midway, midday, midterm
mis-	wrongly, badly	mistake, misbehave
re-	again, back	redo, repay
sub-	under, less than	submarine, subzero
super-	above, greater than	superimpose, superstar
tri-	three	triangle

Following is a list of common suffixes. Knowing the meaning and grammatical function of a suffix can help you determine the meaning of a word.

Noun Suffix	Meaning	Sample Nouns
-acy, -ance, -ence, -hood, -ity, -ment, -ness, -ship	state, quality, or condition of, act or process of	adequacy, attendance, persistence, neighborhood, activity, judgment, brightness, friendship
-ant, -eer, -ent, -er, -ian, -ier, -ist, -or	one who does or makes something	contestant, auctioneer, resident, banker, comedian, financier, dentist, doctor
-ation, -ition, -ion	act or result of	organization, imposition, election

Verb Suffix	Meaning	Sample Verbs
-ate	to become, produce, or treat	validate, salivate, chlorinate
-en	to make, cause to be	weaken, shorten, lengthen
-fy, -ify, -ize	to cause, make	liquefy, glorify, legalize

Adjective Suffix	Meaning	Sample Adjectives
-able, -ible	able, capable of	believable, incredible
-al, -ic,	relating to, characteristic of	natural, romantic
-ful, -ive, -ous	full of, given to, marked by	beautiful, protective, poisonous
-ish, -like	like, resembling	foolish, childlike
-less	lacking, without	careless

A **base** or **root** is the main part of a word to which prefixes and suffixes may be added. Many roots come to English from Latin, such as *-socio-,* meaning "society," or from Greek, such as *-logy-,* meaning "the study of." Knowing Greek and Latin roots can help you determine the meaning of a word such as *sociology,* which means "the study of society."

In the **Building with Classical Roots** sections of this book, you will learn more about some of these Latin and Greek roots and about English words that derive from them. The lists that follow may help you figure out the meaning of new or unfamiliar words that you encounter in your reading.

Greek Root	Meaning	Sample Word
-astr-, -aster-, -astro-	star	astral, asteroid, astronaut
-auto-	self	autograph
-bio-	life	biography
-chron-, chrono-	time	chronic, chronological
-cosm-, -cosmo-	universe, order	microcosm, cosmopolitan
-cryph-, -crypt-	hidden, secret	apocryphal, cryptographer
-dem-, -demo-	people	epidemic, democracy
-dia-	through, across, between	diameter
-dog-, -dox-	opinion, teaching	dogmatic, orthodox
-gen-	race, kind, origin, birth	generation
-gnos-	know	diagnostic
-graph-, -graphy-, -gram-	write	graphite, autobiography, telegram
-log-, -logue-	speech, word, reasoning	logic, dialogue
-lys-	break down	analysis
-metr-, -meter-	measure	metric, kilometer
-micro-	small	microchip
-morph-	form, shape	amorphous
-naut-	sailor	cosmonaut
-phon-, -phone-, -phono-	sound, voice	phonics, telephone, phonograph
-pol-, -polis-	city, state	police, metropolis
-scop-, -scope-	watch, look at	microscopic, telescope
-tele-	far off, distant	television
-the-	put or place	parentheses

Latin Root	Meaning	Sample Word
-cap-, -capt-, -cept-, -cip-	take	capitulate, captive, concept, recipient
-cede-, -ceed-, -ceas-, -cess-	happen, yield, go	precede, proceed, decease, cessation
-cred-	believe	incredible
-dic-, -dict-	speak, say, tell	indicate, diction
-duc-, -duct-, -duit-	lead, conduct, draw	educate, conduct, conduit
-fac-, -fact-, -fect-, -fic-, -fy-	make	faculty, artifact, defect, beneficial, clarify
-ject-	throw	eject
-mis-, -miss-, -mit-, -mitt-	send	promise, missile, transmit, intermittent
-note-, -not-	know, recognize	denote, notion
-pel-, -puls-	drive	expel, compulsive
-pend-, -pens-	hang, weight, set aside	pendulum, pension
-pon-, -pos-	put, place	component, position
-port-	carry	portable
-rupt-	break	bankrupt
-scrib-, -scribe-, -script-	write	scribble, describe, inscription
-spec-, -spic-	look, see	spectator, conspicuous
-tac-, -tag-, -tang-, -teg-	touch	contact, contagious, tangible, integral
-tain-, -ten-, -tin-	hold, keep	contain, tenure, retinue
-temp-	time	tempo, temporary
-ven-, -vent-	come	intervene, convention
-vers-, -vert-	turn	reverse, invert
-voc-, -vok-	call	vocal, invoke

WORKING WITH ANALOGIES

Today practically every standardized examination involving vocabulary, especially the SAT-I, employs the **analogy** as a testing device. For that reason, it is an excellent idea to learn how to read, understand, and solve such verbal puzzles.

What Is an Analogy?

An analogy is a kind of equation using words rather than numbers or mathematical symbols and quantities. Normally, an analogy contains two pairs of words linked by a word or symbol that stands for an equal sign (=). A complete analogy compares the two pairs of words and makes a statement about them. It asserts that the logical relationship between the members of the first pair of words is *the same as* the logical relationship between the members of the second pair of words. This is the only statement a valid analogy ever makes.

Here is an example of a complete analogy. It is presented in two different formats.

Format 1   **Format 2**
maple is to tree as rose is to flower   maple : tree :: rose : flower

Reading and Interpreting Analogies

As our sample indicates, analogies are customarily presented in formats that need some deciphering in order to be read and understood correctly. There are a number of these formats, but you need concern yourself with only the two shown.

Format 1: Let's begin with the format that uses all words:

maple is to tree as rose is to flower

Because this is the simplest format to read and understand, it is the one used in the student texts of VOCABULARY WORKSHOP. It is to be read exactly as printed. Allowing for the fact that the word pairs change from analogy to analogy, this is how to read every analogy, no matter what the format is.

Now you know how to read an analogy. Still, it is not clear exactly what the somewhat cryptic statement "maple is to tree as rose is to flower" means. To discover this, you must understand what the two linking expressions *as* and *is to* signify.

- The word *as* links the two word pairs in the complete analogy. It stands for an equal sign (=) and means "is the same as."

- The expression *is to* links the two members of each word pair, so it appears twice in a complete analogy. In our sample, *is to* links *maple* and *tree* (the two words in the first pair) and also *rose* and *flower* (the two words in the second word pair). Accordingly, the expression *is to* means "has the same logical relationship to" the two words it links.

Putting all this information together, we can say that our sample analogy means:

> The logical relationship between a *maple* and a *tree* is *the same as* (=) the logical relationship between a *rose* and a *flower.*

Now you know what our sample analogy means. This is what every analogy means, allowing for the fact that the word pairs will vary from one analogy to another.

Format 2: Our second format uses symbols, rather than words, to link its four members.

> maple : tree :: rose : flower

This is the format used on the SAT-I and in the *TEST PREP Blackline Masters* that accompany each Level of VOCABULARY WORKSHOP. In this format, a single colon (:) replaces the expression *is to*, and a double colon (::) replaces the word *as*. Otherwise, format 2 is the same as format 1; that is, it is read in exactly the same way ("maple is to tree as rose is to flower"), and it means exactly the same thing ("the logical relationship between a *maple* and a *tree* is the same as the logical relationship between a *rose* and a *flower*").

Completing Analogies

So far we've looked at complete analogies. However, standardized examinations do not provide the test taker with a complete analogy. Instead, the test taker is given the first, or key, pair of words and then asked to *complete* the analogy by selecting the second pair from a given group of four or five choices, usually lettered *a* through *d* or *e*.

Here's how our sample analogy would look on such a test:

1. maple is to tree as
a. acorn is to oak
b. hen is to rooster
c. rose is to flower
d. shrub is to lilac

or

1. maple : tree ::
a. acorn : oak
b. hen : rooster
c. rose : flower
d. shrub : lilac

It is up to the test taker to complete the analogy correctly.

Here's how to do that in just four easy steps!

Step 1: *Look at the two words in the key (given) pair, and determine the logical relationship between them.*

In our sample analogy, *maple* and *tree* form the key (given) pair of words. They indicate the key (given) relationship. Think about these two words for a moment. What is the relationship of a maple to a tree? Well, a maple is a particular kind, or type, of tree.

Step 2: *Make up a short sentence stating the relationship that you have discovered for the first pair of words.*

For our model analogy, we can use this sentence: "A maple is a particular kind (type) of tree."

Step 3: *Extend the sentence you have written to cover the rest of the analogy, even though you haven't completed it yet.*

The easiest way to do this is to repeat the key relationship after the words *just as*, leaving blanks for the two words you don't yet have. The sentence will now read something like this:

A maple is a kind (type) of tree, just as a _?_ is a kind of _?_ .

Step 4: *Look at each of the lettered pairs of words from which you are to choose your answer. Determine which lettered pair illustrates the same relationship as the key pair.*

The easiest and most effective way to carry out step 4 is to substitute each pair of words into the blanks in the sentence you made up to see which sentence makes sense. Only one will.

Doing this for our sample analogy, we get:

a. A maple is a kind of tree, just as an acorn is a kind of oak.
b. A maple is a kind of tree, just as a hen is a kind of rooster.
c. A maple is a kind of tree, just as a rose is a kind of flower.
d. A maple is a kind of tree, just as a shrub is a kind of lilac.

Look at these sentences. Only *one* of them makes any sense. Choice *a* is clearly wrong because an acorn is *not* a kind of oak. Choice *b* is also wrong because a hen is *not* a kind of rooster. Similarly, choice *d* is incorrect because a shrub is *not* a kind of lilac, though a *lilac* is a kind of shrub. In other words, the two words are in the wrong order. That leaves us with choice *c*, which says that a rose is a kind of flower. Well, that makes sense; a rose is indeed a kind of flower. So, choice *c* must be the pair of words that completes the analogy correctly.

Determining the Key Relationship

Clearly, determining the nature of the key relationship is the most important and the most difficult part of completing an analogy. Since there are literally thousands of key relationships possible, you cannot simply memorize a list of them. The table on page 16, however, outlines some of the most common key relationships. Study the table carefully.

Table of Key Relationships

Complete Analogy	Key Relationship
big is to **large** as **little** is to **small**	**Big** means the same thing as **large**, just as **little** means the same thing as **small**.
tall is to **short** as **thin** is to **fat**	**Tall** means the opposite of **short**, just as **thin** means the opposite of **fat**.
brave is to **favorable** as **cowardly** is to **unfavorable**	The tone of **brave** is **favorable**, just as the tone of **cowardly** is **unfavorable**.
busybody is to **nosy** as **klutz** is to **clumsy**	A **busybody** is by definition someone who is **nosy**, just as a **klutz** is by definition someone who is **clumsy**.
cowardly is to **courage** as **awkward** is to **grace**	Someone who is **cowardly** lacks **courage**, just as someone who is **awkward** lacks **grace**.
visible is to **see** as **audible** is to **hear**	If something is **visible**, you can by definition **see** it, just as if something is **audible**, you can by definition **hear** it.
invisible is to **see** as **inaudible** is to **hear**	If something is **invisible**, you cannot **see** it, just as if something is **inaudible**, you cannot **hear** it.
frigid is to **cold** as **blistering** is to **hot**	**Frigid** is the extreme of **cold**, just as **blistering** is the extreme of **hot**.
chef is to **cooking** as **tailor** is to **clothing**	A **chef** is concerned with **cooking**, just as a **tailor** is concerned with **clothing**.
liar is to **truthful** as **bigot** is to **fair-minded**	A **liar** is by definition not likely to be **truthful**, just as a **bigot** is by definition not likely to be **fair-minded**.
starvation is to **emaciation** as **overindulgence** is to **corpulence**	**Starvation** will cause **emaciation**, just as **overindulgence** will cause **corpulence**.
practice is to **proficient** as **study** is to **knowledgeable**	**Practice** will make a person **proficient**, just as **study** will make a person **knowledgeable**.
eyes are to **see** as **ears** are to **hear**	You use your **eyes** to **see** with, just as you use your **ears** to **hear** with.
sloppy is to **appearance** as **rude** is to **manner**	The word **sloppy** can refer to one's **appearance**, just as the word **rude** can refer to one's **manner**.
learned is to **knowledge** as **wealthy** is to **money**	Someone who is **learned** has a great deal of **knowledge**, just as someone who is **wealthy** has a great deal of **money**.

Exercises   In each of the following, circle the item that best completes the analogy. Then explain the key relationship involved.

1. contempt is to **scorn** as
a. dignity is to ridicule
b. hate is to love
c. reversal is to success
d. understanding is to comprehension

2. blunt is to **sharp** as
a. absurd is to ridiculous
b. short is to brief
c. conservative is to radical
d. tall is to fat

3. cowardly is to **courage** as
a. awkward is to gracefulness
b. fabulous is to intelligence
c. drunk is to intoxication
d. funny is to humor

4. hammer is to **tool** as
a. computer is to machine
b. horse is to cow
c. singer is to soprano
d. trunk is to branch

VOCABULARY AND WRITING

When you study vocabulary, you make yourself not only a better reader but also a better writer. The greater the number of words at your disposal, the better you will be able to express your thoughts. Good writers are always adding new words to their personal vocabularies, the pool of words that they understand *and* know how to use properly. They use these words both when they write and when they revise.

There are several factors to consider when choosing words and setting the tone of your writing. First, your choice of words should suit your purpose and your audience. If you are writing an essay for your history teacher, you will probably want to choose words that are formal in tone and precise in meaning. If you are writing a letter to a friend, however, you will probably choose words that are more informal in tone and freer in meaning. Your **audience** is the person or people who will be reading what you write, and your **purpose** is the reason why you are writing. Your purpose, for example, might be to explain; or it might be to describe, inform, or entertain.

Almost any kind of writing—whether a school essay, a story, or a letter to a friend—can be improved by careful attention to vocabulary. Sometimes you will find, for example, that one word can be used to replace a phrase of five or six words. This is not to say that a shorter sentence is always better. However, readers usually prefer and appreciate **economy** of expression. They grow impatient with sentences that plod along with vague, unnecessary words rather than race along with fewer, carefully chosen ones. Writing can also be improved by attention to **diction** (word choice). Many writers use words that might make sense in terms of *general* meaning but that are not precise enough to convey *nuances* of meaning. In the **Writer's Challenge** sections of this book, you will have an opportunity to make word choices that will more clearly and precisely convey the meaning you intend.

Exercises   *Read the following sentences, paying special attention to the words and phrases underlined. From the words in the box, find better choices for the underlined words and phrases.*

1. The jury found that the charges against the defendant were without any good reason or cause.

| groundless | true | doubtful | ridiculous |

2. Our club treasurer is the most vertical and trustworthy person I have ever met.

| friendly | literate | upright | talented |

3. Having to speak in front of an audience is likely to confuse or agitate a person who tends to be shy.

| please | reassure | annoy | fluster |

4. Once the floodwaters go or move backward, we will be able to assess the damage to our house.

| dry out | go away | recede | rise |

5. An Academy Award is sure to boost an actor's relative rank or standing in Hollywood.

| pay | status | reputation | ego |

This test contains a sampling of the words that are to be found in the exercises in this Level of VOCABULARY WORKSHOP. It will give you an idea of the types of words to be studied and their level of difficulty. When you have completed all the units, the Final Mastery Test at the end of this book will assess what you have learned. By comparing your results on the Final Mastery Test with your results on the Diagnostic Test below, you will be able to judge your progress.

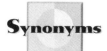

Synonyms — *In each of the following groups, circle the word or phrase that **most nearly** expresses the meaning of the word in **boldface** type in the given phrase.*

1. **incessant** hammering
   a. noisy   b. constant   c. unpleasant   d. occasional

2. **incinerate** the refuse
   a. transport   b. utilize   c. bury   d. burn

3. **succumb** to temptation
   a. yield   b. ignore   c. resist   d. enjoy

4. **spurious** argument
   a. logical   b. strong   c. clever   d. false

5. **biased** opinion
   a. strong   b. prejudiced   c. hasty   d. fair

6. **supplant** an official
   a. elect   b. criticize   c. replace   d. keep in office

7. **tenacious** fighters
   a. persistent   b. dangerous   c. skilled   d. savage

8. **meandering** stream
   a. rushing   b. twisting   c. babbling   d. polluted

9. discarded **dross**
   a. idol   b. waste   c. clothing   d. machinery

10. **auspicious** beginning
    a. slow   b. unpleasant   c. favorable   d. strong

11. **fortify** a city
    a. destroy   b. enter   c. build   d. strengthen

12. **sterling** qualities
    a. inadequate   b. hidden   c. despised   d. excellent

13. **plaintiff** in the lawsuit
    a. judge   b. prosecutor   c. accuser   d. accused

14. **pensive** mood
    a. talkative   b. thankful   c. angry   d. thoughtful

15. an **eminent** teacher
    a. famous   b. youthful   c. elderly   d. experienced

16. hoodwink their opponents

a. deceive b. defeat c. size up d. greet

17. apex of fame

a. reward b. result c. bottom point d. top

18. venomous remarks

a. complimentary b. spiteful c. intelligent d. humorous

19. in a **circumspect** manner

a. careful b. surrounding c. loud d. crude

20. paramount consideration

a. musical b. chief c. theatrical d. final

21. causing **obesity**

a. harm b. fatness c. diet d. economy

22. warped mind

a. clever b. twisted c. determined d. educated

23. auxiliary patrol

a. new b. untrained c. assisting d. chief

24. diligent instructor

a. skillful b. learned c. experienced d. untiring

25. lucrative contract

a. poor b. profitable c. long-term d. expensive

26. feign interest

a. pretend b. increase c. lose d. stimulate

27. malign someone

a. praise b. slay c. protect d. slander

28. gave **asylum** to the refugees

a. shelter b. money c. freedom d. sympathy

29. shoddy material

a. inferior b. colorful c. drab d. sturdy

30. fabricate a product

a. steal b. consume c. put together d. purchase

Antonyms

*In each of the following groups, circle the word or phrase that is most nearly opposite in meaning to the word in **boldface** type in the given phrase.*

31. bogus currency

a. foreign b. counterfeit c. genuine d. worthless

32. devitalize a program

a. weaken b. cancel c. strengthen d. revise

33. slipshod work

a. sloppy b. profitable c. difficult d. careful

34. forestall a riot

a. witness b. prevent c. incite d. enjoy

35. a **momentous** decision
    a. serious   b. untimely   c. trivial   d. puzzling

36. a **bleak** forecast
    a. rosy   b. suspicious   c. believable   d. frightening

37. an **arduous** task
    a. easy   b. endless   c. awful   d. unfinished

38. **chide** the children
    a. dress   b. compliment   c. scold   d. raise

39. **alien** customs
    a. unusual   b. pleasant   c. native   d. colorful

40. **buoyant** outlook
    a. cheerful   b. puzzling   c. immature   d. somber

41. a **perilous** journey
    a. leisurely   b. thrilling   c. costly   d. safe

42. **rancid** butter
    a. unspoiled   b. expensive   c. imported   d. genuine

43. **abridge** a novel
    a. write   b. expand   c. publish   d. read

44. **erratic** behavior
    a. consistent   b. insulting   c. irregular   d. tactful

45. a **humane** act
    a. surprising   b. generous   c. praiseworthy   d. cruel

46. a **ghastly** sight
    a. remarkable   b. horrible   c. pleasant   d. curious

47. a **lucid** explanation
    a. muddled   b. long   c. clear   d. trustworthy

48. **squander** an allowance
    a. save   b. waste   c. refuse   d. demand

49. **relinquish** power
    a. hand over   b. give up   c. hold on to   d. wish for

50. a **candid** statement
    a. curious   b. misleading   c. frank   d. bitter

Definitions

Note carefully the spelling, pronunciation, part(s) of speech, and definition(s) of each of the following words. Then write the word in the blank space(s) in the illustrative sentence(s) following. Finally, study the lists of synonyms and antonyms given at the end of each entry.

1. admonish
(ad män' ish)

(*v.*) to caution or advise against something; to scold mildly; to remind of a duty

The librarian had to _____ the noisy students several times before they settled down.

SYNONYMS: warn, call on the carpet
ANTONYMS: praise, pat on the back

2. breach
(brēch)

(*n.*) an opening, gap, rupture, rift; a violation or infraction; (*v.*) to create an opening, break through

Because of a serious _____ of the rules, two players were ejected from the game.

Our troops were unable to _____ the enemy's lines during the battle.

ANTONYMS: (*v.*) close, seal

3. brigand
(brig' ənd)

(*n.*) a bandit, robber, outlaw, highwayman

Ancient caravans passing through desolate areas were sometimes attacked by _____.

4. circumspect
(sər' kəm spekt)

(*adj.*) careful, cautious

It is important for a diplomat to behave in a manner that is both discreet and _____.

SYNONYMS: wary, prudent, guarded
ANTONYMS: incautious, rash, reckless, heedless

5. commandeer
(käm ən dēr')

(*v.*) to seize for military or official use

Under certain circumstances the U.S. government has the right to _____ private property.

SYNONYMS: take over, requisition, expropriate

6. cumbersome
(kəm' bər səm)

(*adj.*) clumsy, hard to handle; slow-moving

The bus was filled to capacity with holiday shoppers carrying large and _____ packages.

SYNONYMS: unwieldy, ponderous
ANTONYMS: manageable, easy to handle

7. deadlock
(ded' läk)

(*n.*) a standstill resulting from the opposition of two equal forces or factions; (*v.*) to bring to such a standstill

After fifteen innings, the score remained a frustrating 3-to-3 _____.

The refusal of labor and management to modify their demands
_____ the contract negotiations.
SYNONYMS: (n.) standoff, stalemate, impasse
ANTONYMS: (n.) agreement, accord, breakthrough

8. debris
(də brē')

(n.) scattered fragments, wreckage
After the storm, the beach was littered with driftwood and
other _____ .
SYNONYMS: rubble, detritus, flotsam and jetsam

9. diffuse
(v., dif yüz';
adj., dif yüs')

(v.) to spread or scatter freely or widely; (adj.) wordy, long-
winded, or unfocused; scattered or widely spread
The scent of lilacs slowly _____
through the open window.

The speech was so long and _____ that
most members of the audience were thoroughly confused by it.
SYNONYMS: (v.) disperse; (adj.) rambling, verbose, prolix
ANTONYMS: (v.) concentrate; (adj.) brief, concise, succinct

10. dilemma
(di lem' ə)

(n.) a difficult or perplexing situation or problem
During the crisis the President found himself caught in a
painful _____ .
SYNONYMS: predicament, quandary, pickle, bind
ANTONYM: cinch

11. efface
(e fās')

(v.) to wipe out; to keep oneself from being noticed
Time had _____ almost all signs of
the struggle that took place on that famous battlefield.
SYNONYMS: blot out, erase, obliterate, expunge

12. muddle
(məd' əl)

(v.) to make a mess of; *muddle through*: to get by; (n.) a
hopeless mess
Too much stress and too little sleep will almost certainly
_____ a person's ability to concentrate.

The _____ was principally caused
by their failure to carry out the general's orders properly.
SYNONYMS: (v.) jumble, mess up; (n.) confusion, disorder
ANTONYMS: (n.) orderliness, tidiness, neatness

13. opinionated
(ə pin' yən āt id)

(adj.) stubborn and often unreasonable in holding to one's own
ideas, having a closed mind.
My boss is not too _____ to listen to
a reasonable proposal.
SYNONYMS: obstinate, pigheaded, inflexible
ANTONYMS: open-minded, reasonable

14. perennial
(pə ren′ ē əl)

(*adj.*) lasting for a long time, persistent; (*n.*) a plant that lives for many years

Pizza is a _____ favorite of young and old alike in the United States.

A garden of _____ is relatively easy to maintain.

SYNONYMS: (*adj.*) enduring, recurring
ANTONYMS: (*adj.*) brief, short-lived, fleeting, ephemeral

15. predispose
(prē dis pōz′)

(*v.*) to incline to beforehand

My genetic makeup seems to _____ me to colds and sore throats.

SYNONYM: make susceptible to
ANTONYMS: immunize against, shield from

16. relinquish
(rē liŋ′ kwish)

(*v.*) to let go, give up

Severe illness forced me to _____ my role in the school play.

SYNONYMS: surrender, abandon
ANTONYMS: hold on to, keep, retain, cling to

17. salvage
(sal′ vij)

(*v.*) to save from fire or shipwreck; (*n.*) property thus saved

Fortunately, we were able to _____ a few things from the fire.

_____ from sunken ships can be of great value to archaeologists and historians.

SYNONYMS: (*v.*) rescue, recover, retrieve, reclaim
ANTONYMS: (*v.*) abandon, scrap, junk

18. spasmodic
(spaz mäd′ ik)

(*adj.*) sudden and violent but brief; fitful; intermittent

_____ flashes of lightning and booming thunderclaps were accompanied by torrential rain.

SYNONYMS: irregular, occasional
ANTONYMS: steady, continuous, chronic

19. spurious
(spyü′ rē əs)

(*adj.*) not genuine, not true, not valid

Manufacturers who make _____ claims for their products may face fines or lawsuits.

SYNONYMS: false, counterfeit, fraudulent, bogus
ANTONYMS: genuine, authentic, bona fide, valid

20. unbridled
(ən brīd′ əld)

(*adj.*) uncontrolled, lacking in restraint

Sometimes the _____ enthusiasm of sports fans can get a little out of hand.

SYNONYMS: unrestrained, unchecked
ANTONYMS: restrained, held in check, muted

 **Completing the Sentence**

From the words for this unit, choose the one that best completes each of the following sentences. Write the word in the space provided.

1. He is so _____ that he won't even consider the ideas or suggestions offered by other people.

2. The nurse rushed into the hospital corridor to _____ the visitors who were creating a disturbance.

3. Though all modern scholars accept *Macbeth* as Shakespeare's work, one or two of the scenes may be _____ .

4. I added a few drops of food coloring to the liquid and watched as they slowly _____ through it.

5. Before I make an investment, I study all aspects of the situation in a most methodical and _____ manner.

6. The water pouring through the _____ in the dam threatened to flood the entire valley.

7. Many a teenager's room is strewn with clothing, CDs, and all sorts of _____ .

8. Though his partner lost everything, he was able to _____ a few dollars from the wreckage of the bankrupt business.

9. The two sides in the lawsuit reached a(n) _____ when neither was willing to meet the other partway.

10. The idea of a(n) _____ like Robin Hood who helps the poor appeals strongly to the popular imagination.

11. The records of our club were in such a(n) _____ that we couldn't even determine which members had paid their dues.

12. In order to capture the fleeing criminals, the police _____ our car and raced after the vanishing truck.

13. Some people are subject to sudden seizures, during which their heads and legs may jerk about in a wild and _____ manner.

14. Though my memory is getting dimmer and dimmer with the slow passage of time, I doubt that the exciting events of my childhood will ever be totally _____ from my mind.

15. The doctor became more and more fearful that her patient's weakened condition would _____ him to pneumonia.

16. The rug made such a(n) _____ bundle that it took four of us to carry it up the stairs.

17. A man of towering pride and _____ ambition, he stopped at nothing to achieve his goals as quickly and directly as possible.

18. Once Great Britain had given up her vast overseas empire, she found that she had also _____ her position as a world power.

19. Since we do not want to replace the plants in our garden every year, we favor _____ over annuals.

20. If I don't get a job, I won't have the money to do what I want; and if I do get a job, I won't have the time. What a(n) _____!

Synonyms

*Choose the word from this unit that is **the same** or **most nearly the same** in meaning as the **boldface** word or expression in the given phrase. Write the word on the line provided.*

1. requisition a vehicle _____

2. a **rambling** and confusing letter _____

3. make susceptible to infection _____

4. obliterated by erosion _____

5. an **uncontrolled** appetite for luxury _____

6. frustrated by **slow-moving** procedures _____

7. captured by **bandits** _____

8. a **stalemate** in the peace talks _____

9. able to **rescue** cherished mementos _____

10. plagued by a **fitful** cough _____

11. an unexpected **predicament** _____

12. recurring campaign issues _____

13. made a **mess** of the filing system _____

14. a **violation** of security procedures _____

15. cleared the **wreckage** _____

Antonyms

*Choose the word from this unit that is **most nearly opposite** in meaning to the **boldface** word or expression in the given phrase. Write the word on the line provided.*

16. a **valid** argument _____

17. tends to make **reckless** decisions _____

18. open-minded neighbors _____

19. retained title to the plot of land _____

20. praised my friends for their behavior _____

Choosing the Right Word

*Circle the **boldface** word that more satisfactorily completes each of the following sentences.*

1. How can you expect to succeed at your new job when you are (**diffused, predisposed**) to believe that it is "not right" for you?

2. An economy in which the marketplace is considered "open" is one in which competition is more or less (**muddled, unbridled**).

3. My mother broke the (**debris, deadlock**) in the quarrel between my brother and me by saying that neither of us could use the car.

4. Thus, the nation was faced with a (**dilemma, brigand**) in which either to advance or to retreat might endanger its vital interests.

5. The senator refused to (**efface, relinquish**) the floor to any other speaker before he had finished his statement.

6. For the very reason that we are the most powerful nation in the world, we must be extremely (**circumspect, opinionated**) in our foreign policy.

7. Developing nations in all parts of the world face the (**perennial, spurious**) problem of gaining a higher level of economic growth.

8. The robber barons were a group of nineteenth-century captains of industry who amassed wealth by means that a (**brigand, salvager**) might use.

9. Instead of trying to (**admonish, commandeer**) the support of the student body, we must earn it by showing our sincerity and ability.

10. Our city government seems to have (**breached, muddled**) into a first-rate financial crisis.

11. The evidence intended to show that some races or nationalities are superior to others proved to be completely (**spurious, cumbersome**).

12. If only I could (**predispose, efface**) the memory of the look of shock and disappointment on my mother's face!

13. Like the rings a pebble makes in a pool of water, the good feelings generated by the speech (**diffused, relinquished**) through the crowd.

14. Even her refusal to dance with him did not seem to make a (**deadlock, breach**) in his gigantic conceit.

15. The organization of some government agencies is so (**cumbersome, perennial**) that it is all but impossible to know who is responsible for various activities.

16. The dean (**effaced, admonished**) the members of the team for neglecting their homework assignments.

17. After the fire, investigators searched through the (**debris, dilemma**) for clues that might reveal the cause.

18. Since she is so convinced that there is only one right way—her way—I find her too (**circumspect, opinionated**) for my liking.

19. Is it too much to expect that I will be able to (**commandeer, salvage**) a few shreds of self-respect from my humiliating failure?

20. His attempts to rid his administration of inefficiency were so (**unbridled, spasmodic**) that he came to be called the "reformer by fits and starts."

Read the following passage, in which some of the words you have studied in this unit appear in **boldface** type. Then complete each statement given below the passage by circling the letter of the item that is **the same** or **almost the same** in meaning as the highlighted word.

Knox the Ox

(Line)

Henry Knox, born in Boston in 1750, was renowned, not for tactical genius or stirring speeches, but for the unwavering determination to overcome any obstacle, resolve any **dilemma**. This quality, along with his impressive girth, earned him the nickname "Knox the Ox."

(5) Henry Knox faced adversity early in life. His father died when Henry was only 12, and the boy had to go to work in a bookstore. By the time he turned 21, he owned his *own* bookstore. This was an ideal business for him because a strong interest in military affairs **predisposed** him to spend much of his time reading,

(10) particularly about artillery.

In 1775, Knox joined the Continental Army and was made a colonel because of his considerable knowledge and his experience in a Boston militia. One of

(15) his first assignments was to transport 59 captured British cannons from Fort Ticonderoga, in New York, to Boston to fortify that besieged city. These **cumbersome** weapons weighed nearly

(20) 60 tons.

Knox applied both his ox-like determination and the power of *real* oxen to the task of pulling the cannons on wooden sledges. The procession of

Cannons at the restored Fort Ticonderoga

(25) men, horses, and oxen crossed the frozen Hudson River and made the 300-mile journey to Boston. Despite three months of hardship, they managed to **muddle through**.

George Washington's troops put the cannons to good use and succeeded in forcing the British to **relinquish** control of Boston Harbor and evacuate the city. Knox became

(30) a friend and advisor to George Washington, who named him the new nation's secretary of war. The remarkable Knox the Ox continued to serve his country until 1794.

---

1. The meaning of **dilemma** (line 3) is
a. problem
b. quarrel
c. mystery
d. question

2. Predisposed (line 8) most nearly means
a. taught
b. cautioned
c. tempted
d. inclined

3. Cumbersome (line 19) is best defined as
a. large
b. unwieldy
c. dangerous
d. heavy

4. Muddle through (line 27) means
a. get by
b. enjoyed
c. regretted
d. messed up

5. Relinquish (line 29) most nearly means
a. tighten
b. accept
c. abandon
d. negotiate

Definitions

Note carefully the spelling, pronunciation, part(s) of speech, and definition(s) of each of the following words. Then write the word in the blank space(s) in the illustrative sentence(s) following. Finally, study the lists of synonyms and antonyms given at the end of each entry.

1. adjourn
(ə jərn')

(*v.*) to stop proceedings temporarily; move to another place

The judge _____ the hearing until ten o'clock the following morning.

SYNONYMS: postpone, suspend, discontinue
ANTONYMS: open, call to order

2. alien
(ā' lē ən)

(*n.*) a citizen of another country; (*adj.*) foreign, strange

Movies about _____ from outer space have been extremely popular for decades.

An _____ species of plant or animal can upset the balance of an ecosystem.

SYNONYMS: (*adj.*) exotic, unfamiliar
ANTONYMS: (*adj.*) native, endemic, familiar

3. comely
(kəm' lē)

(*adj.*) having a pleasing appearance

The proud parents and their _____ children posed for a family portrait.

SYNONYMS: good-looking, attractive, bonny
ANTONYMS: plain, homely, ugly, repulsive

4. compensate
(käm' pən sāt)

(*v.*) to make up for; to repay for services

The manufacturer was ordered to _____ customers injured by the defective product.

SYNONYMS: pay back, reimburse, recompense
ANTONYMS: fail to reward, stiff

5. dissolute
(dis' ə lüt)

(*adj.*) loose in one's morals or behavior

The mad Roman emperor Caligula led an extravagant and _____ life.

SYNONYMS: dissipated, debauched, immoral, corrupt
ANTONYMS: virtuous, chaste, moral, seemly, proper

6. erratic
(e rat' ik)

(*adj.*) not regular or consistent; different from what is ordinarily expected; undependable

Students who have an _____ attendance record may find themselves disciplined by the principal.

SYNONYMS: irregular, inconsistent, unpredictable
ANTONYMS: steady, consistent, dependable

7. expulsion
(ek spəl′ shən)

(*n.*) the process of driving or forcing out

The story of the _____ of Adam and Eve from the Garden of Eden is told in Genesis.

SYNONYMS: ejection, ouster, eviction
ANTONYMS: admittance, admission

8. feint
(fānt)

(*n.*) a deliberately deceptive movement; a pretense; (*v.*) to make a deceptive movement; to make a pretense of

The chess master's opening _____ gave her an immediate advantage.

His uncanny ability to _____ and counterpunch made the champ unbeatable.

SYNONYMS: (*n.*) trick, ruse, subterfuge, dodge, bluff

9. fodder
(fäd′ ər)

(*n.*) food for horses or cattle; raw material for a designated purpose

Every experience in life is _____ for a novelist's imagination.

SYNONYMS: feed, provender

10. fortify
(fôr′ tə fī)

(*v.*) to strengthen, build up

The soldiers _____ the garrison against the expected attack.

SYNONYMS: reinforce, shore up
ANTONYMS: weaken, undermine, sap, impair

11. illegible
(i lej′ ə bəl)

(*adj.*) difficult or impossible to read

The effects of air pollution have rendered the inscriptions on many old gravestones _____.

SYNONYMS: unreadable, indecipherable, scribbled
ANTONYMS: readable, decipherable, distinct, clear

12. jeer
(jēr)

(*v.*) to make fun of rudely or unkindly; (*n.*) a rude remark of derision

To _____ at someone with a disability is absolutely inexcusable.

Umpires and other referees quickly become immune to the _____ of angry fans.

SYNONYMS: (*v.*) laugh at, mock, taunt
ANTONYMS: (*n.*) applause, plaudits, accolades

13. lucrative
(lü′ krə tiv)

(*adj.*) bringing in money; profitable

Many people find that they can turn a favorite hobby into a highly _____ business.

SYNONYMS: gainful, moneymaking
ANTONYMS: unprofitable, losing, in the red

14. mediocre
(mē dē ō′ kər)

(*adj.*) average, ordinary, undistinguished

The team's number-one draft pick turned out to be a rather
_____ player, not a star who
could lead them to the championship.

SYNONYM: run-of-the-mill
ANTONYMS: exceptional, outstanding, distinguished

15. proliferate
(prō lif′ ə rāt)

(*v.*) to reproduce, increase, or spread rapidly

Because malignant cells _____,
early detection of cancer is absolutely crucial to
successful treatment.

SYNONYMS: multiply, mushroom, burgeon
ANTONYMS: decrease, diminish, dwindle, slack off

16. subjugate
(səb′ jü gāt)

(*v.*) to conquer by force, bring under complete control

"We must act quickly," the general said, "in order to
_____ the rebel forces."

SYNONYMS: subdue, vanquish, master
ANTONYMS: be conquered, submit, surrender

17. sully
(səl′ ē)

(*v.*) to soil, stain, tarnish, defile, besmirch

The Watergate scandal _____
the image of politicians in the minds of many voters.

SYNONYMS: pollute, taint, smear
ANTONYMS: cleanse, purify, decontaminate

18. tantalize
(tan′ tə līz)

(*v.*) to tease, torment by teasing

When I am on a diet, the treats in bakery windows seem to
have been put there to _____ me.

SYNONYMS: tempt, lead on, make one's mouth water
ANTONYMS: satisfy, fulfill, gratify

19. terse
(tərs)

(*adj.*) brief and to the point

The manuscript for my short story was returned to me with
a _____ letter of rejection.

SYNONYMS: concise, succinct, crisp, short and sweet
ANTONYMS: verbose, wordy, diffuse, prolix

20. unflinching
(ən flin′ chiŋ)

(*adj.*) firm, showing no signs of fear, not drawing back

Everyone admires the _____
courage with which firefighters and other rescue workers
carry out their dangerous jobs.

SYNONYMS: resolute, steadfast, unwavering
ANTONYMS: irresolute, wavering, vacillating

Completing the Sentence

From the words for this unit, choose the one that best completes each of the following sentences. Write the word in the space provided.

1. To enlarge the areas under their control, kings of old sent out their armies to _____ their neighbors.

2. Our laws protect not only citizens but also _____ legally residing in this country.

3. When the national economy is expanding, new housing developments begin to _____; when times are lean, construction slacks off.

4. In spite of all the adverse criticism her ideas have received, she remains _____ in her determination to improve our community.

5. Despite all my efforts to make this a(n) _____ enterprise, it continues to be a decidedly unprofitable organization.

6. Since there is a charge for every word used in it, a telegram is usually as _____ as possible.

7. The farmer must provide storage facilities for the _____ he plans to set aside for his cattle during the long winter.

8. The thoroughly disgraceful behavior of a few dissipated officers effectively _____ the honor of the entire unit.

9. How can you be so cruel as to _____ those poor dogs by offering them tidbits that you will never let them have?

10. Their so-called peace initiative proved to be nothing more than a clever _____ designed to lull the enemy into a false sense of security.

11. Though he had a great sinker ball, he was so _____ on the mound that fans started to call him "Wild Pitch Hickok."

12. Our doctor's handwriting is so _____ that my brother used one of his prescriptions as a teacher's pass.

13. When it is time to end one of our meetings, a member must make a motion to _____.

14. Though she is not a beautiful woman by conventional standards, she is certainly _____ and appealing.

15. The speaker advised us not to imitate the _____ kind of person who squanders time and money in the vain pursuit of pleasure.

16. He was a changed young man after his _____ from West Point for "conduct unbecoming an officer and a gentleman."

17. Their only response to my warnings was to _____ at me scornfully and go ahead with their plans.

18. Some people drink quantities of orange juice and swallow vitamin C tablets in a valiant attempt to _____ themselves against winter colds.

19. A(n) _____ student is one who neither fails any subject nor receives any marks that are above average.

20. The fact that you say you are truly sorry does not _____ for the pain I have suffered as a result of your cruelty.

Synonyms

*Choose the word from this unit that is **the same** or **most nearly the same** in meaning as the **boldface** word or expression in the given phrase. Write the word on the line provided.*

1. found myself in **unfamiliar** territory _____

2. ordered to **reimburse** the victims of the swindle _____

3. tried to **master** my hot temper _____

4. a reputation for being **unpredictable** _____

5. ordered the **ouster** of seven career diplomats _____

6. **dodged** to the left and ran for a touchdown _____

7. an ample supply of **feed** for our livestock _____

8. written in an **indecipherable** scrawl _____

9. **suspend** the discussion because of the late hour _____

10. plans to seek more **gainful** employment _____

11. dandelions that seem to **multiply** overnight _____

12. conduct that **taints** the company's reputation _____

13. **tempted** by promises of adventure _____

14. **unwavering** in the pursuit of justice _____

15. **taunted** by the bully _____

Antonyms

*Choose the word from this unit that is **most nearly opposite** in meaning to the **boldface** word or expression in the given phrase. Write the word on the line provided.*

16. a person with a **plain** face _____

17. **undermined** the building's foundation _____

18. issued a **verbose** report on the economy _____

19. a thoroughly **virtuous** individual _____

20. judged the work to be **exceptional** _____

Choosing the Right Word

*Circle the **boldface** word that more satisfactorily completes each of the following sentences.*

1. Though a trained veteran is often a well-tuned fighting machine, a raw recruit is sometimes no better than cannon (**feint, fodder**).

2. To keep my self-respect, I must stand (**comely, unflinching**) before the authorities and tell them the truth as I see it.

3. After the formal dinner was over, we (**adjourned, tantalized**) to the den in order to continue our conversation in a more relaxed atmosphere.

4. As soon as I entered that charming little cottage, I noticed that everything in it was neat and (**erratic, comely**).

5. At one point in our fencing match, my opponent unexpectedly (**sullied, feinted**) to the left and threw me completely off guard.

6. Instead of all those long, flowery passages, why don't you try to write more in the (**mediocre, terse**) and direct style of a good newspaper reporter?

7. I can understand how poor people sometimes feel (**tantalized, jeered**) by the wealth and luxuries they see displayed on TV programs.

8. His behavior is so (**erratic, terse**) that we never know what to expect from him.

9. When I first noticed how (**illegible, lucrative**) my roommate's handwriting was, I suggested that he sign up immediately for a course in penmanship.

10. I would be unwilling to vote for the (**expulsion, fodder**) of club members just because they are behind in their dues.

11. The desire to force everyone to accept the same set of ideas is completely (**illegible, alien**) to the spirit of democracy.

12. We all experience fear and panic, but the leader of a great nation must be able to (**tantalize, subjugate**) such emotions.

13. In my opinion, his writing is so bad that he will have to improve a great deal just to reach the level of (**mediocrity, compensation**).

14. "No," she said, "I won't (**sully, adjourn**) your ears by repeating those mean and nasty rumors."

15. All great athletes should know that the same fans who are cheering them today may be (**jeering, subjugating**) them tomorrow.

16. For centuries people have turned to various kinds of religious literature to (**fortify, proliferate**) themselves against the shocks of daily life.

17. Even though I must work hard for a living, I feel that the company I'm with amply (**subjugates, compensates**) me for my time and effort.

18. *The Rake's Progress* paints a grim and uncompromising picture of some of the more (**dissolute, alien**) and degrading aspects of human behavior.

19. Over the years I've noticed one thing about rumors: Where the facts are few, fictions (**proliferate, fortify**).

20. A best-selling book that is then made into a movie may be more (**dissolute, lucrative**) than the proverbial pot of gold at the end of the rainbow.

*Read the following passage, in which some of the words you have studied in this unit appear in **boldface** type. Then complete each statement given below the passage by circling the letter of the item that is **the same** or **almost the same** in meaning as the highlighted word.*

Pushing the Limits

(Line)

Martha Graham was born in Allegheny, Pennsylvania, in 1894. She was the oldest of three sisters. She considered herself plain and her sisters **comely**, but she **compensated for** this with her athleticism and forceful personality. In 1909, the family moved to Santa Barbara, California. It was there that the 17-year-old Martha had an experience that changed her life. She saw a poster advertising a performance by the (5) dancer Ruth St. Denis. Martha was so fascinated by the exotic, gorgeously costumed image of the dancer that she begged her parents to take her to the performance. Once she saw St. Denis on stage, she knew that she too would become a dancer.

In 1916, she enrolled at the Denishawn School, run by St. Denis and her husband Ted (10) Shawn. In 1923, she set out on her own. She took a **lucrative** job in New York as a solo dancer in a revue and became a Broadway star. Then, in 1929, she started her own dance company and began to choreograph. (15)

Everything was **fodder** for her creative imagination. She drew on childhood memories, her experiences as a dancer, and the innovative ideas in art and music that were swirling around her. Graham created a new language of (20) movement that was thoroughly **alien** to classical ballet technique. It was angular and even distorted, a vehicle for expressing intense emotion. Many of her works were based on ancient Greek legends and biblical and religious (25)

Martha Graham, dancer and choreographer

themes. Other dances dealt with life on the American frontier. She was **unflinching** in the pursuit of her vision of what dance should be, always pushing the limits.

Martha Graham stopped performing at age 74 but continued to choreograph until her death in 1991, at age 96. Today, the Graham technique is part of the training and skills of dancers everywhere. (30)

---

1. The meaning of **comely** (line 2) is
a. popular
b. attractive
c. polite
d. homely

2. Compensated for (line 3) means
a. apologized for
b. explained
c. disregarded
d. made up for

3. Lucrative (line 11) is best defined as
a. profitable
b. glamorous
c. temporary
d. part-time

4. The meaning of **fodder** (line 16) is
a. provender
b. inspiration
c. raw material
d. decoration

5. Alien (line 21) most nearly means
a. familiar
b. subordinate
c. complementary
d. foreign

6. Unflinching (line 26) is best defined as
a. resolute
b. vacillating
c. loyal
d. original

Definitions

Note carefully the spelling, pronunciation, part(s) of speech, and definition(s) of each of the following words. Then write the word in the blank space(s) in the illustrative sentence(s) following. Finally, study the lists of synonyms and antonyms given at the end of each entry.

1. abridge
(ə brij′)

(*v.*) to make shorter

Travel by air _____ the time needed to reach far-distant places.

SYNONYMS: shorten, condense, abbreviate
ANTONYMS: expand, enlarge, augment

2. adherent
(ad hēr′ ənt)

(*n.*) a follower, supporter; (*adj.*) attached, sticking to

The senator's loyal _____ campaigned long and hard for her reelection.

Before we could repaint the walls of our living room, we had to remove an _____ layer of wallpaper.

SYNONYM: (*n.*) disciple
ANTONYMS: (*n.*) opponent, adversary, critic, detractor

3. altercation
(ôl tər kā′ shən)

(*n.*) an angry argument

A noisy _____ in the next apartment kept me awake for hours.

SYNONYMS: quarrel, dispute, squabble
ANTONYMS: agreement, accord

4. cherubic
(che rü′ bik)

(*adj.*) resembling an angel portrayed as a little child with a beautiful, round, or chubby face; sweet and innocent

How well those photographs of the month-old twins capture the _____ expressions on their faces!

SYNONYMS: angelic, seraphic, beatific
ANTONYMS: impish, devilish, diabolic, fiendish

5. condone
(kən dōn′)

(*v.*) to pardon or overlook

Our parents have always made it crystal clear to us that they do not _____ rude behavior.

SYNONYMS: ignore, wink at, turn a blind eye to
ANTONYMS: censure, condemn, disapprove, deprecate

6. dissent
(di sent′)

(*v.*) to disagree; (*n.*) disagreement

Justices have an option to _____ from a ruling issued by a majority of the Supreme Court.

Some people give voice to their _____ on issues of public policy by writing letters to newspapers.

SYNONYMS: (*v.*) differ, dispute
ANTONYMS: (*v.*) agree, concur; (*n.*) unanimity, harmony

7. eminent
(em' ə nənt)

(*adj.*) famous, outstanding, distinguished; projecting

A group of _____ scientists met to discuss long-term changes in Earth's climate.

SYNONYMS: illustrious, renowned
ANTONYMS: obscure, nameless, unsung, lowly, humble

8. exorcise
(ek' sôr sīz)

(*v.*) to drive out by magic; to dispose of something troublesome, menacing, or oppressive

We must do all we can to _____ the evils of hatred and prejudice from our society.

SYNONYMS: expel, dispel

9. fabricate
(fab' rə kāt)

(*v.*) to make, manufacture; to make up, invent

Threads from the cocoons of caterpillars called *silkworms* are used to _____ silk.

SYNONYMS: put together, devise, contrive, concoct
ANTONYMS: take apart, undo, destroy, demolish

10. irate
(ī rāt')

(*adj.*) angry

Long delays caused by bad weather are likely to make even the most unflappable travelers _____.

SYNONYMS: incensed, infuriated, enraged, livid
ANTONYMS: calm, composed, cool, unruffled

11. marauder
(mə rôd' ər)

(*n.*) a raider, plunderer

Edgar Allan Poe's story "The Gold Bug" concerns treasure buried by the _____ Captain Kidd.

SYNONYMS: looter, pirate, freebooter

12. obesity
(ō bē' sə tē)

(*n.*) excessive fatness

Sooner or later, _____ leads to all sorts of serious health problems.

SYNONYMS: serious overweight, extreme corpulence
ANTONYMS: emaciation, gauntness, scrawniness

13. pauper
(pô' pər)

(*n.*) an extremely poor person

During the Great Depression, many people were reduced to leading the desperate lives of _____.

SYNONYM: destitute person
ANTONYMS: millionaire, tycoon

14. pilfer
(pil' fər)

(*v.*) to steal in small quantities

An employee who _____ from the petty cash box will get caught sooner or later.

SYNONYMS: filch, rob, swipe, purloin

15. rift
(rift)

(*n.*) a split, break, breach

Failure to repay a loan can be the cause of an angry _____ between longtime friends.

SYNONYMS: crack, fissure, gap, cleft
ANTONYM: reconciliation

16. semblance
(sem' bləns)

(*n.*) a likeness; an outward appearance; an apparition

Despite a bad case of stage fright, I tried to maintain a _____ of calm as I sang my solo.

SYNONYMS: appearance, air, aura, veneer, facade
ANTONYMS: dissimilarity, contrast, total lack

17. surmount
(sər maùnt')

(*v.*) to overcome, rise above

Wilma Rudolph _____ childhood illness and physical disabilities to win three Olympic gold medals.

SYNONYMS: conquer, triumph over
ANTONYMS: be vanquished, be defeated, succumb to

18. terminate
(tər' mə nāt)

(*v.*) to bring to an end

If you fail to perform your job satisfactorily, your boss may _____ your employment.

SYNONYMS: conclude, finish, discontinue
ANTONYMS: begin, commence, initiate

19. trite
(trīt)

(*adj.*) commonplace; overused, stale

When you write an essay or a story, be especially careful to avoid using _____ expressions.

SYNONYMS: banal, hackneyed, corny
ANTONYMS: original, novel, fresh, innovative

20. usurp
(yü sərp')

(*v.*) to seize and hold a position by force or without right

The general who led the coup _____ the office of the duly elected president.

SYNONYMS: seize illegally, commandeer, supplant

Completing the Sentence

From the words for this unit, choose the one that best completes each of the following sentences. Write the word in the space provided.

1. Though I was hurt by the tactless comment, I tried to show pleasure in it by twisting my lips into a feeble _____ of a smile.

2. During a recent interdenominational service in our community center, the _____ of various faiths met to worship as one.

3. "That child may have an angel's _____ features, but at heart he is a little devil," I exclaimed in disgust.

4. A few of us who disagreed strongly with the committee's conclusions felt compelled to raise our voices in _____ .

5. Although I am not a particularly argumentative person, last week I found myself involved in a heated _____ with a salesclerk.

6. The only way I could _____ the argument peacefully was to walk away abruptly.

7. "I think," said the salesclerk, "that the phrase 'hot under the collar' aptly describes the typical _____ customer that we have to deal with."

8. No one but a heartless scoundrel would _____ nickels and dimes from a charity's collection fund.

9. Although they have enough money to live on, the loss of most of their great wealth has left them feeling like _____ .

10. "I am willing to wink at a harmless prank," the dean remarked, "but I will not _____ outright vandalism."

11. It is a real tribute to the ingenuity of the human mind that for thousands of years people have been _____ new and interesting theories of the universe.

12. After so many years of distinguished service in the United States Senate, he can properly be called a(n) _____ statesman.

13. It is only through the exercise of their intelligence that people can begin to _____ the difficulties they encounter in daily living.

14. The only lasting cure for _____ is to eat a great deal less and exercise a great deal more.

15. In this clever spoof of horror movies, the local witch doctor encounters hilarious difficulties when he tries to _____ an evil demon that has taken up residence in the heroine's body.

16. A screenplay or television drama with the same old boy-meets-girl plot can certainly be criticized as _____ .

17. After driving the lawful ruler out of the country for good, the villainous duke _____ the throne and crowned himself king.

18. In order to fit the newspaper article into the space available, the editor had to _____ it by omitting secondary details.

19. Bands of _____ broke through the frontier defenses of the province and began to plunder the rich farmlands of the interior.

20. As the layer of clouds that hung over the city began to break up, the sun came pouring through the _____ .

Synonyms *Choose the word from this unit that is **the same** or **most nearly the same** in meaning as the **boldface** word or expression in the given phrase. Write the word on the line provided.*

1. vowed to capture the notorious **freebooter**   _____

2. tried to **dispel** our feelings of gloom and doom   _____

3. maintained an **outward appearance** of friendliness   _____

4. programs that aid **destitute persons**   _____

5. **supporters** of the free market system   _____

6. **filched** small change from the cash register   _____

7. refuses to **turn a blind eye to** corrupt practices   _____

8. bravely faced the **enraged** crowd   _____

9. **commandeered** the reins of power   _____

10. a positively **angelic** appearance   _____

11. gets into one **quarrel** after another   _____

12. tried to **make up** a credible alibi   _____

13. a painful **split** between old allies   _____

14. **conquered** every obstacle they faced   _____

15. **condensed** the long and detailed report   _____

Antonyms *Choose the word from this unit that is **most nearly opposite** in meaning to the **boldface** word or expression in the given phrase. Write the word on the line provided.*

16. a major novel by an **obscure** writer   _____

17. a prevailing mood of **harmony** among the members   _____

18. treatment for the patient's **emaciation**   _____

19. **initiated** talks between the warring parties   _____

20. a **fresh** approach to a familiar story   _____

Choosing the Right Word

*Circle the **boldface** word that more satisfactorily completes each of the following sentences.*

1. Either party has the right to (**terminate, surmount**) the agreement that has been made whenever the partnership proves unprofitable.

2. In a dictatorship, people who (**abridge, dissent**) from the official party line usually wind up in prison—or worse.

3. I am very much flattered that you have referred to me as "an (**eminent, obese**) educator," but I prefer to think of myself as just a good teacher.

4. The robber barons of an earlier era often acted more like (**adherents, marauders**) than ethical businessmen in their dealings with the public.

5. You had no right to (**exorcise, usurp**) for yourself the role of gracious host at my party!

6. The few words that she grudgingly muttered were the only (**semblance, altercation**) of an apology that she offered for her rude behavior.

7. I feel like a (**usurper, pauper**) now that my part-time job has come to an end and I no longer have any spending money.

8. Like all literary sneak thieves, he has a truly nasty habit of (**pilfering, fabricating**) other people's ideas and then claiming them as his own.

9. The fact that many citizens are (**trite, irate**) over the new taxes does not mean that these taxes are unjustifiable.

10. My cousin has so much imagination that he can (**dissent, fabricate**) an excuse that even an experienced principal would believe!

11. One can't become a good writer just by (**surmounting, adhering**) closely to rules laid down in standard grammar books.

12. What began as a minor quarrel grew into a serious (**altercation, exorcism**) and then into an ugly brawl.

13. Their (**irate, cherubic**) faces and ethereal voices almost made me believe that the music they were singing was coming from heaven.

14. The fact that Abraham Lincoln was able to (**surmount, terminate**) the handicap of a limited education does not mean that you should quit school.

15. I do not entirely (**usurp, condone**) your misconduct, but I can understand, to a degree, why you behaved as you did.

16. Unless we repair the (**rifts, semblances**) in our party and present a united front, we will go down to crushing defeat in the upcoming election.

17. It is the sacred duty of all Americans to oppose any attempt to (**abridge, condone**) or deny the rights guaranteed to us in the Constitution.

18. Anyone who wants to dine at that outrageously expensive restaurant had better carry a credit card or a truly (**obese, eminent**) wallet.

19. His speech was so (**cherubic, trite**) that one could almost anticipate the phrases he would use next.

20. The comforting presence of relatives did much to (**exorcise, pilfer**) the patient's feelings of alarm at the thought of undergoing major surgery.

*Read the following passage, in which some of the words you have studied in this unit appear in **boldface** type. Then complete each statement given below the passage by circling the letter of the item that is **the same** or **almost the same** in meaning as the highlighted word.*

Angel Island

(Line)

Chinese immigrants came to America for the same reasons that other immigrants came: to seek a better life. They began to arrive in the late 1840s, drawn by the promise of California's gold fields. Later they helped build the railroads. Like other immigrants before and since, many newly arrived Chinese were willing to work for

(5) very low wages. **Irate** critics accused them of taking jobs away from American-born workers and European immigrants. These protests led to the passage of the Chinese Exclusion Act of 1882. Although the law barred most Chinese

(10) from entering the country, it contained exceptions for the wives and children of certain groups of Chinese, such as merchants and teachers. Soon a demand developed for papers **fabricated** to prove the existence of

(15) such relatives.

Poems carved into walls at Angel Island by Chinese immigrants

Angel Island, located in San Francisco Bay, once served as a hideout for **marauders**. But from 1910 to 1940, it was used to enforce the exclusion laws. It became known as the

(20) "Guardian of the Western Gate." Unlike Ellis Island, which was truly a port of entry, Angel Island was a place of detention. New immigrants were held there, sometimes for months, until their claims could be checked. They endured repeated questioning about every detail of their lives in China. Many expressed their hopes and fears in poems written on the walls of their barracks. Despite the laws, thousands of

(25) Chinese, including so-called paper sons and daughters, were able to **surmount** the obstacles that barred their way.

In 1943, Congress **terminated** the 1882 act. People of Chinese descent, along with people from many other parts of Asia, were finally free to come to America. Today a portion of the old station on Angel Island stands as a memorial

(30) to their struggle.

---

1. The meaning of **irate** (line 5) is
  a. severe   c. incensed
  b. unruffled   d. biased

2. Fabricated (line 14) most nearly means
  a. purchased   c. intended
  b. concocted   d. written

3. Marauders (line 17) is best defined as
  a. celebrities   c. spies
  b. pirates   d. fugitives

4. The meaning of **surmount** (line 25) is
  a. overcome   c. protest
  b. bypass   d. face

5. Terminated (line 27) most nearly means
  a. replaced   c. rejected
  b. amended   d. ended

Analogies *In each of the following, circle the item that best completes the comparison.*

1. adjourn is to **terminate** as
a. fabricate is to usurp
b. compensate is to repay
c. efface is to flourish
d. proliferate is to abridge

2. adherent is to **supporter** as
a. doctor is to patient
b. champion is to defender
c. mother is to daughter
d. admirer is to critic

3. semblance is to **likeness** as
a. dilemma is to solution
b. expulsion is to acceptance
c. altercation is to dispute
d. salvage is to piracy

4. pilfer is to **steal** as
a. compensate is to cancel
b. surmount is to remind
c. commandeer is to reward
d. sully is to tarnish

5. exorcise is to **expulsion** as
a. breach is to compensation
b. proliferate is to reduction
c. subjugate is to liberation
d. diffuse is to dispersion

6. native is to **alien** as
a. pleasant is to spurious
b. mediocre is to remarkable
c. awkward is to irate
d. cautious is to circumspect

7. rift is to **breach** as
a. deadlock is to solution
b. dilemma is to examination
c. debris is to wreckage
d. salvage is to shipwreck

8. eminent is to **favorable** as
a. spurious is to favorable
b. unflinching is to unfavorable
c. erratic is to favorable
d. mediocre is to unfavorable

9. fortify is to **weaken** as
a. commandeer is to suggest
b. dissent is to agree
c. admonish is to caution
d. tantalize is to command

10. spasmodic is to **continuous** as
a. dissolute is to dissipated
b. comely is to early
c. erratic is to consistent
d. diffuse is to spurious

11. illegible is to **read** as
a. invisible is to see
b. immobile is to touch
c. inaudible is to avoid
d. inflammable is to count

12. abridge is to **expand** as
a. relinquish is to retain
b. feint is to delay
c. pilfer is to condone
d. subjugate is to conquer

13. angry is to **irate** as
a. glum is to predisposed
b. comely is to ugly
c. unflinching is to rude
d. fat is to obese

14. jeer is to **contempt** as
a. applaud is to horror
b. smile is to beauty
c. yawn is to boredom
d. wink is to curiosity

15. spurious is to **genuine** as
a. lucrative is to wealthy
b. trite is to original
c. cumbersome is to costly
d. terse is to brief

16. circumspect is to **favorable** as
a. admonish is to favorable
b. reckless is to unfavorable
c. cumbersome is to favorable
d. lucrative is to unfavorable

17. pauper is to **millionaire** as
a. cherub is to imp
b. brigand is to robber
c. militant is to adherent
d. marauder is to doctor

18. hay is to **fodder** as
a. tulip is to perennial
b. pig is to pauper
c. feint is to boxing
d. adherent is to muddle

Word Associations

In each of the following groups, circle the word that is best defined or suggested by the given phrase.

1. citizen of a foreign country
a. eminent   b. debris   c. deadlock   d. alien

2. noisy, heated quarrel
a. semblance   b. altercation   c. muddle   d. expulsion

3. careful to consider all possibilities
a. cumbersome   b. circumspect   c. spurious   d. perennial

4. seize for military purposes
a. sully   b. pilfer   c. commandeer   d. diffuse

5. loose in one's morals or behavior
a. spasmodic   b. dissolute   c. comely   d. erratic

6. one who lives by plunder or robbery
a. commandeer   b. debris   c. adherent   d. brigand

7. bring to a conclusion
a. terminate   b. relinquish   c. compensate   d. jeer

8. rescue property in danger
a. proliferate   b. salvage   c. abridge   d. usurp

9. make indistinct by wearing away
a. fabricate   b. breach   c. efface   d. adjourn

10. rise superior to
a. usurp   b. surmount   c. fabricate   d. exorcise

11. distract attention from the intended point of attack
a. condone   b. admonish   c. feint   d. tantalize

12. holding stubbornly to one's own judgment
a. cherubic   b. opinionated   c. trite   d. predisposed

13. choice between two undesirable courses of action
a. salvage   b. brigand   c. obesity   d. dilemma

14. without unnecessary words
a. unbridled   b. terse   c. lucrative   d. mediocre

15. differ in opinion
a. tantalize   b. fortify   c. compensate   d. dissent

16. something to be consumed
a. breach   b. expulsion   c. fodder   d. pauper

17. bring to a standstill
a. proliferate   b. dissent   c. deadlock   d. subjugate

18. one who invades the territory of another
a. marauder   b. alien   c. fodder   d. rift

19. wink at
a. muddle   b. abridge   c. condone   d. subjugate

20. characterized by anger
a. illegible   b. unflinching   c. irate   d. terse

Read the following passage, in which some of the words you have studied in Units 1–3 appear in **boldface** type. Then complete each statement given below the passage by circling the item that is **the same** or **almost the same** in meaning as the highlighted word.

Trash Power

(Line)

In the early 1950s concern grew over the tons of trash produced in the United States, and the limited amount of landfill space available for
(5) dumping. By the 1960s and 70s the public could no longer **condone** such enormous waste. Demands came from **eminent** scientists, politicians, and the general
(10) populace to address the problem by means other than landfill dumping. Many possible solutions emerged, including Municipal Solid Waste Incinerators (MSWIs).

(15) By burning trash in very hot incinerators and then harnessing the heat released to turn water into steam, MSWIs were predicted to reduce a city's trash volume by
(20) around 90%, and produce 10% of their own electricity. But problems arose. The incinerators released carbon monoxide and other pollutants into the air and the
(25) residue that remained contained toxic materials. Worse still, it was discovered that at extreme temperatures a family of toxic chemicals called *dioxins* might
(30) form. Airborne dioxins **diffuse** over local ecosystems and eventually reach humans through the food chain. Cancer and other diseases have been linked to them.

(35) Requiring plants to clean up their harmful by-products is costly, yet necessary for the public good. Does this dilemma spell the end for MSWIs? Answer: No. While fewer
(40) trash burners are in use than expected by the waste disposal industry, they may yet **proliferate**. In Europe and Japan efficient, super-clean incinerators are up and
(45) running. If our communities can pay for such plants, or if the cost of building and operating them comes down, our **perennial** effort to reduce trash will surely be **fortified**.
(50) But it is important to remember that all forms of waste management make a difference. Recycling plastic, glass, aluminum, and paper can make our resources last for
(55) years to come. Treating waste with biological and chemical agents often degrades their hazardous content. And most simply, using and consuming fewer products results in
(60) less waste.

---

1. Condone (line 6) most nearly means
   a. venerate
   b. overlook
   c. conceal
   d. support

2. Eminent (line 8) is best defined as
   a. irate
   b. dominant
   c. qualified
   d. renowned

3. The meaning of **diffuse** (line 30) is
   a. disperse
   b. dispense
   c. fall
   d. concentrate

4. Proliferate (line 42) is best defined as
   a. continue
   b. lessen
   c. increase
   d. burgeon

5. Perennial (line 48) most nearly means
   a. intermittent
   b. persistent
   c. devoted
   d. resistant

6. The meaning of **fortified** (line 49) is
   a. defended
   b. enriched
   c. strengthened
   d. multiplied

Choosing the Right Meaning

Read each sentence carefully. Then circle the item that best completes the statement below the sentence.

Some see in TV's power to abridge the distances separating the world's peoples the means of making the earth a "global village." (2)

1. The word **abridge** in line 1 most nearly means

a. curb   b. reduce   c. explore   d. erase

The cumbersome wagon trains that plied the Oregon Trail often took weeks just to cross the prairies of Kansas and Nebraska. (2)

2. The word **cumbersome** in line 1 is best defined as

a. crude   b. swift   c. unprotected   d. slow-moving

In some parts of the world, to decline a dish served at a banquet is considered an unpardonable breach of etiquette. (2)

3. In line 2 the word **breach** most nearly means

a. opening   b. assault   c. violation   d. breakthrough

As its name suggests, Frank Lloyd Wright's cantilevered "Fallingwater" house stands eminent above a waterfall. (2)

4. The word **eminent** in line 2 is best defined as

a. jutting out   b. distinguished   c. illustrious   d. outstanding

In contrast with the economy of expression that so distinguished the author's early works, the later novels are woefully diffuse. (2)

5. The word **diffuse** in line 2 is used to mean

a. uneven   b. spread out   c. dispersed   d. rambling

Antonyms

*In each of the following groups, circle the word or expression that is most nearly the **opposite** of the word in **boldface** type.*

1. tantalize
a. ridicule
b. gratify
c. lure
d. simmer

2. erratic
a. angry
b. inconsistent
c. pleasing
d. constant

3. unflinching
a. novel
b. wavering
c. angry
d. proud

4. lucrative
a. unsaid
b. unheard
c. understood
d. unprofitable

5. obesity
a. emaciation
b. starving
c. overeating
d. disease

6. expulsion
a. compulsion
b. farewell
c. admission
d. breathing out

7. cherubic
a. friendly
b. impish
c. angelic
d. beautiful

8. muddle
a. murkiness
b. darkness
c. neatness
d. confusion

9. relinquish
a. fade
b. follow
c. keep
d. try

10. condone
a. commend
b. cooperate
c. create
d. condemn

11. unbridled
a. restrained
b. checkered
c. interrupted
d. prolonged

12. salvage
a. abandon
b. tame
c. save
d. injure

13. diffuse
a. scatter
b. accept
c. concentrate
d. originate

14. fortify
a. undermine
b. strengthen
c. narrate
d. listen

15. trite
a. original
b. foolish
c. meaningless
d. stale

16. rift
a. opening
b. revenge
c. reconciliation
d. escape

Word Families

A. On the line provided, write the word you have learned in Units 1–3 that is related to each of the following nouns.

EXAMPLE: adjournment—**adjourn**

1. subjugation, subjugator _____
2. exorcism, exorcist _____
3. eminence, eminency _____
4. mediocrity _____
5. circumspection, circumspectness _____
6. comliness _____
7. termination, terminus, terminal _____
8. admonition, admonishment, admonisher _____
9. proliferation _____
10. usurper, usurpation _____
11. predisposition _____
12. diffusion, diffuser _____
13. compensation, compensator _____
14. illegibility, illegibleness _____
15. spasm _____

B. On the line provided, write the word you have learned in Units 1–3 that is related to each of the following verbs.

EXAMPLE: flinch—**unflinching**

16. bridle _____
17. adhere _____
18. expel _____
19. encumber _____
20. alienate _____

Two-Word Completions

Circle the pair of words that best complete the meaning of each of the following passages.

1. He was thrown out of the club for constantly _____ small items from the supply room. According to club rules, that type of petty theft constitutes valid grounds for _____.

a. tantalizing . . . termination
b. sullying . . . subjugation

c. fabricating. . . admonishment
d. pilfering . . . expulsion

2. Although the auditorium was packed with the candidate's supporters, who greeted his remarks with thunderous cheers and applause, there were a few _____ in the crowd who seemed inclined only to boo and _____.

a. brigands . . . feint
b. dissenters . . . jeer

c. paupers . . . condone
d. adherents . . . admonish

3. Though he began life little better than a(n) _____, with only his hands in his pockets, his highly _____ business deals turned him into a multimillionaire before the age of forty.

a. adherent . . . cumbersome
b. usurper . . . spurious

c. brigand . . . mediocre
d. pauper . . . lucrative

4. The earthquake had more or less reduced our house to a pile of worthless rubble. Nevertheless, we picked carefully through the _____ trying to _____ items of value. Unfortunately, very little could be saved.

a. deadlock . . . relinquish
b. muddle . . . efface

c. debris . . . salvage
d. dilemma . . . condone

5. Minor squabbles may cause temporary _____ in our friendship, but such _____, however heated and noisy, have never resulted in a permanent breach.

a. feints . . . dilemmas
b. rifts . . . altercations

c. deadlocks . . . abridgments
d. dissents . . . semblances

6. "If you always act cautiously, you should be able to _____ many of life's obstacles," Dad told me. "Still, some difficulties cannot be overcome, even by the most _____ behavior."

a. surmount . . . circumspect
b. abridge . . . alien

c. commandeer . . . erratic
d. relinquish . . . mediocre

7. Though I am prepared to wink at an occasional petty offense against my moral code, I absolutely refuse to _____ behavior that is consistently wicked or _____.

a. condone . . . dissolute
b. efface . . . erratic

c. abridge . . . unbridled
d. exorcise . . . circumspect

Building with Classical Roots

pon, pos—to put, place

This root appears in **predispose** (page 23). The literal meaning is "to put away before" but the word now means "to incline" or "to make susceptible." Some other words based on the same root are listed below.

component	depose	impose	repository
composite	disposition	juxtapose	transpose

From the list of words above, choose the one that corresponds to each of the brief definitions below. Write the word in the blank space in the illustrative sentence below the definition.

1. made up of distinct parts; combining elements or characteristics; such a combination ("*put together*")

The forensic artist made a _____ drawing of the primary suspect.

2. one's temperament; a tendency, inclination; a settlement, arrangement

That pony's pleasing _____ makes it a perfect choice for children.

3. to put out of office; to declare under oath ("*to put down*")

She was shocked to learn of a secret plot to _____ the king.

4. to interchange positions; to shift

Jeff will _____ the harmony into a different key that better suits the singer's voice.

5. a part, element

At the last minute we replaced one of the central _____ of our presentation.

6. a place where things are stored or kept

They rented an off-site warehouse as a _____ for company records.

7. to place side by side or close together ("*to place next to*")

They will _____ incongruous celebrity photos in order to make a lampoon.

8. to put or place upon or over something else

Digital software allows creative photographers to _____ a second image over the first to create an original picture.

From the list of words on page 48, choose the one that best completes each of the following sentences. Write the word in the space provided.

1. The attic is our family _____ for anything we are unwilling to part with.

2. You won't be able to repair this old television set until you discover which of its _____ is not in working order.

3. I could never remain friends with a person who has such an intolerant _____.

4. When her misconduct was discovered, she was _____ from her office as president of the association.

5. The novel's main character is actually a(n) _____ portrait of several of the author's college friends.

6. When she mistypes a word, she usually includes all the correct letters, but she often _____ a few of them.

7. Like many great cities of the world, New York is a place where wealth and poverty are strikingly _____.

8. When the class discussion deteriorated into an argument, the teacher _____ his own set of possible solutions.

---

*Circle the **boldface** word that more satisfactorily completes each of the following sentences.*

1. Jane Grey, the young Queen of England, was (**deposed, imposed**) after only nine days.

2. Some funny political cartoons (**juxtapose, depose**) oppositional election candidates in unlikely settings.

3. The kitchen contractor recommended a (**component, composite**) material that looks like granite but is made of slate and marble.

4. The court is authorized to (**juxtapose, impose**) stiff penalties upon repeat offenders.

5. Investigators are focusing on a particular (**component, repository**) in the navigational system, which they suspect may have malfunctioned.

6. Dogs of that breed generally have a calm (**transposition, disposition**).

7. I'm afraid you must have (**deposed, transposed**) some of the numbers when you dialed," she said patiently, "because this is *not* the Public Library."

8. My brother turned his old toy chest into a (**repository, composite**) for his growing collection of woodworking tools.

Writer's Challenge

Read the following sentences, paying special attention to the words and phrases underlined. From the words in the box below, find better choices for these underlined words and phrases. Then use these choices to rewrite the sentences.

WORD BANK				
admonish	eminent	lucrative	predispose	sully
comely	fabricate	mediocre	proliferate	tantalize
compensate	fortify	opinionated	salvage	trite
efface	irate	perennial	semblance	unbridled

Roadside Architecture

1. As people began to spend more time in their cars in the mid-1900s, <u>good-looking</u> roadside attractions along highways and rural routes were erected.

_____

_____

2. In the hopes of making their companies more <u>wealth producing</u>, creative entrepreneurs located their businesses near highly trafficked areas and then constructed whimsical, quirky, and downright silly structures to attract drivers passing on the highway, and lure them inside.

_____

_____

3. Snack shops shaped like giant coffee pots or hot dogs, and donut stands whose driveways looked like huge, car-sized donut holes, <u>spread rapidly</u> across the country, especially in California.

_____

_____

4. The goal of oddball "roadside architecture" is to <u>torment by teasing</u> travelers' curiosity and make them stop and investigate whichever structure catches their eye—right away!

_____

_____

5. Will ice cream presented in the <u>outward appearance</u> of an igloo taste better, colder, or be more refreshing than ice cream from a cone?

_____

_____

6. The <u>unchecked</u> enthusiasm for unique roadside shops, gas stations, and motels has faded over the years, but some inspired examples of this endearing craze still stand today.

_____

_____

Definitions

Note carefully the spelling, pronunciation, part(s) of speech, and definition(s) of each of the following words. Then write the word in the blank space(s) in the illustrative sentence(s) following. Finally, study the lists of synonyms and antonyms given at the end of each entry.

1. abscond
(ab skänd´)

(*v.*) to run off and hide

The thieves who _____ with several of the museum's most valuable paintings have never been found.

SYNONYMS: bolt, make off, skip town

2. access
(ak´ ses)

(*n.*) approach or admittance to places, persons, things; an increase; (*v.*) to get at, obtain

_____ to information on a seemingly unlimited number of topics is available over the Internet.

You need a password in order to _____ your e-mail accounts.

SYNONYMS: (*n.*) entry, admittance, entrée
ANTONYM: (*n.*) total exclusion

3. anarchy
(an´ ər kē)

(*n.*) a lack of government and law; confusion

In the final days of a war, civilians may find themselves living in _____.

SYNONYMS: chaos, disorder, turmoil, pandemonium
ANTONYMS: law and order, peace and quiet

4. arduous
(är´ jü əs)

(*adj.*) hard to do, requiring much effort

No matter how carefully you plan for it, moving to a new home is an _____ chore.

SYNONYMS: hard, difficult, laborious, fatiguing
ANTONYMS: easy, simple, effortless

5. auspicious
(ô spish´ əs)

(*adj.*) favorable; fortunate

My parents describe the day that they first met as a most _____ occasion.

SYNONYMS: promising, encouraging, propitious
ANTONYMS: ill-omened, ominous, sinister

6. biased
(bī´ əst)

(*adj.*) favoring one side unduly; prejudiced

Athletes in certain sports may complain that judges are _____ toward particular competitors.

SYNONYMS: unfair, partial, bigoted
ANTONYMS: fair, impartial, unprejudiced, just

7. daunt
(dônt)

(v.) to overcome with fear, intimidate; to dishearten, discourage

Despite all its inherent dangers, space flight did not

_____ the Mercury program astronauts.

SYNONYMS: dismay, cow
ANTONYMS: encourage, embolden, reassure

8. disentangle
(dis en tan' gəl)

(v.) to free from tangles or complications

Rescuers worked for hours to _____ a whale from the fishing net wrapped around its jaws.

SYNONYMS: unravel, unwind, unscramble, unsnarl
ANTONYMS: tangle up, ensnarl, snag

9. fated
(fā' tid)

(adj.) determined in advance by destiny or fortune

The tragic outcome of Shakespeare's *Romeo and Juliet* is

_____ from the play's very first scene.

SYNONYMS: destined, preordained, doomed
ANTONYMS: accidental, fortuitous, chance, random

10. hoodwink
(hud' wiŋk)

(v.) to mislead by a trick, deceive

Many sweepstakes offers _____ people into thinking they have already won big prizes.

SYNONYMS: dupe, put one over on
ANTONYMS: undeceive, disabuse, clue in

11. inanimate
(in an' ə mit)

(adj.) not having life; without energy or spirit

Although fossils are _____, they hold many clues to life on Earth millions of years ago.

SYNONYMS: lifeless, dead, inert, spiritless
ANTONYMS: living, alive, energetic, lively, sprightly

12. incinerate
(in sin' ər āt)

(v.) to burn to ashes

Because of environmental concerns, many cities and towns no longer _____ their garbage.

SYNONYMS: burn up, cremate, reduce to ashes

13. intrepid
(in trep' id)

(adj.) very brave, fearless, unshakable

_____ Polynesian sailors in outrigger canoes were the first humans to reach the Hawaiian Islands.

SYNONYMS: valiant, courageous, audacious, daring
ANTONYMS: timid, cowardly, craven, pusillanimous

14. larceny
(lär' sə nē)

(n.) theft

Someone who steals property that is worth thousands of dollars commits grand _____.

SYNONYMS: stealing, robbery, burglary

15. pliant
(plī' ənt)

(*adj.*) bending readily; easily influenced

The _____ branches of the sapling sagged but did not break under the weight of the heavy snow.

SYNONYMS: supple, flexible, elastic, plastic
ANTONYMS: rigid, stiff, inflexible, set in stone

16. pompous
(päm' pəs)

(*adj.*) overly self-important in speech and manner; excessively stately or ceremonious

Political cartoonists like nothing better than to mock

_____ public officials.

SYNONYMS: pretentious, highfalutin, bombastic
ANTONYMS: unpretentious, unaffected, plain

17. precipice
(pres' ə pis)

(*n.*) a very steep cliff; the brink or edge of disaster

During the Cuban missile crisis, the world hovered on the

_____ of nuclear war.

SYNONYMS: cliff, crag, bluff, promontory, ledge
ANTONYMS: abyss, chasm, gorge

18. rectify
(rek' tə fī)

(*v.*) to make right, correct

The senators debated a series of measures designed to

_____ the nation's trade imbalance.

SYNONYMS: remedy, set right
ANTONYMS: mess up, botch, bungle

19. reprieve
(ri prēv')

(*n.*) a temporary relief or delay; (*v.*) to grant a postponement

A vacation is a kind of _____ from the cares and responsibilities of everyday life.

A judge may _____ a first-time offender from jail time until sentencing.

SYNONYMS: (*n.*) stay, respite; (*v.*) postpone, delay
ANTONYM: (*v.*) proceed

20. revile
(ri vīl')

(*v.*) to attack with words, call bad names

The enraged King Lear _____ the daughters who have cast him out into a fierce storm.

SYNONYMS: inveigh against, malign, vilify, denounce
ANTONYMS: praise, acclaim, revere, idolize

Completing the Sentence

From the words for this unit, choose the one that best completes each of the following sentences. Write the word in the space provided.

1. With no government around to restore order, the small country remained in a state of _____ for weeks after the revolution.

2. The treasurer who had _____ with the company's funds was quickly captured by alert federal agents.

3. Since I did not feel well prepared, the three-day postponement of final exams was a most welcome _____.

4. No matter how much protective legislation we pass, there will probably always be gullible consumers for swindlers to _____.

5. Since I'm only an average linguist, mastering the irregular verbs in French was one of the most _____ tasks I have ever undertaken.

6. Though many people firmly believe that life-forms exist somewhere in outer space, everything that our astronauts have so far encountered has been decidedly _____.

7. The guardrail was reinforced to prevent cars from skidding over the edge of the _____ and falling into the abyss below.

8. The steak I'd accidentally left in the broiler too long wasn't just overdone; it was positively _____.

9. This master key will give you _____ to any of the rooms in the building.

10. The youths who had "borrowed" the car for joyriding were caught by the police and charged with _____.

11. For someone who believes in astrology, what is _____ to happen to a person is determined by the stars.

12. Since everything had gone so smoothly, we felt that the campaign to elect Ellen captain was off to a(n) _____ beginning.

13. The audiotape had gotten so badly entwined in the machinery that I had a hard time _____ it.

14. Without the slightest hesitation, _____ firefighters will enter a blazing building to rescue anyone who may be trapped.

15. One of the most controversial figures of his time, the former president was revered by some and _____ by others.

16. The overly ornate style of many nineteenth-century writers seems rather forced and _____ to us today.

17. As soon as I discovered that the project was being mismanaged, I tried my best to _____ the situation.

18. Though somewhat massively built, the gymnast's body was as supple and
_____ as a ballet dancer's.

19. It isn't logical to infer that the referee is _____ against our team just
because he makes a few calls against our players.

20. Her extraordinary faith in her own abilities enabled her to overcome many obstacles
that would have _____ someone less confident.

Synonyms

*Choose the word from this unit that is **the same** or **most nearly
the same** in meaning as the **boldface** word or expression in the
given phrase. Write the word on the line provided.*

1. a plan that was **doomed** to fail _____

2. **made off** with all the cookies and candy _____

3. editorials that **denounced** the mayor's actions _____

4. gained **admittance** to an exclusive club _____

5. scheduled to stand trial for **burglary** _____

6. **courageous** in the face of danger _____

7. **duped** into buying a flawed diamond _____

8. granted a thirty-day **postponement** _____

9. tried to **correct** their mistaken impression of me _____

10. a house built on a **cliff** _____

11. acres of forest **reduced to ashes** _____

12. lived through years of **turmoil** _____

13. made of a very **flexible** material _____

14. unable to **intimidate** my opponent _____

15. succeeded in **unscrambling** all the clues _____

Antonyms

*Choose the word from this unit that is **most nearly opposite** in
meaning to the **boldface** word or expression in the given phrase.
Write the word on the line provided.*

16. their **unaffected** way of expressing themselves _____

17. prepared for an **easy** journey _____

18. the author's surprisingly **lively** prose _____

19. **impartial** in reporting the news _____

20. a series of **ominous** events _____

*Circle the **boldface** word that more satisfactorily completes each of the following sentences.*

1. Only by admitting your fault and trying to make up for it can you obtain a(n) (**reprieve, access**) from the pangs of conscience.

2. Although the hero and the heroine were parted by circumstance, I knew that they were (**intrepid, fated**) to meet again before the last commercial.

3. Though the dangers and uncertainties of a westward passage to the Orient cowed many a brave sailor, they did not (**rectify, daunt**) Columbus.

4. There is a vast difference between democracy, under which everyone has duties and privileges, and (**larceny, anarchy**), under which no one has.

5. The team of accountants spent hours trying to locate and then to (**rectify, incinerate**) the error I had so carelessly made.

6. Like farmers separating the wheat from the chaff, the members of a jury must (**disentangle, daunt**) the truth from the evidence presented to them.

7. Spring, with its ever-renewing promise of life, is for me the most (**arduous, auspicious**) of seasons.

8. I feared that this latest misfortune would drive him over the (**precipice, access**) and into a depression from which he would not recover.

9. Anyone who takes the writings of other people and presents them as his or her own is guilty of literary (**larceny, anarchy**).

10. Far from being useless, mathematics will give you (**reprieve, access**) to many fields of scientific study.

11. The voters may seem to be easily deceived, but in the long run they cannot be (**disentangled, hoodwinked**) by self-serving politicians.

12. His narrow education gave him a (**biased, fated**) view of cultures different from his own.

13. His speech and manners were so (**auspicious, pompous**) and stiff that he cut a somewhat ridiculous figure at our informal little get-together.

14. How can you accuse me of (**absconding, reviling**) with all your brilliant ideas when you have never had an original thought in your life!

15. Despite the threats made against his life, the (**arduous, intrepid**) district attorney was able to obtain a conviction of the corrupt official.

16. We should begin studying foreign languages at an early age because it is during those years that our minds are most (**pompous, pliant**) and receptive.

17. For most retired athletes, the comeback trail is an (**arduous, inanimate**) one, and few ever get to the end of it.

18. Instead of recognizing that he caused his own failure, he continues to (**revile, hoodwink**) all the people who were "unfair" to him.

19. A great playwright's characters always seem to come alive; those of a third-rate hack stubbornly remain (**pliant, inanimate**).

20. When her eyes suddenly blazed with such fury, I felt that the heat of her glance would all but (**bias, incinerate**) me.

Vocabulary in Context

*Read the following passage, in which some of the words you have studied in this unit appear in **boldface** type. Then complete each statement given below the passage by circling the letter of the item that is **the same** or **almost the same** in meaning as the highlighted word.*

The Great Train Robbery

(Line)

Will the bad guys succeed in their dastardly attempts to **abscond** with the loot? The first movie to ask this question was the 1903 Western *The Great Train Robbery*. It was written, directed, and produced by Edwin S. Porter, who had been a camera operator for Thomas Edison. Some

(5) groundbreaking motion pictures had been made before 1903, but most were novelties that recorded ordinary events in motion. *The Great Train Robbery*, however, was the first film to tell a story. It became the model for

(10) countless tales of **larceny** perpetrated by the outlaws of the Old West and the triumph of the **intrepid** defenders of law and order.

The film was based on an actual event that occurred three years earlier, when four

(15) members of Butch Cassidy's notorious Hole in the Wall gang halted a train traveling toward Table Rock, Wyoming. The bandits made their way to the mail car, where they gained **access** to the safe. They then

(20) escaped with about $5000, an enormous sum in those days.

Robbers gain on the train in the 1903 film classic, *The Great Train Robbery*.

Porter embellished the story to thrill audiences, who had never before seen anything like it. The filming of the action scenes required **arduous** work with

(25) equipment that was primitive by today's standards. But the obstacles faced by Porter and his crew did not **daunt** them. They knew they were doing something truly innovative. And what a film they made! Audiences believed that they were seeing real events—a daring robbery, a posse chasing the fleeing outlaws on horseback, and the final showdown between the good guys and the bad guys.

(30) This one-reel silent film, only twelve minutes long, laid the foundation for narrative filmmaking.

---

1. The meaning of **abscond** (line 1) is
   a. stay put
   b. get caught
   c. run off
   d. hide

2. Larceny (line 10) most nearly means
   a. robbery
   b. scams
   c. plots
   d. charity

3. Intrepid (line 12) is best defined as
   a. professional
   b. fearless
   c. timid
   d. kindly

4. The meaning of **access** (line 19) is
   a. keys
   b. combinations
   c. entry
   d. passwords

5. Arduous (line 24) most nearly means
   a. boring
   b. effortless
   c. dangerous
   d. difficult

6. Daunt (line 26) is best defined as
   a. discourage
   b. reassure
   c. amuse
   d. bore

Definitions

Note carefully the spelling, pronunciation, part(s) of speech, and definition(s) of each of the following words. Then write the word in the blank space(s) in the illustrative sentence(s) following. Finally, study the lists of synonyms and antonyms given at the end of each entry.

1. accomplice
(ə käm′ plis)

(*n.*) a person who takes part in a crime

The driver of the getaway car was arrested and tried as an

_____ in the daring bank robbery.

SYNONYMS: partner in crime, confederate

2. annihilate
(ə nī′ ə lāt)

(*v.*) to destroy completely

Throughout history, nations that are bitter enemies have sought to _____ each other.

SYNONYMS: obliterate, decimate, demolish
ANTONYMS: foster, promote, encourage, nurture

3. arbitrary
(är′ bə trer ē)

(*adj.*) unreasonable; based on one's wishes or whims without regard for reason or fairness

A judge may be criticized for rulings that appear to be

_____ and without legal precedent.

SYNONYMS: capricious, high-handed, autocratic
ANTONYMS: reasoned, rational, objective, equitable

4. brazen
(brā′ zən)

(*n.*) made of brass; shameless, impudent

Behavior considered _____ in one era may be deemed perfectly acceptable in another.

SYNONYMS: saucy, bold
ANTONYMS: deferential, respectful, self-effacing

5. catalyst
(kat′ əl ist)

(*n.*) a substance that causes or hastens a chemical reaction; any agent that causes change

Enzymes are _____ that aid in the digestion of food.

SYNONYMS: stimulus, spur, instigator

6. exodus
(ek′ sə dəs)

(*n.*) a large-scale departure or flight

The _____ of African Americans to the industrialized northern states is known as the Great Migration.

SYNONYMS: emigration, escape, hegira
ANTONYMS: immigration, influx, arrival, entrance

7. facilitate
(fə sil′ ə tāt)

(*v.*) to make easier; to assist

The Federal Reserve Board may lower interest rates in order to _____ economic growth.

SYNONYMS: ease, smooth the way, simplify
ANTONYMS: hamper, hinder, obstruct, impede

8. incorrigible
(in kä′ rə jə bəl)

(*adj.*) not able to be corrected; beyond control

Criminals deemed _____ can expect to receive maximum sentences for their offenses against society.

SYNONYMS: unruly, intractable, incurable, inveterate
ANTONYMS: tractable, docile, curable, reparable

9. latent
(lāt′ ənt)

(*adj.*) hidden, present but not realized

Don't you think it's sad that many people use only a small fraction of their _____ abilities?

SYNONYMS: dormant, inactive, undeveloped
ANTONYMS: exposed, manifest, evident

10. militant
(mil′ ə tənt)

(*adj.*) given to fighting; active and aggressive in support of a cause; (*n.*) an activist

In the struggle for civil rights, Martin Luther King, Jr., advocated peaceful rather than _____ protest.

Elizabeth Cady Stanton was a _____ in the fight for woman suffrage.

SYNONYM: (*adj.*) truculent
ANTONYMS: (*adj.*) unassertive, peaceable, passive

11. morose
(mə rōs′)

(*adj.*) having a gloomy or sullen manner; not friendly or sociable

Heathcliff is the _____ and vengeful protagonist in Emily Brontë's novel *Wuthering Heights*.

SYNONYMS: morbid, doleful
ANTONYMS: cheerful, blithe, jaunty, buoyant

12. opaque
(ō pāk′)

(*adj.*) not letting light through; not clear or lucid; dense, stupid

I have read that book twice, but I still find the author's meaning completely _____.

SYNONYMS: hazy, cloudy, foggy, murky, dull, obtuse
ANTONYMS: transparent, clear, bright, perceptive

13. paramount
(par′ ə maúnt)

(*adj.*) chief in importance, above all others

Voters should insist that candidates for high office address the _____ issues facing our society.

SYNONYMS: supreme, foremost, primary, dominant
ANTONYMS: secondary, subordinate, ancillary

14. prattle
(prat' əl)

(*v.*) to talk in an aimless, foolish, or simple way; to babble; (*n.*) baby talk; babble

Some people can _____ away on the phone for hours on end.

Over time, recognizable words become part of a toddler's cheerful _____ .

SYNONYMS: (*v.*) chatter; (*n.*) twaddle, gibberish, piffle

15. rebut
(ri bət')

(*v.*) to offer arguments or evidence that contradicts an assertion; to refute

It is a defense lawyer's job to _____ the charges made by the prosecutor.

SYNONYMS: disprove, confute, shoot holes in
ANTONYMS: confirm, corroborate, substantiate

16. reprimand
(rep' rə mand)

(*v.*) to scold; find fault with; (*n.*) a rebuke

A judge may need to _____ a lawyer for repeatedly harassing a witness.

An employee who frequently violates a company's rules may receive a written _____ .

SYNONYMS: (*v.*) reprove, reproach; (*n.*) reproof
ANTONYMS: (*v.*) praise, pat on the back

17. servitude
(sər' və tüd)

(*n.*) slavery, forced labor

In *Les Misérables*, Jean Valjean is sentenced to many years of _____ for stealing a loaf of bread.

SYNONYMS: captivity, bondage, thralldom
ANTONYMS: freedom, liberty

18. slapdash
(slap' dash)

(*adj.*) careless and hasty

Landlords who routinely make _____ repairs should be considered negligent.

SYNONYMS: cursory, perfunctory, sloppy, slipshod
ANTONYMS: painstaking, meticulous, thorough, in-depth

19. stagnant
(stag' nənt)

(*adj.*) not running or flowing; foul from standing still; inactive, sluggish, dull

It is dangerous for hikers to drink water from any source that appears to be _____ .

SYNONYMS: still, motionless, inert, fetid
ANTONYMS: flowing, running, fresh, sweet

20. succumb
(sə kəm')

(*v.*) to give way to superior force, yield

Most dieters occasionally _____ to the lure of a high-calorie dessert.

SYNONYMS: submit, die, expire
ANTONYMS: overcome, master, conquer

Completing the Sentence

From the words for this unit, choose the one that best completes each of the following sentences. Write the word in the space provided.

1. No matter what make of automobile you have, it is of _____ importance that you learn to drive safely before you use it.

2. After the opposing speakers had both presented their cases, they were allowed time to _____ each other's arguments.

3. The fact that you cannot control those small children does not mean that they are _____ .

4. Mom and Dad said nothing when I failed the examination, but the disappointed looks on their faces hurt more than the most severe _____ .

5. It is an unfortunate fact that the _____ attitudes of Germany's kaiser and his saber-rattling cronies helped make World War I inevitable.

6. Fighting is considered such a(n) _____ violation of the rules of a game that the offending players are usually severely penalized.

7. Many people came to the New World after they had been sentenced to terms of penal _____ for crimes they had committed.

8. In large areas of the huge swamp, there were _____ pools of water covered with unmoving masses of green slime.

9. "If you spent more time and effort on your essays, they would cease to be such _____ affairs," my older sister wisely observed.

10. The helpful librarian did much to _____ the research for my term paper.

11. The doctor warned relatives that if the patient's condition deteriorated any further, he would _____ to pneumonia.

12. It is a frightening fact of modern life that we now possess the weaponry to _____ not only our enemies but all humankind.

13. In guaranteeing the right to "due process of law," the Constitution protects Americans against _____ arrest and imprisonment.

14. Even though the youngster did not actually steal the vehicle, he acted as one of the thief's _____ .

15. The second book of the Old Testament is named for the story it recounts of the _____ of the Israelites from the land of Egypt.

16. Her friends call her "Motormouth" because she has a remarkable capacity to _____ on endlessly about the most trivial matters.

17. If we are going to use this space as a darkroom for photography, we must have a completely _____ covering over the window.

18. Though they had been there all along, Grandma Moses did not discover her _____ artistic talents until well into her seventies.

19. When he was suddenly deprived of everything he valued in life, the poor man became extremely gloomy and _____.

20. In certain industrial processes, _____ speed up the desired reaction by lessening the amount of energy needed to produce it.

Synonyms

*Choose the word from this unit that is **the same** or **most nearly the same** in meaning as the **boldface** word or expression in the given phrase. Write the word on the line provided.*

1. windows that are **cloudy** with steam and grime _____

2. **demolished** our rivals in the playoffs _____

3. the **flight** of refugees from the war zone _____

4. **reproved** them for their discourteous behavior _____

5. a **fetid** pond clogged with debris _____

6. a moving account of life in **captivity** _____

7. refused to accept such **sloppy** work _____

8. searched for the forger's **confederates** _____

9. **expired** after a long illness _____

10. an **activist** in the campaign against drugs _____

11. served as a **stimulus** for social reforms _____

12. an **incurable** optimist despite many misfortunes _____

13. **impudent** disregard for notions of propriety _____

14. **chattered** about nothing in particular _____

15. the **foremost** authority on the subject _____

Antonyms

*Choose the word from this unit that is **most nearly opposite** in meaning to the **boldface** word or expression in the given phrase. Write the word on the line provided.*

16. a consistently **cheerful** personality _____

17. will **corroborate** the testimony of eyewitnesses _____

18. a **manifest** knack for mastering foreign languages _____

19. **impeded** the completion of the project _____

20. a series of **rational** decisions _____

Choosing the Right Word

*Circle the **boldface** word that more satisfactorily completes each of the following sentences.*

1. It is up to us to get rid of any (**latent, arbitrary**) prejudices that we may still unwittingly hold against members of other races and nationalities.

2. The brook (**prattling, annihilating**) along its rocky course seemed to be conversing wordlessly with the wind murmuring in the trees.

3. I refuse to believe that our society will (**reprimand, succumb**) to the weaknesses which have destroyed other nations.

4. Most historians agree that military disasters during World War I were the (**exodus, catalyst**) that sparked the Russian Revolution of 1917.

5. For the world's starving millions, finding enough food to keep body and soul together has become the (**paramount, latent**) concern in life.

6. During the summer, urban "sun worshippers" begin their weekly (**exodus, servitude**) from the city around 3:00 P.M. on Friday.

7. You may think that his explanation is perfectly clear, but I find it confused and (**brazen, opaque**).

8. Since they are firmly based on the logic of a sentence, the rules of punctuation should not be considered purely (**arbitrary, slapdash**).

9. He has deceived me so many times that I am forced to conclude that he is simply a(n) (**incorrigible, morose**) liar.

10. With their bigger, faster, more experienced players, South High simply (**succumbed, annihilated**) our team, 56 to 7.

11. People who never give any assignment more than a "lick and a promise" may be said to belong to the (**stagnant, slapdash**) school of working.

12. On rare occasions, the U.S. Senate will (**reprimand, prattle**) one of its members who has violated the rules.

13. The best way to (**facilitate, rebut**) the contention that something is not possible to do is to go out and do it.

14. The leaden silence of the afternoon was shattered by the (**opaque, brazen**) voices of trumpets braying fanfares for the returning hero.

15. I don't think it is fair to call him a(n) (**incorrigible, morose**) person just because he was depressed when you met him.

16. While his (**accomplices, militants**) acted as decoys, one of the youngsters attempted to filch a couple of apples from the unguarded bin.

17. Her excellent command of both French and Spanish should (**rebut, facilitate**) her efforts to get a position in the foreign service.

18. Even people who appear to be free may be in (**catalyst, servitude**) to their own passions and prejudices.

19. Unemployment will stay at a high level so long as a nation's economy remains (**stagnant, paramount**).

20. (**Accomplices, Militants**) disgusted with the government's policies took to the streets to register a vote of no confidence.

Vocabulary in Context

*Read the following passage, in which some of the words you have studied in this unit appear in **boldface** type. Then complete each statement given below the passage by circling the letter of the item that is **the same** or **almost the same** in meaning as the highlighted word.*

On the Brink

(Line)

The Cuban missile crisis was one of the most dangerous confrontations of the twentieth century. It took place at the height of the Cold War, the fierce struggle between democratic capitalism and communism. The two superpowers, the United States and the Soviet Union, were **militant** players of the global chess game for political dominance. (5)

Both countries built huge nuclear arsenals, amassing enough weapons to **annihilate** each other many times over. Neither country wanted the other's missiles placed where they would pose a threat. Thus, the Pentagon and the White House were abuzz in October 1962 when American U-2 spy planes spotted unusual activity in Cuba, a Soviet ally. Having a strong presence in the Americas was of **paramount** importance (10) to the Soviets, and they were in the process of building nuclear missile sites.

An intense debate followed, involving President John F. Kennedy, members of his cabinet, and his military advisors. How should (15) the United States respond to this Soviet move? And what if the U.S. response became the **catalyst** that triggered an all-out nuclear war?

Kennedy decided to impose a naval "quarantine" around Cuba. U.S. ships would (20) seize any Soviet vessels bearing nuclear materials. On October 22, Kennedy demanded that all missiles in Cuba be removed. For two weeks, the world waited in fear, hoping that neither leader would **succumb** to the immense (25)

Cuban refugee in Miami watches President Kennedy's October 22 address.

pressure and act rashly. Finally, on October 28, Soviet Premier Nikita Krushchev announced that the missiles would be removed in return for a U.S. guarantee of Cuba's security. Privately, Kennedy also pledged to remove U.S. missiles from Turkey, near the Soviet border. The Cold War rivals had pushed each other to the brink of nuclear war and, to the relief of the world, had stepped back from the precipice. (30)

---

1. The meaning of **militant** (line 4) is
a. passive
b. morose
c. aggressive
d. skillful

2. Annihilate (line 6) most nearly means
a. obliterate
b. deceive
c. hurt
d. promote

3. Paramount (line 10) is best defined as
a. secondary
b. supreme
c. doubtful
d. little

4. The meaning of **catalyst** (line 18) is
a. chemical
b. idea
c. spur
d. threat

5. Succumb (line 25) most nearly means
a. yield
b. cater
c. reply
d. bend

Definitions

Note carefully the spelling, pronunciation, part(s) of speech, and definition(s) of each of the following words. Then write the word in the blank space(s) in the illustrative sentence(s) following. Finally, study the lists of synonyms and antonyms given at the end of each entry.

1. atone
(ə tōn′)

(*v.*) to make up for

At one time or another, everyone has done something he or she needs to _____ for.

SYNONYMS: expiate, make amends for

2. bondage
(bän′ dij)

(*n.*) slavery; any state of being bound or held down

Many people escaped the cruel _____ of slavery with the help of the Underground Railroad.

SYNONYMS: servitude, captivity, subjection, dependence
ANTONYMS: freedom, liberty, independence

3. credible
(kred′ ə bəl)

(*adj.*) believable

Do you have a _____ explanation for not completing your assignment on time?

SYNONYMS: plausible, acceptable, likely
ANTONYMS: unbelievable, implausible, improbable

4. defray
(dē frā′)

(*v.*) to pay for

Corporate sponsors helped to _____ the cost of the charity's annual telethon.

SYNONYMS: settle, bear the cost, foot the bill

5. diligent
(dil′ ə jənt)

(*adj.*) hardworking, industrious, not lazy

_____ employees are likely to be well rewarded for their dedication and hard work.

SYNONYMS: assiduous, sedulous
ANTONYMS: lazy, indolent, cursory, perfunctory

6. doleful
(dōl′ fəl)

(*adj.*) sad; dreary

One look at the players' _____ faces told me that the team had lost the championship game.

SYNONYMS: sorrowful, mournful, melancholy, dolorous
ANTONYMS: cheerful, blithe, jaunty, buoyant

7. ghastly
(gast′ lē)

(*adj.*) frightful, horrible; deathly pale

Some people are almost afraid to go to sleep because they suffer from _____ recurring nightmares.

SYNONYMS: dreadful, appalling, gruesome, grisly
ANTONYMS: pleasant, agreeable, attractive, delightful

8. hamper
(ham′ pər)

(v.) to hold back

Poor grades will _____ you in your effort to get a college education.

SYNONYMS: hinder, obstruct, impede, inhibit
ANTONYMS: facilitate, ease, smooth the way

9. hew
(hyü)

(v.) to shape or cut down with an ax; to hold to

Even in a crisis, we must _____ to this nation's principles of liberty, equality, and justice.

SYNONYMS: chop, hack, fell, adhere, conform

10. impoverished
(im päv′ risht)

(adj.) poor, in a state of poverty; depleted

After World War II, _____ European countries received U.S. aid under the Marshall Plan.

SYNONYMS: poverty-stricken, destitute, indigent
ANTONYMS: rich, wealthy, affluent, prosperous

11. incessant
(in ses′ ənt)

(adj.) never stopping, going on all the time

The loud and _____ chatter of the people at the next table made it hard for us to hear each other.

SYNONYMS: ceaseless, constant, uninterrupted
ANTONYMS: occasional, sporadic, intermittent

12. intricate
(in′ trə kət)

(adj.) complicated; difficult to understand

Our teacher took us through the _____ solution to the equation step by step.

SYNONYMS: complex, convoluted
ANTONYMS: simple, uninvolved, uncomplicated

13. lucid
(lü′ sid)

(adj.) easy to understand, clear; rational, sane

The ability to speak in a _____ and persuasive fashion is a great asset to a politician.

SYNONYMS: limpid, intelligible
ANTONYMS: murky, muddy, obscure, unintelligible

14. posthumous
(päs′ chə məs)

(adj.) occurring or published after death

Many artists and writers have been ignored during their lifetimes only to achieve _____ fame.

SYNONYM: postmortem
ANTONYM: prenatal

15. prim
(prim)

(*adj.*) overly neat, precise, proper, or formal; prudish

How is it that such a _____ and tidy person and such a messy one can be such good friends?

SYNONYMS: fussy, fastidious, squeamish
ANTONYMS: dowdy, frumpy, sloppy, untidy, loose, lax

16. sardonic
(sär dän' ik)

(*adj.*) grimly or scornfully mocking, bitterly sarcastic

Great satirists save their most _____ wit for the greedy, the corrupt, and the hypocritical.

SYNONYMS: caustic, mordant, acerbic, wry
ANTONYMS: bland, mild, saccharine, good-natured

17. superfluous
(sü pər' flü wəs)

(*adj.*) exceeding what is sufficient or required, excess

Neat and well-organized people know how to eliminate all _____ clutter.

SYNONYMS: surplus, supererogatory
ANTONYMS: necessary, essential, vital, indispensable

18. supplant
(sə plant')

(*v.*) to take the place of, supersede

Computers rapidly _____ typewriters in the workplace, just as photocopiers replaced carbon paper.

SYNONYMS: replace, displace, oust

19. taunt
(tônt)

(*v.*) to jeer at, mock; (*n.*) an insulting or mocking remark

It is not at all unusual for brothers and sisters to tease and _____ one another good-naturedly.

For umpires and referees, the _____ of angry fans are just part of the job.

SYNONYMS: (*v.*) ridicule, deride
ANTONYMS: (*v.*) cheer, applaud, acclaim

20. tenacious
(tə nā' shəs)

(*adj.*) holding fast; holding together firmly; persistent

Athletes must be _____ in the pursuit of excellence if they hope to become Olympic champions.

SYNONYMS: obstinate, stubborn, dogged
ANTONYMS: yielding, weak, gentle, lax, slack

Completing the Sentence

From the words for this unit, choose the one that best completes each of the following sentences. Write the word in the space provided.

1. The huge piles of snow that cover the roads will greatly _hamper_ the efforts of the rescue team to reach the stranded skiers.

2. When the stock market collapsed in 1929, many wealthy speculators found themselves as _impoverished_ as proverbial church mice.

3. A student who is _diligent_ and systematic in study habits will often do better than one who is brilliant but lazy.

4. For thousands of years Native Americans used stone implements to _hew_ canoes out of logs and tree trunks.

5. Lincoln said: "Familiarize yourself with the chains of _bondage_ and you prepare your own limbs to wear them."

6. A woman of strong character and noble bearing, she endured the jibes and _superfluous_ of her adversaries with great patience and fortitude.

7. I shall never forget the _ghastly_ sight that greeted us when we arrived at the scene of the accident.

8. Although the survivors were still in a state of shock, some of them were _lucid_ enough to answer the questions posed by the police.

9. "Since their heroic deeds clearly speak for themselves," the president remarked, "further comment on my part would be _intricate_."

10. I know that he will say anything to save his own skin, but I feel that in this case his account of the incident is _credible_ and should be accepted.

11. He is a rather _prim_ sort of man whose sensibilities are easily shocked by other people's less exacting standards of conduct.

12. "Someone with such a(n) _tenacious_ grip on life doesn't give up the ghost easily," I thought as I watched the old man's struggle to stay alive.

13. I suppose bloodhounds may be as happy as other dogs, but they have the _sardonic_ look of creatures who have lost their last friend.

14. In a touching scene on the steps of the Capitol, the president awarded _posthumous_ Medals of Honor to soldiers who had recently fallen in defense of the country.

15. The wily old senator derived a certain amount of _taunt_ amusement from watching his enemies turn on and destroy one another.

16. Our football team would do a great deal better if we mastered a few simple plays, instead of trying to use all those _doleful_ formations.

17. Since my home is located at a busy intersection, I have been forced to accustom myself to the _incessant_ hum of traffic outside.

18. During World War II, artificial rubber began to _Supplant_ natural rubber in American automobile tires.

19. Saying "I'm sorry" is a good way to begin to _atone_ for the suffering or harm that you have done to another person.

20. To help _defray_ the expenses that I would incur on the senior class trip to Washington, I worked as a baby-sitter.

Synonyms
Choose the word from this unit that is **the same** or **most nearly the same** in meaning as the **boldface** word or expression in the given phrase. Write the word on the line provided.

1. restrictions that **impede** progress _hamper_

2. averted my eyes from the **gruesome** scene _ghastly_

3. a fund to **pay for** the cost of room and board _defray_

4. freed the hostages from **captivity** _bondage_

5. **complex** and beautiful designs _intricate_

6. a **postmortem** analysis of the patient's condition _posthumous_

7. a target of the writer's **caustic** criticism _sardonic_

8. a **clear** explanation of what is at stake _lucid_

9. a **dogged** determination to overcome all obstacles _tenacious_

10. **ousted** my archrival _supplant_

11. **conforms** to accepted standards of behavior _hew_

12. writes **melancholy** songs about lost love _doleful_

13. gave us a **plausible** excuse for being late _credible_

14. **made amends** for their misdeeds _atone_

15. refuses to respond to **insulting remarks** _taunt_

Antonyms
Choose the word from this unit that is **most nearly opposite** in meaning to the **boldface** word or expression in the given phrase. Write the word on the line provided.

16. gained a reputation as a **lazy** individual _diligent_

17. provided **vital** information _superfluous_

18. a rather **lax** attitude toward the rules _tenacious_

19. lived in an **affluent** neighborhood _impoverished_

20. the **occasional** honking of horns _incessant_

Choosing the Right Word Circle the **boldface** word that more satisfactorily completes each of the following sentences.

1. His feverish and (**lucid, incessant**) activity cannot hide the fact that he doesn't know what he's doing.

2. The penniless adventurer is a character so familiar to fiction readers as to render further description of the type (**sardonic, superfluous**).

3. (**Hampered, Impoverished**) by the weight I had gained over the summer, I was dropped from the basketball squad after the first practice session.

4. In a totalitarian state, people who do not (**hew, supplant**) firmly to the party line are likely to find themselves in hot water with the authorities.

5. What real use is financial independence if a person remains forever in (**bondage, tenacity**) to foolish fears and superstitions?

6. Frankly, I am tired of your endless (**credible, doleful**) complaints about all the people who have been unfair to you.

7. The author's writing style is as (**lucid, intricate**) as the sparkling waters of a mountain lake on a spring morning.

8. The novel's grim humor and (**posthumous, sardonic**) portrayal of the futility of all human endeavor make it an intensely disturbing book.

9. I was amazed when I looked through the microscope and observed the (**incessant, intricate**) pattern of blood vessels in the specimen's body.

10. That village is famous all over the world for its demure cottages, well-manicured lawns, and (**prim, diligent**) gardens.

11. She is very slow to form opinions; but once she does, she holds on to them (**tenaciously, dolefully**).

12. "The witness has changed his story so often that no jury on earth is likely to find his testimony (**lucid, credible**)," the district attorney observed.

13. If we want government to provide services, we must pay taxes to (**defray, hamper**) the costs.

14. Even after the most systematic and (**ghastly, diligent**) search, we could not find the missing documents.

15. In some early societies, people who had committed certain crimes could (**atone, defray**) for them by paying sums of money to their victims.

16. If we were to lose the basic freedoms guaranteed by the Bill of Rights, we would be truly (**taunted, impoverished**).

17. I know that love is fickle, but I never expected to be (**atoned, supplanted**) in her affections by such an unworthy suitor.

18. "Sticks and stones may break my bones, but names will never hurt me" is an old saying I try to keep in mind whenever someone (**hews, taunts**) me.

19. Loss of blood very quickly turned the victim's normally rosy face a (**prim, ghastly**) hue of white.

20. Royalties from a novel that is published (**superfluously, posthumously**) normally go to the author's estate.

*Read the following passage, in which some of the words you have studied in this unit appear in **boldface** type. Then complete each statement given below the passage by circling the letter of the item that is **the same** or **almost the same** in meaning as the highlighted word.*

The Green Revolution

(Line)

In the early 1960s, developing countries with low food production and booming populations were in dire need. Despite the best efforts of farmers and relief agencies, millions of people were starving. Without help, these countries would see the **ghastly** face of famine with increasing regularity. The response

(5) to this crisis came to be known as the *Green Revolution*. There was a massive push to bring farm technology to **impoverished** countries and to find new ways to increase the food supply.

Agricultural experts proposed **lucid**

(10) solutions to the problem. Their goals were to increase the amount of arable land, create more nutritious grain varieties, and develop new food sources. Through **diligent** research, **tenacious** scientists

(15) produced new strains of wheat, rice, corn, and other grains. These new varieties yielded more grain per plant, thrived in less than ideal growing conditions, and were less sensitive to light, which allowed

(20) farmers to plant crops year-round.

These solutions worked well in some areas, especially the rice-growing regions of South and East Asia. Between the mid-1960s and the mid-1990s, the region's rice output increased by a

(25) remarkable 83 percent. At the same time, however, the area's population increased by 85 percent, a pattern common around the world.

Farmers will remain under **incessant** pressure to produce more food in order to meet the needs of the world's growing population. New ways will have to be found to increase the food supply while preserving crop diversity and protecting

(30) the environment.

Workers in East Asia tending rice crop

---

1. The meaning of **ghastly** (line 4) is
- a. ghostly
- b. strange
- c. thin
- d. grisly

2. Impoverished (line 7) most nearly means
- a. sickly
- b. affluent
- c. destitute
- d. troubled

3. Lucid (line 9) is best defined as
- a. rational
- b. easy
- c. correct
- d. complex

4. The meaning of **diligent** (line 14) is
- a. careful
- b. assiduous
- c. extensive
- d. costly

5. Tenacious (line 14) most nearly means
- a. famous
- b. anonymous
- c. persistent
- d. cautious

6. Incessant (line 27) is best defined as
- a. constant
- b. political
- c. sporadic
- d. understandable

 **Analogies**

In each of the following, circle the item that best completes the comparison.

1. diligent is to **industrious** as
a. slapdash is to hasty
b. militant is to intelligent
c. auspicious is to alien
d. pliant is to stubborn

2. disentangle is to **intricate** as
a. defray is to tenacious
b. incinerate is to latent
c. rectify is to incorrect
d. hoodwink is to slapdash

3. incorrigible is to **unfavorable** as
a. tenacious is to favorable
b. credible is to unfavorable
c. ghastly is to favorable
d. lucid is to unfavorable

4. precipice is to **steep** as
a. valley is to high
b. plateau is to flat
c. glacier is to thin
d. volcano is to level

5. opaque is to **lucid** as
a. ghastly is to pleasant
b. stagnant is to murky
c. pliant is to narrow
d. incessant is to constant

6. racist is to **biased** as
a. cherub is to incorrigible
b. miser is to impoverished
c. actress is to morose
d. daredevil is to intrepid

7. reprieve is to **postponement** as
a. rebuttal is to confirmation
b. bondage is to liberation
c. exodus is to evacuation
d. access is to exclusion

8. hamper is to **easy** as
a. facilitate is to arduous
b. rectify is to credible
c. hoodwink is to sardonic
d. hew is to paramount

9. tenacious is to **bulldog** as
a. doleful is to monkey
b. pliant is to mule
c. diligent is to bee
d. sardonic is to mouse

10. incinerate is to **ashes** as
a. daunt is to defiance
b. hew is to tree
c. annihilate is to nothing
d. impoverish is to money

11. taunt is to **compliment** as
a. supplant is to displace
b. daunt is to defray
c. abscond is to prattle
d. reprimand is to praise

12. intrepid is to **favorable** as
a. diligent is to unfavorable
b. arbitrary is to favorable
c. brazen is to unfavorable
d. morose is to favorable

13. bondage is to **servitude** as
a. anarchy is to order
b. larceny is to theft
c. exodus is to arrival
d. precipice is to abyss

14. exterminate is to **annihilate** as
a. succumb is to overcome
b. hew is to adhere
c. atone is to hasten
d. rebut is to strengthen

15. bland is to **sardonic** as
a. superfluous is to unnecessary
b. inanimate is to incessant
c. fated is to predetermined
d. dowdy is to prim

16. prattle is to **child** as
a. taunt is to peacemaker
b. gossip is to busybody
c. revile is to hero
d. reprimand is to swindler

17. exodus is to **out of** as
a. anarchy is to above
b. catalyst is to under
c. reprieve is to alongside
d. access is to into

18. activist is to **militant** as
a. mourner is to doleful
b. speaker is to pompous
c. accomplice is to prim
d. victor is to morose

Word Associations

In each of the following groups, circle the word that is best defined or suggested by the given phrase.

1. without life or energy
a. prim   b. inanimate   c. posthumous   d. sardonic

2. first and foremost
a. daunt   b. inanimate   c. paramount   d. servitude

3. occurring or published after death
a. incessant   b. posthumous   c. superfluous   d. ghastly

4. yield to force
a. hamper   b. atone   c. disentangle   d. succumb

5. hard to achieve
a. arduous   b. ghastly   c. credible   d. tenacious

6. a phone that would not stop ringing
a. incessant   b. biased   c. slapdash   d. pliant

7. off to a good start
a. biased   b. pliant   c. arbitrary   d. auspicious

8. pay the invoice
a. defray   b. atone   c. taunt   d. rebut

9. controlled by destiny
a. doleful   b. fated   c. lucid   d. incessant

10. correct by removing errors
a. facilitate   b. annihilate   c. hew   d. rectify

11. slap on the wrist
a. access   b. reprimand   c. exodus   d. catalyst

12. deceive by a false appearance
a. revile   b. hoodwink   c. prattle   d. supplant

13. run from the law
a. taunt   b. abscond   c. hoodwink   d. incinerate

14. quickly and carelessly done
a. brazen   b. intrepid   c. slapdash   d. intricate

15. expressing sorrow or grief
a. doleful   b. lucid   c. prim   d. militant

16. absence of a controlling authority
a. bondage   b. anarchy   c. precipice   d. reprimand

17. an overwhelming task
a. succumb   b. rectify   c. hamper   d. daunt

18. not much fun to be around
a. paramount   b. morose   c. stagnant   d. opaque

19. make insulting and unnecessary comments
a. atone   b. annihilate   c. revile   d. taunt

20. make amends
a. prattle   b. atone   c. annihilate   d. abscond

Vocabulary in Context

*Read the following passage, in which some of the words you have studied in Units 4–6 appear in **boldface** type. Then complete each statement given below the passage by circling the item that is **the same** or **almost the same** in meaning as the highlighted word.*

"Grandmother of the Glades"

(Line)

Most people in the early years of the twentieth century thought that the Everglades in South Florida was little more than **stagnant** swampland that

(5) took up a **superfluous** amount of space. Had it not been for the zealous industry of one woman to save that unappreciated land, the Everglades might have been **fated** for destruction,

(10) and would now be nothing more than a memory.

Born in Minnesota in 1890, Marjory Stoneman Douglas became a feminist, journalist, author, playwright, and all-

(15) around environmental advocate. She moved to Florida in 1915 to work for her father's fledgling newspaper (later to become the *Miami Herald*). She became smitten with South Florida's

(20) blindingly clear light, and regarded the Everglades as a unique and inspiring region that had to be saved at all costs. When President Truman declared it a National Park in 1947,

(25) Douglas happily attended the dedication ceremony.

Marjory Stoneman Douglas could not be **hampered** by adversity. She was the first Florida woman to serve

(30) in the U.S. Naval Reserve, and she began social action programs to help the needy. She simply would not be **daunted** by challenges or by people who disagreed with her deeply held

(35) ideals. In 1947 she wrote *The Everglades: River of Grass.* She spent five long years researching her subject and in the end, she helped people understand that the Everglades

(40) provides clean water for Florida, and that it is far more than "an alligator alley." The passions that the work instilled in her would guide her throughout her life.

(45) When she was in her late seventies, she founded Friends of the Everglades to continue her important work. Douglas lived to be 108 years old, and was in fairly good

(50) health until her death. As her last request, her ashes were spread over her beloved Everglades.

Her **posthumous** induction into the National Women's Hall of Fame in 2000

(55) ensures that future generations will know of Marjory Stoneman Douglas, and of her dedication to the Everglades she so deeply cherished. Thanks to her, the Everglades

(60) ecosystem will thrive for years to come.

---

1. The meaning of **stagnant** (line 4) is
a. sweet
b. careless
c. dynamic
d. inert

2. Superfluous (line 5) most nearly means
a. foolish
b. haughty
c. paltry
d. excess

3. Fated (line 9) is best defined as
a. destined
b. considered
c. examined
d. adapted

4. The meaning of **hampered** (line 28) is
a. aided
b. expected
c. impeded
d. exceeded

5. Daunted (line 33) most nearly means
a. entangled
b. vulnerable
c. intimidated
d. destined

6. Posthumous (line 53) is best defined as
a. believable
b. after-death
c. poverty-stricken
d. good-natured

Choosing the Right Meaning

Read each sentence carefully. Then circle the item that best completes the statement below the sentence.

Far from being the pliant figurehead that many politicians expected, Lincoln as president firmly proved himself his own man. (2)

1. The word **pliant** in line 1 is best defined as
   a. elastic   b. flexible   c. indeterminate   d. easily influenced

Environmentalists expressed concern that unchecked development would leave the region impoverished of wildlife. (2)

2. The word **impoverished** in line 2 most nearly means
   a. indigent   b. rich   c. depleted   d. unpopulated

The young playwright was overwhelmed by the sudden access of fame occasioned by the phenomenal success of her second play. (2)

3. In line 1 the word **access** is best defined as
   a. passage   b. increase   c. diminishment   d. entry

Is he really so opaque, I wondered, or is he merely pretending ignorance, the better to dupe me? (2)

4. The best definition for the word **opaque** in line 1 is
   a. obtuse   b. transparent   c. murky   d. unclear

After a period of servitude in a penal colony, he became an evangelical minister and died in the odor of sanctity. (2)

5. In line 1 the word **servitude** most nearly means
   a. service   b. forced labor   c. illness   d. slavery

Antonyms

*In each of the following groups, circle the word or expression that is most nearly the **opposite** of the word in **boldface** type.*

1. succumb
a. release
b. conquer
c. sicken
d. resign

2. pompous
a. unreal
b. unpretentious
c. unsophisticated
d. unbalanced

3. superfluous
a. inglorious
b. indispensable
c. insufficient
d. incapable

4. revile
a. hide
b. praise
c. find
d. harden

5. servitude
a. bondage
b. liberty
c. poverty
d. cowardice

6. intrepid
a. fat
b. timid
c. nasty
d. ignorant

7. annihilate
a. destroy
b. repeat
c. foster
d. argue

8. diligent
a. worried
b. painstaking
c. indolent
d. concerned

9. disentangle
a. clarify
b. declare
c. snag
d. reject

10. doleful
a. cheerful
b. facile
c. sad
d. angry

11. morose
a. dark
b. blithe
c. frozen
d. kind

12. arbitrary
a. lazy
b. reasoned
c. correct
d. dull

13. exodus
a. exit
b. entrance
c. movement
d. home

14. rectify
a. salute
b. explain
c. correct
d. bungle

15. reprimand
a. praise
b. answer
c. find fault with
d. punish

16. prim
a. sloppy
b. empty
c. tidy
d. lonely

Word Families

A. On the line provided, write the word you have learned in Units 4–6 that is related to each of the following nouns.
EXAMPLE: atonement—**atone**

1. rectification, rectifier _____

2. lucidity, lucidness _____

3. opacity, opaqueness _____

4. incorrigibility, incorrigibleness _____

5. militancy, militance, militantness _____

6. credibility, credit _____

7. pomposity, pompousness _____

8. intricacy _____

9. stagnancy, stagnation _____

10. incineration, incinerator _____

11. annihilation, annihilator _____

12. tenacity, tenaciousness _____

13. diligence, diligentness _____

14. superfluity, superfluousness _____

15. latency _____

B. On the line provided, write the word you have learned in Units 4–6 that is related to each of the following verbs.
EXAMPLE: animate—**inanimate**

16. catalyze _____

17. bias _____

18. bind _____

19. militarize _____

20. impoverish _____

Two-Word Completions

Circle the pair of words that best complete the meaning of each of the following passages.

1. Shakespeare's Timon of Athens is a bitter misanthrope who spends much of his time on stage _____ the world and those in it with _____ taunts and caustic jests.
   a. reviling . . . sardonic
   b. reprimanding . . . posthumous
   c. rebutting . . . prim
   d. daunting . . . lucid

2. Though learning a foreign language never comes easily for me, I've found that I can _____ the process if I imitate the ant in the old fable and apply myself to the task as _____ as possible.
   a. defray . . . credibly
   b. rectify . . . brazenly
   c. hamper . . . tenaciously
   d. facilitate . . . diligently

3. "A(n) _____ is supposed to _____ the commission of a crime," the burglar growled at his sidekick. (The latter had just set off the alarm system to the bank the pair were robbing.) "But all *you* can seem to do," the burglar continued, "is make this job more difficult!"
   a. catalyst . . . revile
   b. accomplice . . . facilitate
   c. rebuttal . . . incinerate
   d. precipice . . . reprimand

4. Tourists always gasp in amazement when _____ Mexican daredevils climb to the top of a lofty _____ in Acapulco and dive fearlessly into the sea hundreds of feet below.
   a. brazen . . . access
   b. intrepid . . . precipice
   c. prim . . . catalyst
   d. pliant . . . exodus

5. His lies sounded so much like the truth that I was completely taken in by them. If they hadn't seemed so _____, I don't think I would have been _____ quite so easily.
   a. intrepid . . . impoverished
   b. intricate . . . disentangled
   c. credible . . . hoodwinked
   d. ghastly . . . annihilated

6. "I'm trying to help you, not _____ you," I said. "I want to make your task easier, not more _____."
   a. reprieve . . . slapdash
   b. hamper . . . arduous
   c. revile . . . pliant
   d. supplant . . . latent

7. They could no longer sit idly by while a gross injustice went uncorrected. For that reason, they joined a group of _____ reformers actively trying to get the government to _____ the situation.
   a. militant . . . rectify
   b. incorrigible . . . disentangle
   c. biased . . . taunt
   d. morose . . . defray

Building with Classical Roots

ten, tain, tin—to hold, keep

This root appears in **tenacious** (page 67), which means, literally, "full of holding power." Some other words based on the same root are listed below.

abstention	detention	retinue	tenor
detain	pertain	sustenance	tenure

From the list of words above, choose the one that corresponds to each of the brief definitions below. Write the word in the blank space in the illustrative sentence below the definition.

1. the means of support or subsistence; nourishment

During her ordeal, she drew _____ from her abiding faith.

2. the time during which something is held; a permanent right to an office or position after a trial period

The Constitution limits a President's _____ to two consecutive 4-year terms of office.

3. to have reference to; to be suitable; to belong, as an attribute or accessory

An attorney can only introduce evidence that directly _____ to the case.

4. a body of followers, group of attendants

The delegation consisted of the king and his loyal _____ of advisors and protectors.

5. the act of doing without; refraining

The doctor advised the patient to observe total _____ from fatty foods to prevent another heart attack.

6. confinement; holding in custody

The temporary holding cells in that impoverished country were dank and filthy places of _____ .

7. the flow of meaning through something written or spoken, drift; the highest adult male voice

He auditioned for the lead _____ role in the opera *Tosca*.

8. to prevent from going on, delay, hold back; hold as a prisoner

"This traffic jam may _____ us for so long that we miss our flight," he complained.

From the list of words on page 78, choose the one that best completes each of the following sentences. Write the word in the blank space provided.

1. When their food supplies ran out, the desperate survivors turned to roots and berries for _____.

2. The librarian suggested references in which I might search for materials that _____ to the topic of my research paper.

3. They showed their dissatisfaction with both candidates running for office by widespread _____ from voting.

4. "My main goal during my _____ in office," pledged the new mayor, "is to ensure that our city will meet the needs of all its citizens."

5. We gathered from the _____ of his remarks that he doesn't share our opinion on this issue.

6. The detectives _____ the suspect for more questioning after they noticed a discrepancy in his story.

7. After-hours _____ is a prevalent method of punishment in schools.

8. The basketball star had a steady _____ of hangers-on who turned his head with endless praise.

---

*Circle the **boldface** word that more satisfactorily completes each of the following sentences.*

1. Although we objected to the prickly (**tenure, tenor**) of the review, the astute critic did make several valuable observations.

2. Total (**abstention, detention**) from caffeine includes avoiding chocolates and cola-flavored soft drinks, as well as tea and coffee.

3. The employee was denied (**tenure, sustenance**) on the grounds of his uneven performance record.

4. International rules demand that (**retinue, detention**) centers for prisoners of war must meet certain minimal standards of cleanliness and humane treatment.

5. "Your comments are very interesting," the teacher acknowledged, "but they do not actually (**detain, pertain**) to the issue we are trying to resolve."

6. The queen's (**retinue, abstention**) accompanied her in a fleet of smaller boats that sailed ahead of and behind the royal barge.

7. The koala takes its (**sustenance, tenor**)—both food and water—from the leaves of the eucalyptus tree.

8. U.S. Customs officials have the authority to (**pertain, detain**) anyone who tries to enter the United States without appropriate identity documents, such as a current passport or visa.

Read the following sentences, paying special attention to the words and phrases underlined. From the words in the box below, find better choices for these underlined words and phrases. Then use these choices to rewrite the sentences.

		WORD BANK		
access	bondage	doleful	paramount	revile
anarchy	brazen	exodus	pompous	servitude
arduous	catalyst	ghastly	rectify	succumb
atone	credible	militant	reprieve	tenacious

The Amistad Case

1. In 1839, fifty-three Africans held prisoner on the slave ship *Amistad* staged a rebellion in an attempt to escape a life of <u>forced submission</u>.

_____

_____

2. Believing they had won a <u>stay</u> from their unjust fate, the Africans ordered the crew to sail the ship to Africa.

_____

_____

3. Pretending to have <u>given way</u> to the revolt, the crew redirected the *Amistad* without revealing that they were in fact heading toward New England.

_____

_____

4. Upon arrival in America, the *Amistad* was seized, the slave traders freed, and the African "cargo" placed in <u>a state of incarceration</u>.

_____

_____

5. Enraged abolitionists used the *Amistad* situation as a <u>spur</u> to bring attention to the evils of slavery. They pressed for trial.

_____

_____

6. Former president John Quincy Adams took on the <u>exceedingly difficult</u> task of defending the fifty-three Africans in a country where slavery still existed. He won them their freedom.

_____

_____

7. The <u>above all others</u> issue Adams argued was that international slave trading was illegal, and therefore anyone trying to escape it should be seen as free.

_____

_____

 **Analogies**

In each of the following, circle the item that best completes the comparison.

1. Proliferate is to **stagnate** as
a. facilitate is to hamper
b. relinquish is to pilfer
c. supplant is to replace
d. rebut is to mock

2. prim is to **dissolute** as
a. spurious is to bogus
b. unbridled is to unflinching
c. terse is to curt
d. lucid is to muddled

3. circumspect is to **caution** as
a. inanimate is to life
b. credible is to doubt
c. intricate is to simplicity
d. tenacious is to persistence

4. subjugate is to **bondage** as
a. incarcerate is to prison
b. terminate is to servitude
c. fabricate is to doghouse
d. incinerate is to debt

5. pauper is to **impoverished** as
a. comedian is to sardonic
b. dancer is to obese
c. superstar is to eminent
d. orator is to pompous

6. doleful is to **grief** as
a. intrepid is to fear
b. irate is to anger
c. brazen is to envy
d. morose is to joy

7. spasmodic is to **incessant** as
a. hasty is to slapdash
b. biased is to opinionated
c. lucrative is to profitable
d. latent is to overt

8. chore is to **arduous** as
a. detail is to superfluous
b. novel is to posthumous
c. note is to legible
d. burden is to cumbersome

9. hew is to **ax** as
a. rectify is to ruler
b. efface is to eraser
c. hoodwink is to pistol
d. defray is to thread

10. diligent is to **erratic** as
a. alien is to foreign
b. cherubic is to angelic
c. novel is to trite
d. comely is to lively

 **Choosing the Right Meaning**

Read each sentence carefully. Then circle the item that best completes the statement below the sentence.

Fearing that readers would not grasp what he was up to with his "whale" story, some friends admonished Melville against publishing *Moby Dick*. (2)

1. The word **admonished** in line 2 most nearly means
a. scolded   b. reminded   c. cautioned   d. prevented

"Why be content just to muddle through the course," my math teacher asked, "when you might excel if you only put your mind to it?" (2)

2. In line 1 the phrase **muddle through** is used to mean
a. mess up   b. get by   c. drop   d. fail dismally

In the first act of Hamlet, the Prince is visited by the semblance of his murdered father. (1)

3. In line 1 the word **semblance** most nearly means
a. memory   b. relative   c. facade   d. apparition

The author's prim style is poorly matched to the story of overwrought passions it recounts.   (2)

4. The best definition for the word **prim** in line 1 is

    a. precise   b. exacting   c. crisp   d. fussy

Rather than trust in an increasingly erratic public transportation system, some commuters have turned to private bus services.   (2)

5. The word **erratic** in line 1 is best defined as

    a. undependable   b. untimely   c. unexpected   d. expensive

Two-Word Completions

Circle the pair of words that best complete the meaning of each of the following sentences.

1. Though some of our most _____ writers and artists became famous while they were alive, to others such renown was accorded only

_____.

    a. eminent . . . posthumously   c. intrepid . . . superfluously
    b. lucrative . . . incorrigibly   d. opaque . . . illegibly

2. In a society that is totally free of prejudice and bigotry, the demons of racial and religious _____ have forever been totally _____ from the minds and hearts of the people.

    a. anarchy . . . reprieved   c. debris . . . salvaged
    b. bias . . . exorcised   d. larceny . . . annihilated

3. When the negotiations for a new contract become _____, the representatives of labor and management in some cases attempt to

_____ a settlement by calling on the services of an impartial outside mediator.

    a. disentangled . . . hamper   c. rectified . . . commandeer
    b. defrayed . . . fabricate   d. deadlocked . . . facilitate

4. Though we had no difficulty _____ small valuables from the old wreck, our efforts to raise the hull itself were _____ by swift currents and heavy seas.

    a. accessing . . . compensated   c. salvaging . . . hampered
    b. breaching . . . tantalized   d. foddering . . . predisposed

5. I regarded the rival who had _____ me in my true love's affections with as much displeasure and dismay as a legitimate heir would look upon the upstart _____ who had stolen his throne.

    a. fortified . . . brigand   c. supplanted . . . usurper
    b. terminated . . . cherub   d. condoned . . . marauder

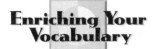

Enriching Your Vocabulary

Read the passage below. Then complete the exercise at the bottom of the page.

A Legal Inheritance of Words

The doors open, and the jury files in. Suspense builds as they take their seats. Innocent or guilty? What will their verdict be?

Trials, whether civil or criminal, can make for high drama, gripping the public's attention and resulting in landmark decisions that touch many aspects of American life. Among these historic cases: the *Amistad* trial (1839-1840); the Leopold and Loeb murder trial (1924); the Rosenbergs spy trial (1951); and *Brown vs. Board of Education* (1954), in which the Supreme Court ruled segregated schools unconstitutional.

In the United States, persons who believe they have been wronged may sue, provided there is enough evidence to support a case. The one bringing the legal complaint is the *plaintiff* (Unit 15), who must prove "with a preponderance of the evidence" that the accused is guilty; the *defendant* (the accused) is innocent until proven guilty.

Courtroom scene from the film *To Kill a Mockingbird* (1962)

Films, television shows, plays, and books based on aspects of our legal system abound. As a result, many legal terms have found their way into everyday English. Some, such as *plaintiff,* largely maintain their legal meaning, while others enjoy broader usage. For example, *reprieve* (Unit 4) is a legal term meaning to postpone punishment. However, when a teacher postpones a difficult exam, students might consider *that* a wonderful reprieve.

In Column A below are 6 more words with legal origins. With or without a dictionary, match each word with its meaning in Column B.

Column A

_____ **1.** indictment
_____ **2.** subpoena
_____ **3.** affidavit
_____ **4.** arraign
_____ **5.** contraband
_____ **6.** defraud

Column B

a. a written statement made under oath before a person authorized to administer legally binding oaths

b. to swindle, deceive

c. a formal written statement usually presented by a grand jury charging one or more persons with an offense

d. goods prohibited by law for import or export; smuggled goods

e. (*n.*) a written legal order requiring a person to appear in court to give legal testimony; (*v.*) to serve or summon with such a written order

f. to bring an accused person before a court of law to hear and answer the legal charge made against him or her

Definitions

Note carefully the spelling, pronunciation, part(s) of speech, and definition(s) of each of the following words. Then write the word in the blank space(s) in the illustrative sentence(s) following. Finally, study the lists of synonyms and antonyms given at the end of each entry.

1. adieu
(ə dü′; a dyü′)

(*int.*) "Farewell!"; (*n.*) a farewell

As my friends boarded the airplane, I waved and shouted, "_____! Have a safe trip."

When the hour grew late, the last of the dinner guests made their _____ to their gracious hosts.

SYNONYMS: (*int.*) "So long"; (*n.*) good-bye
ANTONYMS: (*int.*) "Hello"; (*n.*) greeting

2. advent
(ad′ vent)

(*n.*) an arrival; a coming into place or view

The _____ of spring is particularly welcome after a long, harsh winter.

SYNONYM: approach
ANTONYMS: departure, going away, exodus

3. apex
(ā′ peks)

(*n.*) the highest point, tip

If you want to reach the _____ of the Washington Monument, you can take the stairs or an elevator.

SYNONYMS: peak, summit, acme, crowning point
ANTONYMS: bottom, nadir

4. assimilate
(ə sim′ ə lāt)

(*v.*) to absorb fully or make one's own; to adopt as one's own; to adapt fully

A well-read person _____ knowledge of a wide range of subjects.

SYNONYMS: digest, incorporate, blend in

5. bogus
(bō′ gəs)

(*adj.*) false, counterfeit

Cashiers receive special training so that they will be able to identify _____ currency.

SYNONYMS: phony, fake, spurious
ANTONYMS: genuine, authentic

6. exorbitant
(eg zôr′ bə tənt)

(*adj.*) unreasonably high; excessive

Management rejected the union's demands for higher wages and better benefits as _____.

SYNONYMS: extreme, inordinate, overpriced
ANTONYMS: inexpensive, affordable, reasonable

7. interim
(in′ tər əm)

(*n.*) the time between; (*adj.*) temporary, coming between two points in time

In the _____ between landing and takeoff, the ground crew cleaned and refueled the plane.

The team played well under an _____ coach for the final three months of the season.

SYNONYMS: (*n.*) interval, interlude; (*adj.*) provisional, stopgap

8. inundate
(in′ ən dāt)

(*v.*) to flood, overflow; to overwhelm by numbers or size

Torrential rains and high tides _____ the streets of the picturesque seaside community.

SYNONYMS: submerge, deluge, swamp

9. malign
(mə līn′)

(*v.*) to speak evil of, slander; (*adj.*) evil

In every office, there are gossips who are only too willing to _____ their coworkers.

Iago reveals his _____ motives to the audience in a series of soliloquies.

SYNONYMS: (*v.*) defame, vilify, badmouth; (*adj.*) wicked
ANTONYMS: (*v.*) praise, commend; (*adj.*) kind, benevolent

10. meander
(mē an′ dər)

(*v.*) to wander about, wind about; (*n.*) a sharp turn or twist

When I travel, I like to _____ through unfamiliar towns and cities.

Lombard Street in San Francisco is famous for its many

_____.

SYNONYMS: (*v.*) ramble, roam, zigzag, twist

11. metropolis
(mə träp′ ə ləs)

(*n.*) a large city; the chief city of an area

Archaeologists have learned much about the Mayans from the ruins of the _____ Palenque.

SYNONYM: large urban center
ANTONYMS: hamlet, village

12. momentous
(mō men′ təs)

(*adj.*) very important

A _____ decision by the Supreme Court in 1954 declared public school segregation unconstitutional.

SYNONYMS: consequential, weighty, portentous
ANTONYMS: inconsequential, trivial, slight, unimportant

13. obstreperous
(əb strep′ ər əs)

(*adj.*) noisy; unruly, disorderly

Our teacher will not tolerate _____ behavior in the classroom.

SYNONYMS: wild, rowdy, uncontrolled, riotous
ANTONYMS: quiet, well-behaved, docile

14. pensive
(pen′ siv)

(*adj.*) thoughtful; melancholy

We admired the skill with which the artist captured the child's _____ expression.

SYNONYMS: dreamy, reflective, contemplative, wistful

15. perilous
(per′ ə ləs)

(*adj.*) dangerous

Episodes of old-time movie serials usually ended with the hero or heroine in _____ circumstances.

SYNONYMS: risky, chancy, hazardous, unsafe
ANTONYMS: safe, secure, harmless

16. shoddy
(shäd′ ē)

(*adj.*) of poor quality; characterized by inferior workmanship

That designer watch I bought from a street vendor turned out to be a _____ knockoff.

SYNONYMS: flimsy, cheap, tacky, imitative
ANTONYMS: well-made, solid, durable, superior

17. sprightly
(sprīt′ lē)

(*adj.*) lively, full of life; spicy, flavorful

Though Grandmother is well into her eighties, she is still as _____ as a teenager.

SYNONYMS: frisky, peppy, spirited, animated, buoyant
ANTONYMS: sullen, spiritless, dull, morose, sluggish

18. surly
(sər′ lē)

(*adj.*) angry and bad-tempered; rude

Passengers stranded in an airport because their flight is canceled may become quite _____.

SYNONYMS: gruff, sullen, cranky, grouchy, hostile
ANTONYMS: polite, gracious, civil, friendly, genial

19. tirade
(tī′ rād)

(*n.*) a long, angry speech, usually very critical

The dictator's televised _____ against his opponents lasted for four hours.

SYNONYMS: harangue, diatribe, tongue-lashing

20. vagrant
(vā′ grənt)

(*n.*) an idle wanderer, tramp; (*adj.*) wandering aimlessly

During the Great Depression, many people lost everything and were forced to live as _____.

Advertisers continually vie with one another to capture the _____ attention of fickle consumers.

SYNONYMS: (*n.*) drifter, vagabond, hobo, nomad
ANTONYMS: (*n.*) stay-at-home, homebody, resident

Completing the Sentence

From the words for this unit, choose the one that best completes each of the following sentences. Write the word in the space provided.

1. It takes many long hours of study to _____ all the technical information you need to know if you wish to become a computer programmer.

2. Is there anything more unpleasant than to go to a store and find yourself in the hands of a(n) _____ salesperson?

3. The senator departed from his prepared remarks to deliver an intemperate _____ attacking the administration's foreign policy.

4. King's Highway, an old Indian trail, _____ through Brooklyn, crossing many important streets and almost retracing its path at some points.

5. My friend interrupted my _____ mood with the quip "A penny for your thoughts."

6. Baby-sitters often find that children described by their parents as well behaved become _____ brats as soon as those parents leave the house.

7. It is sad to have to bid _____ to friends we have known for many years.

8. The difficult choice between going to college and getting a job is indeed a(n) _____ momentous one for a young person.

9. The people living in the valley will have to leave their homes because the area will be _____ when a new dam is constructed across the river.

10. Shakespeare's wicked characters often assume the guise of kindness to cloak their _____ natures.

11. When the band struck up a(n) _____ tune, even the most reserved party guests began to laugh, dance, and have fun.

12. When the head of your golf club has reached the _____ of the swing, pause for a second before you begin the downward motion.

13. When vacant apartments are in short supply, landlords can often get away with charging _____ rents.

14. The food processor certainly looked impressive, but its construction was so _____ that within a few months it began to fall apart.

15. In the streets of all our great cities, you will find _____ who wander about without homes, jobs, or friends.

16. How can you criticize me for the way I behaved during the emergency when you yourself have never been in so _____ a position?

17. Many students take jobs during the _____ between the end of one school year and the beginning of the next.

18. The appearance of many a main street was transformed with the _____ of fast-food restaurants.

19. "This great _____ has many problems," the mayor said, "but it also has much to offer both residents and visitors."

20. The notorious jewel thief evaded capture for years by adopting numerous clever disguises and _____ identities.

Synonyms

*Choose the word from this unit that is **the same** or **most nearly the same** in meaning as the **boldface** word or expression in the given phrase. Write the word on the line provided.*

1. prepared for the **arrival** of winter _____

2. made of **flimsy** material _____

3. music that suits my **wistful** state of mind _____

4. refused to respond to my opponent's **harangue** _____

5. enjoyed the **animated** conversation _____

6. the **crowning point** of a brilliant career _____

7. **roamed** through the beautiful gardens _____

8. a **portentous** meeting of world leaders _____

9. **deluged** the company with phone calls _____

10. foreign words **incorporated** into English _____

11. provides **drifters** with hot meals and shelter _____

12. tabloids that **slander** the rich and famous _____

13. representatives of the **provisional** government _____

14. received a fond **farewell** from my coworkers _____

15. a group of **rowdy** fans _____

Antonyms

*Choose the word from this unit that is **most nearly opposite** in meaning to the **boldface** word or expression in the given phrase. Write the word on the line provided.*

16. treats strangers in a **friendly** manner _____

17. arrived home after a **safe** journey _____

18. willing to pay **reasonable** fees _____

19. purchased **authentic** Roman coins _____

20. spent their vacation in a **village** _____

Choosing the Right Word

*Circle the **boldface** word that more satisfactorily completes each of the following sentences.*

1. I feel that a symphony orchestra is just as important to a (**vagrant, metropolis**) as a big department store or a major-league sports team.

2. Churchill once said that if a nation tries to avoid everything that is hard and (**shoddy, perilous**), it will weaken its own security.

3. I have no respect for people who are unfailingly courteous to their superiors but (**sprightly, surly**) to the employees under them.

4. Only after Lincoln's death did most people appreciate the great qualities of the man who had been so (**maligned, inundated**) in his own lifetime.

5. The bylaws state that any member who speaks in a(n) (**obstreperous, perilous**) manner is to be quieted by the sergeant at arms.

6. His talk (**maligned, meandered**) aimlessly through memories of his youth, descriptions of his children, and criticisms of the administration.

7. I suffered a substantial financial loss and an even greater loss of faith in human nature when I tried to cash his (**obstreperous, bogus**) check.

8. I know that you're eager to have that pretty dress for the junior prom, but don't you think the price is a little (**perilous, exorbitant**)?

9. We can all agree that Elizabethan drama reached its (**apex, metropolis**) in the matchless plays of Shakespeare.

10. One of the glories of America has been its ability to (**assimilate, inundate**) immigrants from every part of the globe.

11. I don't know which is worse—your failure to keep your promise to me or your (**shoddy, momentous**) excuse for lying about it.

12. The governor appointed a member of the state assembly to serve as a(n) (**bogus, interim**) senator until a new election can be held.

13. When the new recruits refused to budge from their foxholes, the enraged sergeant let loose with a(n) (**apex, tirade**) of insults and abuse.

14. My mother's recipe for lemon meringue pie is a (**pensive, sprightly**) blend of tartness and sweetness.

15. I lay there quietly, looking at the clouds and allowing (**vagrant, surly**) thoughts to pass through my mind.

16. Was any event in American history more (**momentous, exorbitant**) than the decision of the Continental Congress in 1776 to break away from Great Britain?

17. The (**tirade, advent**) of e-mail has revolutionized the way in which people communicate with one another.

18. You have reached the stage of life where you must expect to say (**interim, adieu**) to childhood and take on the responsibilities of a young adult.

19. It was amazing to see how that quiet, (**pensive, exorbitant**) teenager changed into a tough, hard-driving leader.

20. When we asked for suggestions on how to improve our school's athletic program, we were (**assimilated, inundated**) by "bright ideas" from all sides.

Vocabulary in Context

*Read the following passage, in which some of the words you have studied in this unit appear in **boldface** type. Then complete each statement given below the passage by circling the letter of the item that is **the same** or **almost the same** in meaning as the highlighted word.*

Celebrating Lady Liberty

(Line)

The Statue of Liberty, which stands in New York City Harbor, was a gift from France to America. It was designed by the sculptor Auguste Bartholdi and the engineer Gustave Eiffel. Since 1886, Lady Liberty has been an inspirational sight to countless immigrants after their **perilous** ocean journey.

In 1980, a French engineer, Jacques Moutard, was cleaning a copper statue of (5) similar construction in Paris. Noting the smaller statue's poor condition, Moutard wondered if the much larger Liberty was in a similar state. An inspection revealed that it was. Extensive renovations were begun, to be completed in time for the centennial celebration (10) of the statue's dedication, held in 1986.

Fireworks and tall ships celebrate Lady Liberty's first hundred years.

First, an elaborate scaffold was erected around the statue. The copper skin was then carefully cleaned, and the rusted iron ribs of the frame were replaced with stainless steel ones. The viewing (15) area, located in the crown just above Liberty's noble, **pensive** face, was rebuilt. Supports for her upraised arm were strengthened, and finally, a new torch covered with gold leaf was installed. Renovations were complete by late 1985, and the (20) scaffold was taken down early in 1986.

The **momentous** celebration took place on July 4, 1986. A parade of magnificent tall sailing vessels from around the world entered the harbor of the great **metropolis** and sailed up the (25) Hudson River. That night, a spectacular fireworks display lit up the sky, delighting the throngs of people who had **inundated** the southern tip of Manhattan—all in honor of the newly renovated statue. She is indeed a powerful and lasting symbol of the American ideals of liberty and democracy. (30)

---

1. The meaning of perilous (line 4) is
a. arduous
b. joyous
c. cramped
d. hazardous

2. Pensive (line 17) most nearly means
a. reflective
b. smiling
c. stern
d. comely

3. Momentous (line 22) is best defined as
a. elaborate
b. somber
c. important
d. costly

4. The meaning of metropolis (line 25) is
a. town
b. region
c. city
d. state

5. Inundated (line 27) most nearly means
a. flooded
b. entered
c. surrounded
d. visited

Definitions

Note carefully the spelling, pronunciation, part(s) of speech, and definition(s) of each of the following words. Then write the word in the blank space(s) in the illustrative sentence(s) following. Finally, study the lists of synonyms and antonyms given at the end of each entry.

1. assurance
(ə shŭr′ əns)

(*n.*) a pledge; freedom from doubt, self-confidence

The airport was built with the _____ that all the people displaced by its construction would be fairly compensated.

SYNONYMS: promise, sureness, poise, self-possession
ANTONYMS: uncertainty, doubt, insecurity

2. asylum
(ə sī′ ləm)

(*n.*) an institution for the care of children, elderly people, etc.; a place of safety

Some refugees are political fugitives who have fled their homeland to seek _____ in another country.

SYNONYMS: sanatorium, sanctuary, refuge

3. console
(*v.*, kən sōl′;
n., kän′ sōl)

(*v.*) to comfort; (*n.*) the keyboard of an organ; a control panel for an electrical or mechanical device

A neighbor tried to _____ the sobbing child whose cat had wandered away.

The _____ of the large church organ had an assortment of keys, knobs, and pedals.

SYNONYMS: (*v.*) soothe, solace, alleviate
ANTONYMS: (*v.*) distress, aggravate, bother, vex, torment

4. dilate
(dī′ lāt)

(*v.*) to make or become larger or wider; to expand upon

The ophthalmologist said she would _____ the pupil before examining the injured eye.

SYNONYMS: enlarge, expand, swell, prolong
ANTONYMS: contract, compress, constrict

5. dross
(drôs)

(*n.*) refuse, waste products

The _____ from the manufacturing process turned out to be highly toxic.

SYNONYMS: rubbish, trash, detritus, dregs, scum

6. dwindle
(dwin′ dəl)

(*v.*) to lessen, diminish

During the coldest weeks of winter, the pile of firewood slowly _____ until there were no logs left.

SYNONYMS: decrease, shrink, fade, peter out
ANTONYMS: increase, enlarge, swell, proliferate

7. flippant
(flip′ ənt)

(*adj.*) lacking in seriousness; disrespectful, saucy

Parents and other adults are often upset by a teenager's
_____ responses.

SYNONYMS: frivolous, impudent, impertinent, insolent
ANTONYMS: serious, respectful, deferential, obsequious

8. immunity
(i myü′ nə tē)

(*n.*) resistance to disease; freedom from some charge or obligation

Most babies are vaccinated so that they develop an
_____ to measles.

SYNONYMS: exemption, impunity
ANTONYMS: vulnerability, susceptibility, exposure

9. institute
(in′ stə tüt)

(*v.*) to establish, set up; (*n.*) an organization for the promotion of learning

Congress has been reluctant to _____
new guidelines for campaign spending.

After graduating from high school, I plan to attend an
accredited _____ of technology.

SYNONYMS: (*v.*) found, bring about; (*n.*) academy
ANTONYMS: (*v.*) terminate, discontinue, demolish, raze

10. liability
(lī ə bil′ ə tē)

(*n.*) a debt; something disadvantageous

A limited attention span is his biggest _____
as a student.

SYNONYMS: handicap, difficulty, impediment, drawback
ANTONYMS: advantage, asset

11. preposterous
(prē päs′ tər əs)

(*adj.*) ridiculous, senseless

The theory that Stonehenge was constructed by alien life-forms
is utterly _____.

SYNONYMS: nonsensical, absurd, incredible
ANTONYMS: sensible, reasonable, realistic, plausible

12. pugnacious
(pəg nā′ shəs)

(*adj.*) quarrelsome, fond of fighting

The fox terrier is a particularly _____
breed of dog known for its aggressive behavior.

SYNONYMS: argumentative, combative, belligerent
ANTONYMS: peace-loving, friendly, amicable, congenial

13. rabid
(rab′ id)

(*adj.*) furious, violently intense, unreasonably extreme; mad; infected with rabies

Police arrived in force to quell the riot set off by
_____ soccer fans.

SYNONYMS: fanatical, zealous, raving, infuriated, berserk
ANTONYMS: moderate, restrained, blasé, indifferent

14. realm
(relm)

(*n.*) a kingdom; a region or field of study

While astronomy falls within the _____ of science, astrology does not.

SYNONYMS: domain, duchy, bailiwick, jurisdiction

15. rejuvenate
(ri jü' və nāt)

(*v.*) to make young again; to make like new

A few minutes of conversation with my best friend helped to _____ my flagging spirits.

SYNONYMS: revitalize, renew
ANTONYMS: wear out, exhaust, enervate, debilitate

16. remunerate
(ri myü' nə rāt)

(*v.*) to reward, pay, reimburse

The couple promised to _____ the artist handsomely for a portrait of their child.

SYNONYMS: compensate, satisfy, profit, benefit

17. sparse
(spärs)

(*adj.*) meager, scant; scattered

Unlike its neighboring metropolis, the area has quite a _____ population.

SYNONYMS: thin, scanty, few and far between
ANTONYMS: plentiful, abundant, profuse, teeming

18. sterling
(stər' liŋ)

(*adj.*) genuine, excellent; made of silver of standard fineness

The reviewer noted the young actor's _____ performance in *A Midsummer Night's Dream*.

SYNONYMS: first-rate, outstanding, worthy, pure
ANTONYMS: mediocre, shoddy, second-rate, sham

19. venture
(ven' chər)

(*n.*) a risky or daring undertaking; (*v.*) to expose to danger; to dare

An overseas voyage was a daunting _____ during the age of exploration.

It takes courage to _____ out into unknown territory.

SYNONYMS: (*n.*) gamble; (*v.*) try, chance, undertake
ANTONYMS: (*v.*) withdraw, retire, shrink from, shy away

20. warp
(wôrp)

(*v.*) to twist out of shape; (*n.*) an abnormality

The carpenter explained that humidity caused the kitchen door to _____.

Criminal behavior often shows a striking lack of judgment or a _____ in thinking.

SYNONYMS: (*v.*) bend, distort, misshape; (*n.*) irregularity
ANTONYMS: (*v.*) straighten, unbend, rectify

Completing the Sentence

From the words for this unit, choose the one that best completes each of the following sentences. Write the word in the space provided.

1. Because his army was stronger than his rival's, the pretender to the throne was able to seize power throughout the entire _____.

2. Calling upon her many years of experience, the retired warden discussed with great _____ the topic of the evening—"Can Criminals Be Rehabilitated?"

3. Can any amount of money _____ someone for years sacrificed to a hopeless cause?

4. You will need experience, ability, financing, and good luck to have any chance of succeeding in so risky a business _____.

5. Despite intense heat, meager rainfall, and _____ vegetation, many animals have adapted to life in the desert.

6. Weary from months of hard work, she was hopeful that a week at a spa would _____ her.

7. As days passed without a phone call, a note, or an e-mail, his hopes for a reconciliation _____ until he no longer thought about her at all.

8. All the riches of this world, said the minister, are so much worthless _____ without spiritual values and faith.

9. He is such a(n) _____ sports enthusiast that he spends almost all of his spare time either playing ball or watching ball games on TV.

10. As the snake came into view and slithered across her path, the archaeologist's eyes _____ with fear.

11. The wooden staircase we had worked so hard to build was now irregularly curved because the boards had _____.

12. Doctors hope to lessen the number, length, and severity of common colds, even if they cannot provide complete _____ from them.

13. The idea that an incoming President can miraculously solve all of the nation's problems is simply _____.

14. Although I cannot support her in the election, I fully appreciate her many _____ qualities.

15. The philanthropist devoted his time, energy, and funds to establishing a(n) _____ for promoting world peace.

16. The English word *bedlam* was taken from the name of an infamous _____ for the insane in medieval London.

17. When my pet hamster died suddenly, my friends were unable to _____ me during my hours of grief.

18. When we are discussing a serious problem like drug abuse, I feel that
_____ remarks are in bad taste.

19. He is an excellent ball handler and a very good shot; his only serious
_____ as a basketball player is lack of speed.

20. I consider myself a very peaceful person, but if anyone approaches me in a(n)
_____ manner, I am prepared to defend myself.

Synonyms

*Choose the word from this unit that is **the same** or **most nearly the same** in meaning as the **boldface** word or expression in the given phrase. Write the word on the line provided.*

1. a potion to **revitalize** and energize _____

2. seek **refuge** from incessant strife _____

3. free from all **debt** _____

4. the **refuse** of molten metal _____

5. build **resistance** to bee stings _____

6. a **quarrelsome** person ready to take offense _____

7. **comfort** the family in their sorrow _____

8. **distorted** her judgment _____

9. **compensate** the babysitter for his time _____

10. cause blood vessels to **expand** _____

11. **bring about** a change in policy _____

12. fall within the queen's **domain** _____

13. resent their **impertinent** attitude _____

14. **chance** a long pass for a touchdown _____

15. the **fanatical** ravings of a rabble-rouser _____

Antonyms

*Choose the word from this unit that is **most nearly opposite** in meaning to the **boldface** word or expression in the given phrase. Write the word on the line provided.*

16. walked with an air of **uncertainty** _____

17. a **plausible** explanation for the noise _____

18. gradually **increase** in size _____

19. an area of **abundant** resources _____

20. a person of **mediocre** reputation _____

Choosing the Right Word

*Circle the **boldface** word that more satisfactorily completes each of the following sentences.*

1. The outworn ideas of the past cannot be (**rejuvenated, dilated**) simply by expressing them in snappy, modern slang.

2. Today scientists smile wryly at the (**preposterous, pugnacious**) notion that the earth is flat, but in earlier times it was an accepted fact.

3. We must clear away the (**immunity, dross**) of false ideas from our minds and take a long, hard look at reality.

4. Generally, (**pugnacious, sterling**) behavior on the football field is more effective in drawing penalties than in gaining ground.

5. As usual, there are plenty of *talkers,* but the supply of *doers* is (**flippant, sparse**).

6. Patriotism is a fine quality, but not when it is (**dwindled, warped**) into a hatred of other nations.

7. A sound understanding of the principles of freedom and self-government is the best way to gain (**immunity, liability**) from totalitarian propaganda.

8. Many Americans think that the United States should continue to provide (**assurance, asylum**) for people fleeing from tyranny in other lands.

9. I agree with some of the speaker's ideas, but I find his (**rabid, sparse**) enthusiasm for crackpot causes hard to take.

10. I support the team captain because of the (**sterling, preposterous**) leadership she has given us during the long, hard season.

11. Do you expect me to be (**instituted, consoled**) by the fact that I was not the only one to fail the exam?

12. When you write so imaginatively about "life on other planets," you are entering the (**realm, dross**) of science fiction.

13. In spite of all his talk about his great wealth, I noticed that the penny-pincher did not offer to (**console, remunerate**) us for expenses.

14. I would not agree to run for public office before receiving (**assurance, asylum**) of support from important groups in the community.

15. An unwillingness to listen to suggestions from others is a grave (**liability, realm**) in a leader.

16. No doubt the instructor knows a great deal about ecology, but is there any need for her to (**venture, dilate**) on threats to the environment at such great length?

17. How quickly interest in the program (**dwindles, rejuvenates**) when students realize that it calls for so much work, with little chance for glory!

18. In order to meet stricter industry standards, manufacturers will have to (**institute, remunerate**) new systems of quality control.

19. I know better than to (**warp, venture**) into a canoe that a novice will paddle upstream against a crosswind.

20. I like humor as well as anyone, but I don't believe in being (**flippant, rabid**) on so solemn an occasion.

*Read the following passage, in which some of the words you have studied in this unit appear in **boldface** type. Then complete each statement given below the passage by circling the letter of the item that is **the same** or **almost the same** in meaning as the highlighted word.*

A Brilliant Failure

(Line)

No pioneer or explorer ever departs with an ironclad **assurance** of success, or even of survival itself. And so it was when British adventurer Ernest Shackleton (1874–1922) set out to be the first person to cross the Antarctic continent on foot.

(5) In December, 1914, Shackleton and his crew set sail on the *Endurance*, a sailing ship with coal-fired steam engines. On their way to Antarctica, they navigated through dense, shifting pack ice, "a gigantic and interminable jigsaw puzzle devised by nature," which eventually trapped the

(10) *Endurance*. The twenty-eight men, sixty-nine sledge dogs, and one cat camped aboard the ice-bound ship for weeks. In late January, the ice shifted; the *Endurance* **warped**, cracked, split apart, and sank beneath the icy waters.

(15) Shackleton and his crew camped on the ice, living on food they salvaged from the *Endurance*. As supplies **dwindled**, they hunted penguins and seals. But the unstable ice provided only temporary **asylum**. The men climbed into three

(20) open lifeboats, struggling through blizzards and heaving seas until they reached tiny Elephant Island. There, Shackleton boldly decided to sail for help, taking with him five men. They had few navigation tools, meager supplies, and no shelter, but **consoled** themselves with

(25) the belief that they would reach a whaling station 800 miles away.

Seventeen days later, their **venture** paid off. Shackleton reached the whaling station and returned to Elephant Island with a rescue team. Miraculously, every crew member survived. So, although the voyage failed in its goal—Antarctica was not traversed on foot until 1957—it was a success in terms of the resourcefulness

(30) of the crew.

Ernest Shackleton's ship, *Endurance*, trapped in the ice of Antarctica in 1916.

1. The meaning of **assurance** (line 1) is
   a. waste
   b. argument
   c. undertaking
   d. pledge

2. Warped (line 13) most nearly means
   a. renewed
   b. bent
   c. expanded
   d. contracted

3. The meaning of **dwindled** (line 17) is
   a. increased
   b. spoiled
   c. decreased
   d. distorted

4. Asylum (line 19) most nearly means
   a. distress
   b. uncertainty
   c. resistance
   d. sanctuary

5. Consoled (line 24) is best defined as
   a. expanded
   b. comforted
   c. teased
   d. renewed

6. The meaning of **venture** (line 26) is
   a. gamble
   b. difficulty
   c. refuge
   d. domain

Definitions

Note carefully the spelling, pronunciation, part(s) of speech, and definition(s) of each of the following words. Then write the word in the blank space(s) in the illustrative sentence(s) following. Finally, study the lists of synonyms and antonyms given at the end of each entry.

1. auxiliary
(ôg zil′ yə rē)

(*adj.*) giving assistance or support; (*n.*) a helper, aid

If the main motor fails, the instructions say to turn on the _____ motor.

Someone second in command is an _____ to the person in charge.

SYNONYMS: (*adj.*) additional, back-up; (*n.*) reserve, accessory
ANTONYMS: (*adj.*) main, primary, principal

2. candid
(kan′ did)

(*adj.*) frank, sincere; impartial; unposed

It is safe to be _____ about our faults with friends and loved ones.

SYNONYMS: forthright, plainspoken, unbiased
ANTONYMS: insincere, evasive, misleading, artful

3. cubicle
(kyü′ bə kəl)

(*n.*) a small room or compartment

The tiniest _____ is usually assigned to the newest employee.

SYNONYMS: enclosure, hole-in-the-wall
ANTONYMS: vast hall, auditorium

4. drudgery
(drəj′ ə rē)

(*n.*) work that is hard and tiresome

Trade unions lobby to relieve the endless _____ of factory workers.

SYNONYMS: toil, labor, grind
ANTONYMS: play, frolic, amusement, recreation, fun

5. envoy
(en′ voi; än′ voi)

(*n.*) a representative or messenger (as of a government)

On more than one occasion, a former President has been asked to act as a special _____ to the United Nations.

SYNONYMS: agent, ambassador, emissary, minister

6. escalate
(es′ kə lāt)

(*v.*) to elevate; to increase in intensity

A small dispute can _____ into a major conflict unless the opposing parties sit down and talk.

SYNONYMS: climb, raise, ascend, mount
ANTONYMS: decrease, lessen, descend, defuse

7. expedient
(ek spē′ dē ənt)

(*n.*) a means to an end; (*adj.*) advantageous, useful

As an _____, we chose to use a rock as a makeshift hammer.

An opportunist is someone who is always ready to do whatever is most _____.

SYNONYMS: (*n.*) contrivance, device; (*adj.*) serviceable
ANTONYMS: (*adj.*) inconvenient, untimely, disadvantageous

8. feign
(fān)

(*v.*) to pretend

Children sometimes _____ illness to avoid going to school.

SYNONYMS: fake, sham, affect, simulate

9. flair
(flâr)

(*n.*) a natural quality, talent, or skill; a distinctive style

An opera singer needs a _____ for the dramatic as well as a good voice.

SYNONYMS: aptitude, bent, knack, gift, style, panache
ANTONYMS: inability, incapacity

10. grievous
(grē′ vəs)

(*adj.*) causing sorrow or pain; serious

Reporters should take careful notes when interviewing to avoid making _____ errors in print.

SYNONYMS: painful, heartrending, onerous, flagrant
ANTONYMS: joyful, uplifting, cheery, upbeat, comforting

11. heterogeneous
(het ə rə jē′ nē əs)

(*adj.*) composed of different kinds, diverse

Most college admissions officers actively seek a student body that is both talented and _____.

SYNONYMS: miscellaneous, mixed, variegated
ANTONYMS: uniform, homogeneous, of a piece

12. horde
(hôrd)

(*n.*) a vast number (as of people); a throng

When the doors opened, a _____ of shoppers headed towards the sales racks.

SYNONYMS: crowd, mass, multitude, host, swarm
ANTONYMS: few, handful

13. impel
(im pel′)

(*v.*) to force, drive forward

Hunger often _____ people to leave their homes in search of food.

SYNONYMS: urge, push, spur, propel, incite
ANTONYMS: discourage, check, restrain, curb

14. incredulous
(in krej′ ə ləs)

(*adj.*) disbelieving, skeptical

When the testimony of a witness contradicts the evidence, you can expect _____ stares from the jury.

SYNONYMS: dubious, mistrustful, doubting
ANTONYMS: believing, trustful, gullible

15. inscribe
(in skrīb′)

(*v.*) to write or engrave; to enter a name on a list

The young man asked the jeweler to _____ the locket with his fiancée's name.

SYNONYMS: imprint, enroll, enlist
ANTONYMS: erase, rub out, delete, efface, obliterate

16. monologue
(män′ ə läg)

(*n.*) a speech by one actor; a long talk by one person

By means of a _____, a playwright shares a character's private thoughts with the audience.

SYNONYMS: soliloquy, recitation
ANTONYMS: dialogue, conversation, colloquy

17. prognosis
(präg nō′ səs)

(*n.*) a forecast of the probable course and outcome of a disease or situation

Doctors are particularly happy to deliver a _____ of a speedy recovery.

SYNONYMS: prediction, projection

18. rasping
(ras′ piŋ)

(*adj.*) with a harsh, grating sound; (*n.*) a harsh sound

Chronic bronchitis can lead to a _____ cough that is difficult to cure.

The _____ of metal scraping against metal sets my teeth on edge.

SYNONYMS: (*adj.*) scratchy, scraping, abrasive, gravelly
ANTONYMS: (*adj.*) sonorous, smooth, satiny, silky, mellow

19. repugnant
(rē pəg′ nənt)

(*adj.*) offensive, disagreeable, distasteful

Despite their _____ lack of cleanliness, pigs are endearing to many people.

SYNONYMS: hateful, odious, revolting, repulsive
ANTONYMS: pleasing, attractive, tempting, wholesome

20. scuttle
(skət′ əl)

(*v.*) to sink a ship by cutting holes in it; to get rid of something in a decisive way; to run hastily, scurry; (*n.*) a pail

Pirates would not wish to _____ a captured galleon before looting its cargo.

Years ago, it was possible to buy a _____ of coal at the corner grocery store.

SYNONYMS: (*v.*) abandon, discard, scrap, ditch, dump
ANTONYMS: (*v.*) keep afloat, salvage, rescue, preserve

Completing the Sentence

From the words for this unit, choose the one that best completes each of the following sentences. Write the word in the space provided.

1. The New York City Marathon begins with a(n) _____ of runners swarming across the Verrazano-Narrows Bridge.

2. In many cities, groups of private citizens have volunteered to serve as _____ police to help combat crime.

3. It is a(n) _____ population that accounts for the wide variety of cultures found in some neighborhoods.

4. While some people relish Limburger cheese, others find its strong odor truly _____ .

5. It is all very well to be _____ , but there are times when you should keep certain thoughts and opinions to yourself.

6. In times of rapid inflation, prices of goods _____ at a dizzying rate.

7. An unwilling pupil is apt to look upon hours of practice at the piano as so much boredom and _____ .

8. A(n) _____ for color and texture is an indispensable asset to an aspiring dress designer.

9. We must have the courage and the clear-sightedness to realize that what is _____ is not always right.

10. A strong sense of fair play should _____ you to admit your mistake.

11. My rather lame excuse for failing to complete my homework was greeted with a(n) _____ snort by the teacher.

12. The names of all four members of the record-breaking relay team are _____ on the trophy awarded to our school.

13. I maintain that my _____ in the dormitory is so small that I have to walk into the hallway to change my mind or stretch my imagination.

14. I can't help but admire your ability to _____ interest when someone prattles on endlessly about nothing.

15. I hope you will listen attentively to your parent's dire _____ of the probable effect a third bowl of chili will have on your digestion.

16. In his opening _____ , the talk-show host often pokes fun at political candidates and elected officials.

17. Her voice is so _____ that I find it painful to listen to her speak.

18. When Lincoln had been in the White House about a year, he suffered a(n) _____ loss in the death of his son Willie.

19. A special _____ was named by the President to negotiate a settlement in the war-torn region.

20. Hopelessly cut off from the main fleet, the captain of the vessel decided to _____ his ship rather than allow it to fall into enemy hands.

Synonyms

*Choose the word from this unit that is **the same** or **most nearly the same** in meaning as the **boldface** word or expression in the given phrase. Write the word on the line provided.*

1. spurred by driving ambition _____

2. worn down by years of daily **toil** _____

3. pretend happiness at a rival's success _____

4. scrap an impractical idea _____

5. an **agent** of a foreign government _____

6. the **scratchy** tone of an old vinyl record _____

7. rely on the **back-up** speakers _____

8. an extraordinary **aptitude** for numbers _____

9. continue to **climb** rapidly _____

10. skeptical of stories about aliens _____

11. an endless **recitation** of petty complaints _____

12. an optimistic **forecast** for economic recovery _____

13. the names **engraved** on a monument _____

14. a **swarm** of angry mosquitoes _____

15. a crafty scheme or **means to an end** _____

Antonyms

*Choose the word from this unit that is **most nearly opposite** in meaning to the **boldface** word or expression in the given phrase. Write the word on the line provided.*

16. a **misleading** statement of opinion _____

17. directed to a **vast hall** _____

18. a **homogeneous** mixture of items _____

19. a **joyful** cry from the heart _____

20. an unusually **pleasing** sensation _____

Choosing the Right Word

Circle the **boldface** word that more satisfactorily completes each of the following sentences.

1. I must admit now that I was hurt when the coach took me out in the last minutes of the game, but I tried to (**scuttle, feign**) indifference.

2. I don't consider it (**drudgery, rasping**) to prepare meals every day because I love good food and good cooking.

3. I work in an office compartment, travel in a midget car, and sleep in a tiny bedroom. My life seems to take place in a series of (**envoys, cubicles**)!

4. How can you say that the TV interview was spontaneous and (**heterogeneous, candid**) when it was all carefully rehearsed?

5. Instead of sending your little sister as a(n) (**envoy, horde**) to explain what went wrong, why don't you stand up and speak for yourself?

6. The building is equipped with a(n) (**repugnant, auxiliary**) generator, ready to go into service whenever the main power source is cut off.

7. Despite the doctor's gloomy (**prognosis, flair**) when I entered the hospital, I was up and about in a matter of days.

8. "The noble Brutus has told you Caesar was ambitious; if it were so, it was a (**grievous, candid**) fault."

9. Since the person I was trying to interview wouldn't let me get a word in edgewise, our conversation quickly turned into a (**prognosis, monologue**).

10. People who boast of their high moral principles are often the ones who will (**scuttle, escalate**) them most quickly to serve their own interests.

11. An army without strong leadership and firm discipline is no more than an armed (**horde, drudgery**).

12. After examining the price tag, I gingerly replaced the coat on the rack, (**incredulous, grievous**) at the preposterous sum the store was asking for it.

13. Political analysts, students of statecraft, and historians tried to determine what caused a minor border incident to (**escalate, feign**) into a full-scale war.

14. Was it patriotism, a desire to show off, or just self-interest that (**inscribed, impelled**) the foreign minister to take those terrible risks?

15. The expression of satisfaction that comes over her face when she talks of the failures of other people is highly (**expedient, repugnant**) to me.

16. As soon as I heard (**incredulous, rasping**) noises coming from the workshop, I knew that someone was using a saw or a file.

17. It's one thing to be interested in writing; it's quite another to have a (**flair, monologue**) for it.

18. Cut off from all supplies, the soldiers had to use various (**expedients, cubicles**) to keep their equipment in working order.

19. The poet Browning tells us that if we were to open his heart, we would find the word "Italy" (**inscribed, impelled**) inside it.

20. I searched in vain through the (**auxiliary, heterogeneous**) pile of odds and ends for the spare part I had inadvertently thrown away.

Vocabulary in Context

*Read the following passage, in which some of the words you have studied in this unit appear in **boldface** type. Then complete each statement given below the passage by circling the letter of the item that is **the same** or **almost the same** in meaning as the highlighted word.*

Bee-havior

(Line)

Of the 20,000 species of bees in the world, only one makes honey. The honeybee is a social insect that lives and works with others in large groups or colonies. A typical honeybee colony is made up of one queen bee and her offspring: **hordes** of female worker bees and several hundred male drones. Their home is a hive, which contains a honeycomb. A close examination of a (5) honeycomb shows a series of six-sided **cubicles**, or cells, that are used for storing honey and raising young bees. Generally, the cells with the young bees are in the center of the hive and the storage cells are on the periphery.

Laying eggs is the queen bee's only (10) function. The drones' sole responsibility is to mate with the queen—in most cases, the queen of another colony. Unlike the queen and the drones, the worker bees have **heterogeneous** functions. For example, the (15) worker bees gather nectar, convert the nectar to honey, and feed both the young honeybees and the drones. They also keep the hive clean, build new honeycombs, and stand guard at the hive entrance to ward off (20) predators. For the worker bees, there is no

Most beekeepers work in protective clothing.

relief from **drudgery**. Their labor is necessary to the success of the hive, and without them, the queen's offspring would perish.

Some people raise bees commercially for their honey. Others keep bees as a hobby. Contrary to popular belief, honeybees are relatively easy to handle, and (25) their sting is relatively harmless, if painful. Experienced beekeepers do not **scuttle** away from swarming bees. Knowing that quick movements disturb bees, they move slowly and deliberately. While most wear protective clothing, a few brave souls prefer to handle their bees with bare hands!

---

1. The meaning of **hordes** (line 4) is
a. varieties   c. pairs
b. masses   d. lines

2. Cubicles (line 6) most nearly means
a. enclosures   c. temples
b. organisms   d. designs

3. Heterogeneous (line 15) is best defined as
a. outrageous   c. similar
b. important   d. diverse

4. Drudgery (line 22) most nearly means
a. tension   c. toil
b. pleas   d. misfortune

5. The meaning of **scuttle** (line 26) is
a. scurry   c. tremble
b. shout   d. whisper

Analogies

In each of the following, circle the item that best completes the comparison.

1. apex is to **triangle** as
a. floor is to ceiling
b. diameter is to circle
c. ditch is to road
d. crest is to wave

2. dilate is to **widen** as
a. malign is to praise
b. venture is to claim
c. remunerate is to reward
d. dwindle is to spin

3. flippant is to **unfavorable** as
a. candid is to favorable
b. heterogeneous is to unfavorable
c. obstreperous is to favorable
d. auxiliary is to unfavorable

4. meander is to **winding** as
a. venture is to straight
b. warp is to twisted
c. scuttle is to straight
d. dilate is to twisted

5. bully is to **pugnacious** as
a. officer is to bogus
b. auxiliary is to momentous
c. thinker is to pensive
d. envoy is to rabid

6. vagrant is to **wander** as
a. spoilsport is to travel
b. spendthrift is to economize
c. daredevil is to cower
d. busybody is to meddle

7. surly is to **politeness** as
a. candid is to honesty
b. flippant is to seriousness
c. repugnant is to cruelty
d. sprightly is to liveliness

8. feign is to **pretend** as
a. institute is to instruct
b. inscribe is to worship
c. inundate is to flood
d. impel is to restrain

9. "Welcome!" is to **advent** as
a. "Adieu!" is to disaster
b. "Adieu!" is to defeat
c. "Adieu!" is to delay
d. "Adieu!" is to departure

10. asylum is to **safety** as
a. drudgery is to pleasure
b. assurance is to doubt
c. venture is to risk
d. interim is to success

11. incredulous is to **belief** as
a. informal is to attire
b. insensitive is to feeling
c. invincible is to victory
d. insincere is to skill

12. malign is to **hateful** as
a. console is to kind
b. assimilate is to expedient
c. warp is to merciful
d. rejuvenate is to grievous

13. immunity is to **liability** as
a. prognosis is to disease
b. metropolis is to hamlet
c. flair is to dross
d. monologue is to tirade

14. escalate is to **up** as
a. dilate is to down
b. institute is to down
c. remunerate is to down
d. dwindle is to down

15. sprightly is to **favorable** as
a. sterling is to unfavorable
b. sparse is to favorable
c. surly is to unfavorable
d. shoddy is to favorable

16. bogus is to **authentic** as
a. candid is to frank
b. pensive is to thoughtful
c. momentous is to trivial
d. rasping is to grating

17. cubicle is to **small** as
a. realm is to large
b. metropolis is to small
c. expedient is to large
d. horde is to small

18. exorbitant is to **reasonable** as
a. pugnacious is to excited
b. perilous is to safe
c. incredulous is to distasteful
d. preposterous is to bright

Word Associations

In each of the following groups, circle the word that is best defined or suggested by the given phrase.

1. farewell
   a. interim   b. immunity   c. prognosis   d. adieu

2. Leave the dregs behind
   a. realm   b. liability   c. envoy   d. dross

3. bend out of shape
   a. inundate   b. warp   c. assimilate   d. meander

4. causing severe pain or suffering
   a. candid   b. heterogeneous   c. momentous   d. grievous

5. extremely unpleasant
   a. candid   b. sprightly   c. repugnant   d. expedient

6. having no fixed course
   a. rasping   b. vagrant   c. bogus   d. pugnacious

7. suitable for achieving a desired end
   a. flippant   b. expedient   c. exorbitant   d. pensive

8. person who represents one government in dealings with another
   a. dross   b. envoy   c. liability   d. console

9. hastily or poorly done
   a. rabid   b. obstreperous   c. surly   d. shoddy

10. utter false reports
   a. feign   b. dilate   c. malign   d. meander

11. undertaking involving risk or danger
   a. institute   b. auxiliary   c. venture   d. envoy

12. long, violently critical speech
   a. advent   b. tirade   c. dross   d. horde

13. enter on a list
   a. escalate   b. scuttle   c. impel   d. inscribe

14. the very summit
   a. auxiliary   b. console   c. cubicle   d. apex

15. urge forward
   a. impel   b. rejuvenate   c. warp   d. venture

16. the time between dusk and dawn
   a. interim   b. dross   c. envoy   d. realm

17. area of control
   a. monologue   b. cubicle   c. flair   d. realm

18. provide payment
   a. dwindle   b. remunerate   c. assimilate   d. institute

19. involving danger
   a. flippant   b. sterling   c. perilous   d. incredulous

20. contrary to common sense
   a. pensive   b. sparse   c. sterling   d. preposterous

Vocabulary in Context

Read the following passage, in which some of the words you have studied in Units 7–9 appear in **boldface** type. Then complete each statement given below the passage by circling the item that is **the same** or **almost the same** in meaning as the highlighted word.

Nutria Explosion

(Line)

A nutria is not a vitamin, a Japanese car, a cancer-preventing vegetable, nor is it even a subatomic particle. No, no, no. Nutrias are **pugnacious**
(5) twenty-pound, semiaquatic rodents with webbed feet. Their whiskered faces resemble those of a beaver, while the **sparse** hair on their tails is more reminiscent of a rat.

(10)   Nutrias are indigenous to South America, but were introduced to the United States in the 1930s by fur traders looking for a cheap version of mink. In 1937 tabasco sauce tycoon
(15) I. A. McIlhenny imported thirteen pairs of nutrias to Avery Island, Louisiana to start a fur farm. But nutria fur never caught on, and all the animals were released into the wild.
(20) With a reproductive rate of five to eight young per litter, and up to three litters yearly, the North American nutria population did not **dwindle**. Before long, there were a million
(25) "giant rats" in Louisiana, and they spread to Mississippi, Alabama, Texas, and Florida. In addition, nutrias were introduced throughout the Gulf of Mexico to control specific
(30) types of aquatic vegetation in lakes

and ponds, but since nutrias are **rabid** consumers of all vegetation, this process failed. At their population **apex**, nutrias numbered
(35) about ten million nationwide.

Many North American ecosystems cannot **assimilate** nutrias, and they damage wetlands, erode beach dunes, compete with indigenous
(40) species such as muskrat and water foul for food, and eat farmers' crops. They make their nests out of plant materials in burrows dug into river banks, and can eat up to twenty-five
(45) percent of their body weight per day. In Louisiana, people are being urged to "Save the Coast, Eat Nutrias"—as in nutria sausage, barbequed nutria, and nutria chili.

(50)   The nutria explosion reminds us that with a global transportation network, it is becoming increasingly easy for people and animals to move from place to place—sometimes with
(55) unexpected results.

---

1. Pugnacious (line 4) most nearly means
a. inquisitive   c. combative
b. active   d. adventurous

2. Sparse (line 8) is best defined as
a. scanty   c. dense
b. rare   d. coarse

3. The meaning of **dwindle** (line 23) is
a. explode   c. stabilize
b. vanish   d. shrink

4. Rabid (line 32) most nearly means
a. zealous   c. speedy
b. diseased   d. constant

5. Apex (line 34) is best defined as
a. lowest   c. peak
b. median   d. worst

6. The meaning of **assimilate** (line 37) is
a. incorporate   c. adopt
b. segregate   d. withstand

Choosing the Right Meaning

Read each sentence carefully. Then circle the item that best completes the statement below the sentence.

"I should have been a pair of ragged claws
Scuttling across the floors of silent seas."
(T. S. Eliot, "The Love Song of J. Alfred Prufrock")   (2)

1. The word **scuttling** in line 2 most nearly means

   a. slinking   b. scraping   c. scurrying   d. salvaging

As a longtime friend of one of the participants, I don't think I can be an entirely candid judge of the debate.   (2)

2. The word **candid** in line 2 is used to mean

   a. forthright   b. sincere   c. unposed   d. impartial

The rich flavor of the fish was heightened by the sprightly sauce with which it was served.   (2)

3. In line 1 the word **sprightly** is best defined as

   a. spicy   b. secret   c. animated   d. frisky

Scouts came upon a Pawnee hunting party encamped near a meander of the Platte River.   (2)

4. In line 1 the word **meander** most nearly means

   a. incline   b. turn   c. rapids   d. wandering

Though the few defenders remaining fought bravely and well, they were inundated by wave upon wave of shock troops.   (2)

5. In line 1 the word **inundated** is best defined as

   a. overwhelmed   b. saturated   c. relieved   d. harried

Antonyms

In each of the following groups, circle the word or expression that is most nearly the **opposite** of the word in **boldface** type.

1. monologue
a. convention
b. recitation
c. conversation
d. invocation

2. obstreperous
a. kind
b. docile
c. selfish
d. disorderly

3. sparse
a. lasting
b. first
c. plentiful
d. important

4. flippant
a. respectful
b. brief
c. attractive
d. expensive

5. repugnant
a. peaceful
b. brief
c. attractive
d. expensive

6. malign
a. hide
b. pretend
c. praise
d. repulse

7. drudgery
a. dull work
b. hard work
c. artistry
d. fun

8. heterogeneous
a. scientific
b. variegated
c. contrary
d. uniform

9. bogus
a. mandatory
b. homemade
c. machine-made
d. genuine

10. surly
a. clean
b. clear
c. clever
d. polite

11. rabid
a. slow
b. restrained
c. extreme
d. foolish

12. incredulous
a. skeptical
b. gullible
c. faithful
d. disloyal

13. dwindle
a. diverge
b. decrease
c. increase
d. ignite

14. scuttle
a. sink
b. rescue
c. torpedo
d. drift

15. liability
a. truth
b. advantage
c. impossibility
d. drawback

16. advent
a. preparation
b. arrival
c. interim
d. departure

Word Families

A. *On the line provided, write the word you have learned in Units 7–9 that is related to each of the following nouns.*

EXAMPLE: dilation—**dilate**

1. expediency, expedience _____
2. institution, institutionalization, institutor _____
3. repugnance, repugnancy _____
4. escalation, escalator _____
5. assimilation, assimilator _____
6. consolation, consoler _____
7. candor, candidness _____
8. surliness _____
9. remuneration, remunerator _____
10. sprightliness _____
11. inscription, inscriber _____
12. inundation _____
13. rejuvenation, rejuvenator _____
14. flippancy _____
15. exorbitance _____

B. *On the line provided, write the word you have learned in Units 7–9 that is related to each of the following verbs.*

EXAMPLE: expedite—**expedient**

16. assure _____
17. prognosticate _____
18. imperil _____
19. immunize _____
20. rasp _____

Two-Word Completions

Circle the pair of words that best complete the meaning of each of the following passages.

1. "Over the years, consumer prices have soared, while the real purchasing power of the dollar has _____," the speaker said. "If the cost of living continues to _____, the value of our money must surely shrink even more."
   a. dwindled . . . dwindle
   b. escalated . . . dwindle
   c. escalated . . . escalate
   d. dwindled . . . escalate

2. "They're asking far too much for this _____ merchandise," I remarked. "I'd be a fool to pay such an _____ price for goods that are so badly made."
   a. bogus . . . rasping
   b. sterling . . . expedient
   c. shoddy . . . exorbitant
   d. grievous . . . auxiliary

3. Roman governors had at their command both regular legionary troops and _____ units drawn from the native population to repel the _____ of savage barbarians that from time to time swarmed into the provinces of the Empire like an invasion of locusts.
   a. pugnacious . . . tirades
   b. heterogeneous . . . envoys
   c. vagrant . . . realms
   d. auxiliary . . . hordes

4. Some people really enjoy doing all the tiresome and time-consuming chores associated with housework, but to me such _____ is truly _____.
   a. drudgery . . . repugnant
   b. immunity . . . obstreperous
   c. liability . . . boorish
   d. assurance . . . pensive

5. After fighting my way all year along the noisy, crowded streets of a bustling modern _____ like Tokyo or New York, I find it quite a pleasure to _____ aimlessly along a winding country road.
   a. realm . . . dilate
   b. metropolis . . . meander
   c. asylum . . . impel
   d. cubicle . . . venture

6. As soon as the robins and the crocuses herald the _____ of spring, our personnel department is _____ with a veritable deluge of letters from college students asking about summer employment.
   a. interim. . . impelled
   b. advent . . . inundated
   c. prognosis . . . rejuvenated
   d. flair . . . consoled

7. Does the old saying, "Nothing _____, nothing gained," mean that someone who expects to be _____ well for his or her efforts must be prepared to take some risks?
   a. scuttled . . . maligned
   b. feigned . . . impelled
   c. ventured . . . remunerated
   d. assimilated . . . inundated

Building with Classical Roots

pol—city, state; **ly**—to loosen, to set free

The root **pol** appears in **metropolis**, "a large city" (page 85). The root **ly** appears in **catalyst**, "any agent that causes change" (page 58). Some other words based on these roots are listed below.

acropolis	**cosmopolitan**	**metropolitan**	**political**
analysis	**electrolysis**	**paralysis**	**psychoanalysis**

From the list of words above, choose the one that corresponds to each of the brief definitions below. Write the word in the blank space in the illustrative sentence below the definition.

1. the breaking apart of a complex whole into its simpler parts for closer study; a statement of the results of this process; a brief summary or outline

Chemical _____ of the debris can help to establish the cause of the fire.

2. common to or representative of the whole world; not national or local; at home everywhere, widespread; conversant with many spheres of interest

Music is truly a _____ art form.

3. partial or complete loss, or temporary interruption, of the ability to move or experience sensation in part or all of the body; any condition of helpless inactivity or powerlessness

A serious spinal cord injury can result in permanent _____.

4. concerned with the structure or affairs of government, politics, citizens, or the state; involving politicians, governmental organizations, or parties on distinct sides in an issue

When I register to vote, I may align myself with a particular _____ party.

5. the fortified upper part or citadel of an ancient Greek city

While in Greece, we visited the "Sacred Rock of Athens" to see the ruins of the ancient _____.

6. decomposition of an electrolyte caused by electric current passing through it; removal of excess hair or other living tissue by destroying it with a needle-like electrode

The first practice of _____ took place in 1869, when St. Louis eye doctor Charles Michel sent a current through a gold needle to remove a swollen ingrown eyelash.

7. relating to a major city; comprised of a central city and its adjacent suburbs and communities

Most _____ newspapers include extensive arts and entertainment listings.

8. a therapeutic examination of the mind, developed by Freud, to discover the unconscious desires, fears, and anxieties that produce mental and emotional disorders; psychiatric treatment based on this theory and its methodology

The man will undergo _____ to try to determine the cause of his emotional confusion.

From the list of words on page 111, choose the one that best completes each of the following sentences. Write the word in the blank space provided.

1. The banker advised us to do a thorough _____ of our family budget.

2. The _____ of President Franklin Roosevelt's legs as a result of polio was hidden from the public for many years.

3. I enjoy seeing the clever _____ cartoons that poke fun at public issues.

4. It may be challenging for so _____ a person to adjust to small-town life.

5. Many city states in ancient Greece were built around a towering _____, which provided a place of refuge for local residents during times of invasion.

6. The new spa includes a hydrotherapy center and a modern _____ clinic.

7. After years of deep _____, the patient developed effective strategies to manage her emotional distress.

8. It is the editorial mission of *New Yorker* magazine to publish articles, stories, and reviews that reflect _____ life in that great city.

---

*Circle the **boldface** word that more satisfactorily completes each of the following sentences.*

1. Throughout Greek history, the (**acropolis, electrolysis**) alternately served as a fortress, a religious center, and a political hub.

2. U.S. anarchist Emma Goldman once complained that "the (**political, metropolitan**) arena leaves one no alternative—one must either be a dunce or a rogue."

3. The doctor recommended (**paralysis, electrolysis**) as a means of removing hair.

4. To appeal to the sophisticated palates of their clientele, certain (**political, cosmopolitan**) restaurants serve items that feature a broad range of culinary influences.

5. In the final (**analysis, psychoanalysis**), I hope to be judged by the friends and family I've loved and the kindnesses I've shown, not by the possessions I may have acquired.

6. Crowds, noise, high prices, and a relentless pace are common complaints about (**cosmopolitan, metropolitan**) life.

7. Sometimes even (**analysis, paralysis**) can be better than actions made in haste.

8. During a recent session of (**psychoanalysis, acropolis**), the patient experienced a dramatic moment of self-discovery.

Writer's Challenge

Read the following sentences, paying special attention to the words and phrases underlined. From the words in the box below, find better choices for these underlined words and phrases. Then use these choices to rewrite the sentences.

WORD BANK				
apex	console	flippant	preposterous	sterling
assurance	dilate	institute	rabid	tirade
asylum	exorbitant	monologue	sparse	venture
auxiliary	flair	perilous	sprightly	warp

Animals that Serve

1. Dogs not only make great family pets, but <u>extremely high quality</u> companions to people with disabilities.

_____

_____

2. Dog schools select the most well-behaved puppies they can find, and train them for months, so that they can help navigate their blind masters through <u>chancy</u> situations.

_____

_____

3. Service dogs also act as <u>additional helpers</u> for the hearing impaired, alerting them to the sounds of telephones, doorbells, smoke alarms, and other vital auditory signals.

_____

_____

4. Dogs trained to work with the disabled are loyal and loving creatures whose goal is to offer <u>self-possession</u> and increased independence to their masters.

_____

_____

5. These <u>spirited and peppy</u> service dogs retire after about eight years.

_____

_____

6. It is easy for retired dogs to find <u>safety and shelter</u>, and at some guide dog schools, the wait list to adopt is up to six years.

_____

_____

7. But while they might be the most famous,dogs are not the only service animals. Smaller animals such as capuchin monkeys have shown a <u>knack</u> for assisting quadriplegics with basic tasks, such as working lights, loading tapes in VCRs, and sipping from cups.

_____

_____

Analogies

In each of the following, circle the item that best completes the comparison.

1. exodus is to **adieu** as
a. anarchy is to good-bye
b. metropolis is to bon voyage
c. advent is to hello
d. servitude is to welcome

2. salvage is to **scuttle** as
a. dilate is to feign
b. proliferate is to dwindle
c. dissent is to escalate
d. abridge is to reprieve

3. spurious is to **bogus** as
a. mournful is to doleful
b. superfluous is to essential
c. exorbitant is to minimal
d. lucid is to opaque

4. compensate is to **remunerate** as
a. taunt is to jeer
b. malign is to supplant
c. hew is to relinquish
d. warp is to rectify

5. arduous is to **difficulty** as
a. inanimate is to strength
b. sterling is to intensity
c. perilous is to danger
d. pompous is to simplicity

6. intrepid is to **daunt** as
a. diligent is to tantalize
b. incredulous is to hoodwink
c. incorrigible is to surmount
d. obstreperous is to rejuvenate

7. shoddy is to **quality** as
a. trite is to novelty
b. spasmodic is to interest
c. eminent is to renown
d. credible is to belief

8. brazen is to **modesty** as
a. candid is to honesty
b. rabid is to enthusiasm
c. biased is to prejudice
d. flippant is to earnestness

9. inundate is to **water** as
a. defray is to wind
b. assimilate is to lightning
c. incinerate is to fire
d. annihilate is to snow

10. institute is to **terminate** as
a. atone is to succumb
b. facilitate is to hamper
c. impel is to inscribe
d. revile is to fortify

Choosing the Right Meaning

Read each sentence carefully. Then circle the item that best completes the statement below the sentence.

After a decade of neglect the once splendid hotel had taken on a decidedly shoddy appearance. (2)

1. The word **shoddy** in line 2 is best defined as
a. flimsy   b. tacky   c. mediocre   d. run-down

It was not his behavior so much as the rabid nature of his talk that gave him away as a madman. (2)

2. In line 1 the word **rabid** is used to mean
a. furious   b. diseased   c. insane   d. odd

In her talk the psychiatrist described the brain as the "console of human perception." (1)

3. In line 1 the word **console** most nearly means
a. monitor   b. comfort   c. origin   d. solace

Consumer advocates demanded that the manufacturer either retract or substantiate the exorbitant claims advanced for the product. (2)

4. In line 2 the word **exorbitant** most nearly means

a. overpriced   b. unproven   c. excessive   d. modest

Scholars and students alike now use computers to access vast stores of information housed in libraries all over the world. (2)

5. The best definition for the word **access** in line 1 is

a. approach   b. gain entry to   c. admit   d. communicate

Two-Word Completions

Circle the pair of words that best complete the meaning of each of the following sentences.

1. Though he has no real _____ for teaching, he's a very hard worker whose _____ and persistence make up handsomely for what he lacks in talent.

a. repugnance . . . tenacity
b. flair . . . diligence
c. bias . . . obesity
d. predisposition . . . mediocrity

2. As order gave way to _____ in that strife-torn country, the stream of refugees seeking _____ from the turbulence of the times swelled to a mighty torrent.

a. liability . . . immunity
b. bondage . . . access
c. deadlock . . . assurance
d. anarchy . . . asylum

3. In a famous _____ towards the end of the play, the deposed and incarcerated king laments the fact that the vast _____ over which he once ruled has shrunk to the dimensions of a narrow prison cell.

a. tirade . . . precipice
b. interim . . . rift
c. monologue . . . realm
d. catalyst . . . debris

4. Instead of giving me the gist of his complaint in a few _____ and pithy sentences, he launched into a long and bitterly abusive _____ against all the people he claimed were "out to get him."

a. lucid . . . venture
b. erratic . . . feint
c. terse . . . tirade
d. opaque . . . altercation

5. After the beauty pageant was over, _____ of reporters swarmed into the backstage area hoping to get a few words with the _____ winner of the contest.

a. dilemmas . . . surly
b. hordes . . . comely
c. muddles . . . prim
d. deadlocks . . . sprightly

Enriching Your Vocabulary

Read the passage below. Then complete the exercise at the bottom of the page.

How Does It Sound?

Every day, thousands of diverse sounds bombard our ears. A modern, ever-changing language must have words that describe, evaluate, and distinguish the different sounds we hear. Many of the sound words that enrich our language imitate the very sounds they name.

SPLASH! That's the perfect word for the sound of a swimmer jumping into the water.

The use of words that imitate sounds is called *onomatopoeia*. Examples include *hiss, buzz, splash, cluck, quack, snort, twitter, chirp, ping, boom, clang, clop,* and *mumble. Rasping* (Unit 9), an adjective for a harsh, grating sound, is another example of onomatopoeia. As you might guess, onomatopoetic words are popular with children, comedians, entertainers, and poets.

Some English words about sound come from science. Many originate in the world of music, with its myriad terms to express concepts of melody, rhythm, color, volume, and harmony. A voice that *quavers* (Unit 11) has a marked shake or trill to it. The *staccato* (Unit 11) sound of popping firecrackers comes from an Italian word that means "detached." Sound words can be purely descriptive; they can be used to make sonic judgments. Others offer emotional connotations, such as pleasure, surprise, anticipation, or grief. Pause for a moment to listen to the hum of spoken language to perceive its special resonance.

In Column A below are 10 more words related to sound. With or without a dictionary, match each word with its meaning in Column B.

Column A

_____ **1.** discordant
_____ **2.** dulcet
_____ **3.** keen
_____ **4.** shrill
_____ **5.** sibilant
_____ **6.** sonorous
_____ **7.** stentorian
_____ **8.** strident
_____ **9.** tremulous
_____ **10.** vociferate

Column B

a. a hissing sound as made by *s, sh, z,* or *zh*

b. extremely loud

c. to utter or shout loudly and vehemently, especially in protest; bawl, clamor

d. pleasant to hear, melodious, sweet-sounding

e. high-pitched or piercing in sound or tone; irritatingly insistent

f. marked by trembling, quivering, or shaking

g. disagreeable in sound; dissonant, out of harmony

h. having or producing a resonant sound that is full, deep, or rich

i. loud, harsh-sounding, grating, shrill, raucous

j. (*v.*) to wail loudly or lament shrilly for the dead

Definitions

Note carefully the spelling, pronunciation, part(s) of speech, and definition(s) of each of the following words. Then write the word in the blank space(s) in the illustrative sentence(s) following. Finally, study the lists of synonyms and antonyms given at the end of each entry.

1. adept
(*adj.*, ə dept';
n., a' dept)

(*adj.*) thoroughly skilled; (*n.*) an expert

Not only is the soloist an accomplished singer, but he is also _____ at playing the saxophone.

An _____ at chess, she hopes to compete in tournaments against top-rated players.

SYNONYMS: (*adj.*) masterful, accomplished, proficient
ANTONYMS: (*adj.*) clumsy, unskilled, maladroit; (*n.*) novice

2. aspire
(ə spīr')

(*v.*) to have ambitious hopes or plans, strive toward a higher goal, desire earnestly; to ascend

An early fascination with ants led the young naturalist to _____ to a career as an entomologist.

SYNONYMS: seek, yearn, aim for, soar

3. bleak
(blēk)

(*adj.*) bare, dreary, dismal

Urban renewal can turn a run-down city with _____ economic prospects into a flourishing metropolis.

SYNONYMS: grim, cheerless, gloomy, desolate, barren
ANTONYMS: rosy, cheerful, sunny, promising, encouraging

4. chide
(chīd)

(*v.*) to blame; scold

The teacher _____ the student for truancy and tardiness.

SYNONYMS: upbraid, reprimand, rebuke, chastise
ANTONYMS: approve, praise, compliment, pat on the back

5. despicable
(di spik' ə bəl)

(*adj.*) worthy of scorn, contemptible

Whatever the provocation, there is no justification for such _____ behavior.

SYNONYMS: low, vile, cheap, sordid, detestable
ANTONYMS: praiseworthy, commendable, meritorious

6. diminutive
(də min' yə tiv)

(*adj.*) small, smaller than most others of the same type

The _____ lapdog was so small that it actually fit in its owner's purse.

SYNONYMS: undersized, miniature, tiny, compact
ANTONYMS: oversized, gigantic, huge, enormous

7. emancipate
(ē man' sə pāt)

(v.) to free from slavery; to release or liberate

Scientific knowledge can _____ humanity from blind superstition.

SYNONYMS: set loose, unchain, unshackle, unfetter
ANTONYMS: enslave, snare, chain, shackle

8. erroneous
(e rō' nē əs)

(adj.) incorrect, containing mistakes

An _____ first impression is not easily corrected.

SYNONYMS: mistaken, fallacious, all wrong
ANTONYMS: accurate, correct, exact, unerring

9. exploit
(v., ek sploit';
n., ek' sploit)

(v.) to make use of, develop; to make improper use of for personal profit; (n.) a feat, deed

A good debater knows how to _____ weaknesses in an opponent's argument.

The _____ of Robin Hood and his Merry Men are so well known that they have become a part of Western culture.

SYNONYMS: (v.) utilize, turn to advantage, misuse

10. extemporaneous
(ek stem pə rā' nē əs)

(adj.) made or delivered on the spur of the moment

The stand-up comedian's outrageous act included about twenty minutes of completely _____ banter.

SYNONYMS: spontaneous, impromptu, off-the-cuff
ANTONYMS: planned, rehearsed, prepared

11. impair
(im pâr')

(v.) to make imperfect, damage, harm

I am fortunate that the scratch on my eye will not permanently _____ my vision.

SYNONYMS: injure, mar, disable, cripple, enervate
ANTONYMS: improve, strengthen, promote, advance

12. invincible
(in vin' sə bəl)

(adj.) not able to be defeated, unbeatable

Napoleon I, emperor of France, was _____ until he launched a disastrous invasion of Russia.

SYNONYMS: unconquerable, indomitable, insuperable
ANTONYMS: vulnerable, conquerable, surmountable

13. languid
(laŋ' gwid)

(adj.) drooping; without energy, sluggish

A big lunch makes me feel _____ for the rest of the day.

SYNONYMS: lazy, sluggish, listless, slack, lethargic
ANTONYMS: lively, energetic, vigorous, enlivening

14. mire
(mīr)

(*n.*) mud; wet, swampy ground; a tough situation; (*v.*) to get stuck

The once verdant expanse of the soccer field has become a rectangle of muck and _____.

Congress will never ratify that bill _____ in controversy.

SYNONYMS: (*n.*) marsh, swamp, bog, slough

15. obtrusive
(əb trü′ siv)

(*adj.*) forward; undesirably prominent; thrust out

I don't blame you for being put off by his _____ attempt to dominate the conversation.

SYNONYMS: brash, impudent, conspicuous, protruding
ANTONYMS: meek, reserved, deferential, recessed

16. preamble
(prē′ am bəl)

(*n.*) an introduction to a speech or piece of writing

The _____ to the Constitution describes the purpose of our national government.

SYNONYMS: opening, preface, prologue, preliminary
ANTONYMS: conclusion, ending, closing, epilogue

17. render
(ren′ dər)

(*v.*) to cause to become; to perform; to deliver officially; to process, extract

The freelance writer presented the managing editor with a bill for services _____.

SYNONYMS: present, furnish, submit, make, effect

18. rugged
(rəg′ əd)

(*adj.*) rough, irregular; severe, stern; strong; stormy

Settlers had a rough time crossing the _____ Appalachian Mountains.

SYNONYMS: rocky, craggy, blunt, harsh, hardy, tough
ANTONYMS: smooth, flat, soft, mild, tender, delicate

19. skeptical
(skep′ tə kəl)

(*adj.*) inclined to doubt; slow to accept something as true

I am _____ of promises made by politicians when they are running for office.

SYNONYMS: dubious, suspicious, incredulous
ANTONYMS: believing, credulous, gullible, ingenuous

20. slipshod
(slip′ shäd)

(*adj.*) untidy in dress, personal habits, etc.; careless, sloppy

The commission attributed the unfortunate collapse of the apartment building to its _____ construction.

SYNONYMS: messy, untidy, slovenly, slapdash, cursory
ANTONYMS: tidy, neat, orderly, careful, painstaking

Completing the Sentence

From the words for this unit, choose the one that best completes each of the following sentences. Write the word in the space provided.

1. I understand math very well, but, according to my teacher, my performance in class is, at best, _____.

2. Why do you take it on yourself to _____ me whenever I say or do anything even slightly out of line?

3. The many inconsistencies in the suspect's story made the police highly _____ of his alibi.

4. The Welsh mining village, with its rows of drab cottages, seemed terribly _____ and uninviting in the cold autumn rain.

5. It is better to openly admit ignorance than to give _____ information.

6. The warmth of the June sun made me feel so _____ that I scarcely had the energy to brush away the flies.

7. To improve their standard of living, the people of an underdeveloped country must learn to _____ the resources of their land.

8. The _____ but powerful halfback from Syracuse was one of the lightest men ever to play professional football.

9. How can you _____ to work in the space program when you haven't even been able to pass your science and math courses?

10. Since it had rained heavily all night, the newly plowed fields were by now an almost impassable _____.

11. We learned that the matchless discipline and superior leadership of the Roman legions made them all but _____.

12. Poor diet, lack of exercise, and insufficient rest have done a great deal to _____ my health.

13. Marching over the _____ terrain under a broiling sun, we were soon on the verge of exhaustion.

14. The honoree's after-dinner speech was so polished and sure that we never guessed it was _____.

15. The master silversmith was extraordinarily _____ in the use of simple hand tools.

16. The fiddler _____ the fast-paced Virginia reel in a very lively fashion.

17. Against the solemn hush of the memorial service, the boisterous laughter we heard was singularly _____.

18. Before we get into the specific details of our proposal, we should write a(n)
_____ that will explain in general terms what we want to do.

19. The social worker said with great emphasis that anyone who would take advantage of an elderly person is utterly _____.

20. There are many millions of people throughout the world still waiting to be _____ from the bonds of grinding poverty.

Synonyms

*Choose the word from this unit that is **the same** or **most nearly the same** in meaning as the **boldface** word or expression in the given phrase. Write the word on the line provided.*

1. a **vile** and cowardly act _____

2. wallow like a pig in the **mud** _____

3. **dubious** about the chances of winning _____

4. **mar** relations between nations _____

5. **liberate** a slave from bondage _____

6. **seek** higher education _____

7. an **accomplished** musician _____

8. not just assertive, but **impudent** _____

9. **utilize** natural resources _____

10. a **slapdash** piece of work _____

11. the opening remarks, or **preface** _____

12. a **gloomy**, overcast November morning _____

13. **reprimand** for misbehavior _____

14. **submit** a verdict of not guilty _____

15. **harsh** living conditions _____

Antonyms

*Choose the word from this unit that is **most nearly opposite** in meaning to the **boldface** word or expression in the given phrase. Write the word on the line provided.*

16. make an **accurate** assumption _____

17. in a **vulnerable** position _____

18. **gigantic** in proportion _____

19. an **energetic** wave of the hand _____

20. deliver a **rehearsed** series of comments _____

Choosing the Right Word

*Circle the **boldface** word that more satisfactorily completes each of the following sentences.*

1. That monologue about the young accountant on her very first day on the job (**rendered, emancipated**) me helpless with laughter.

2. A good scientist will always be (**skeptical, despicable**) about any theory that is not backed up by convincing evidence.

3. The goalie's reflexes were as sharp as ever, but the knee injury had plainly (**impaired, aspired**) his ability to maneuver.

4. It is worse than useless to (**render, chide**) children for misbehaving without giving them an opportunity to behave better.

5. I am not accusing anyone of deliberately lying, but I can prove beyond doubt that the charges are (**rugged, erroneous**).

6. When I asked the student why he wasn't going to the Senior Prom, he answered only with a(n) (**bleak, obtrusive**) smile.

7. After four years as the President's press secretary, I have become a noted (**adept, exploit**) in the art of fielding questions.

8. In Jonathan Swift's fictional country of Lilliput, everyone and everything is pint-sized, or (**diminutive, erroneous**).

9. The visitor's huge bulk, combined with his (**extemporaneous, languid**) manner, made me think of a tired whale.

10. Passengers could not exit the bus without tripping over the (**invincible, obtrusive**) package in the aisle.

11. When we tried to straighten out the mess, we found ourselves (**mired, chided**) in a mass of inaccurate, incomplete, and mixed-up records.

12. In the (**slipshod, extemporaneous**) give-and-take of a televised debate, it is easy for a nervous nominee to make a slip of the tongue.

13. I could see that the merchant's long, sad story about bad luck was only the (**adept, preamble**) to a request for a loan.

14. I would never trust my funds to anyone who is so (**bleak, slipshod**) in managing his own affairs.

15. When Emerson said "Hitch your wagon to a star," he meant that we should (**aspire, mire**) to reach the very highest levels of which we are capable.

16. Sergeant Alvin York was awarded this nation's highest honor for his many daring (**preambles, exploits**) during World War I.

17. The sculptor has done a superb job of representing the strong, rough planes of Lincoln's (**languid, rugged**) features.

18. It is up to all of us to (**impair, emancipate**) ourselves from prejudices and false ideas acquired early in life.

19. Our basketball team, with its well-planned attack, tight defense, and seven-foot center, proved all but (**invincible, skeptical**).

20. Far from admiring the way they got those letters of recommendation, I consider their deception utterly (**diminutive, despicable**).

Vocabulary in Context

Read the following passage, in which some of the words you have studied in this unit appear in **boldface** type. Then complete each statement given below the passage by circling the letter of the item that is **the same** or **almost the same** in meaning as the highlighted word.

Racing with the Sun

(Line)

Australian Hans Tholstrup once read an article about using a solar-powered, ultralight flying machine to successfully cross the English Channel. This **exploit** inspired the adventurer and solar-energy advocate to build a solar car for himself and to see how far it might take him. In 1982 he drove from west to east across the

(5) **bleak**, sun-baked Australian outback on solar power alone.

In 1987 Tholstrup instituted the World Solar Challenge (WSC), a race for solar-powered cars. The WSC covers a distance of 1,864 miles (3,000 km) from Darwin in the far north of Australia to Adelaide in the south. The Challenge is "to design a car

(10) capable of crossing the vast Australian continent, but with only daylight as fuel." The ultimate purpose is to interest highly **adept** engineers and designers into harnessing solar energy.

(15) Each solar-powered car in the WSC has its own solar panel, not larger than 1.6 square meters. Batteries store the generated electricity. With a charge little more than that required to run a hair dryer, the beautifully

(20) streamlined cars glide across **rugged** terrain for four or five pressure-packed days, stopping each evening to camp by the roadside in the Australian desert.

An odd-looking car tools along an Australian highway in the World Solar Challenge race.

The participants in the WSC are diverse.

(25) Team members come from universities and corporations all over the world, each **aspiring** to win the prize. Large, well-funded motor corporations, once **skeptical** of solar power, are now formidable foes. In scrambling to keep up, smaller school teams and individuals often display great ingenuity in building light, efficient cars. Everyone's contribution counts in the larger race to develop

(30) cheap and effective ways to use the sun's power.

1. The meaning of **exploit** (line 2) is
   a. tactic   c. deed
   b. misuse   d. contract

2. Bleak (line 5) most nearly means
   a. grimy   c. desolate
   b. lush   d. rosy

3. Adept (line 12) is best defined as
   a. proficient   c. maladroit
   b. bright   d. energetic

4. The meaning of **rugged** (line 20) is
   a. smooth   c. unconquerable
   b. rough   d. masterful

5. Aspiring (line 26) most nearly means
   a. pondering   c. needing
   b. striving   d. flying

6. Skeptical (line 27) is best defined as
   a. complimentary   c. opposed
   b. logical   d. suspicious

Definitions

Note carefully the spelling, pronunciation, part(s) of speech, and definition(s) of each of the following words. Then write the word in the blank space(s) in the illustrative sentence(s) following. Finally, study the lists of synonyms and antonyms given at the end of each entry.

1. brevity
(brev' ə tē)

(*n.*) shortness

The speech was notable more for its _____ than for its clarity.

SYNONYMS: conciseness, terseness, pithiness
ANTONYMS: verbosity, long-windedness, prolixity

2. comport
(kəm pôrt')

(*v.*) to conduct or bear oneself, behave; to be in agreement

As the students left the building, the principal reminded them to _____ themselves as emissaries of the school.

SYNONYMS: deport oneself, agree, concur

3. concise
(kən sīs')

(*adj.*) expressing much in a few words

As a rule of thumb, editors and readers appreciate writing that is _____ and forceful.

SYNONYMS: brief, succinct, terse, pithy, to the point
ANTONYMS: wordy, verbose, long-winded, prolix

4. demure
(di myùr')

(*adj.*) sober or serious in manner, modest

Despite her _____ appearance, she is a competitive speed skater, always ready for a challenge on ice.

SYNONYMS: shy, diffident, sedate, seemly, decorous
ANTONYMS: bold, forward, assertive, immodest

5. depreciation
(di prē shē ā' shən)

(*n.*) a lessening in value; a belittling

The accountant calculated the _____ of the computer over a period of five years.

SYNONYMS: cheapening, lowering, devaluation
ANTONYMS: increase, appreciation, enhancement

6. deteriorate
(di tir' ē ə rāt)

(*v.*) to lower in quality or value; to wear away

It is painful for anyone, particularly a doctor, to watch someone's health _____ .

SYNONYMS: worsen, decline, degenerate, debase
ANTONYMS: improve, fix up, enhance

7. divulge
(di vəlj′)

(v.) to tell, reveal; to make public

On some occasions, scrupulous reporters cannot
_____ their sources of information.

SYNONYMS: disclose, impart, spill the beans, "leak"
ANTONYMS: hide, conceal, cover up, secrete, keep under wraps

8. enlightened
(en līt′ ənd)

(adj.) free from ignorance and false ideas; possessing sound understanding

An _____ society is ruled by
knowledge and reason rather than superstition and prejudice.

SYNONYMS: knowing, informed, aware, cultivated
ANTONYMS: ignorant, unaware, untaught, benighted

9. forestall
(fōr stôl′)

(v.) to prevent by acting first

Sometimes it is possible to _____
a cold by taking Vitamin C.

SYNONYMS: hinder, thwart, preclude, ward off
ANTONYMS: welcome, accept, allow, submit, abide by

10. garble
(gär′ bəl)

(v.) to distort in such a way as to make unintelligible

If you've played "telephone," you know how easy it is to
inadvertently _____ a message.

SYNONYMS: jumble, scramble, confuse, misrepresent
ANTONYMS: clarify, elucidate, articulate

11. proponent
(prō pō′ nənt)

(n.) one who puts forward a proposal; one who supports a cause or belief

Lucretia Coffin Mott and Elizabeth Cady Stanton were
among the first _____ of women's
suffrage in the United States.

SYNONYMS: supporter, advocate, exponent
ANTONYMS: opponent, critic, foe, adversary

12. quaver
(kwā′ vər)

(v.) to shake, tremble; to trill

My voice _____ whenever I try to
reach the high notes.

SYNONYMS: quiver, vibrate, shiver, quake, palpitate

13. recoil
(v., ri koil′;
n., rē′ koil)

(v.) to spring back, shrink; (n.) the act of springing back

In The Speckled Band, sleuth Sherlock Holmes points out that
"violence does, in truth, _____ upon the violent."

When the engineer accidentally released the giant spring,
its powerful _____ sent him
sprawling.

SYNONYMS: (v.) flinch; (n.) kickback
ANTONYMS: (v.) advance, proceed, gain ground

14. recoup
(ri küp′)

(v.) to make up for, regain

I plan to _____ my family's lost fortune by working hard, earning extra money, and investing wisely.

SYNONYMS: recover, retrieve
ANTONYMS: lose, default, forfeit, kiss goodbye

15. reek
(rēk)

(n.) an unpleasant smell; (v.) to give off unpleasant smells; to give a strong impression

The unmistakable _____ of spoiled food greeted us as we entered the long-abandoned cabin.

In *How the Other Half Lives* (1890), Jacob Riis describes tenements in urban neighborhoods that _____ of poverty.

SYNONYMS: (n.) stench; (v.) stink, smell
ANTONYMS: (n.) perfume, fragrance, bouquet

16. relentless
(ri lent′ ləs)

(adj.) unyielding, harsh, without pity

The novel *Les Misérables* recounts ex-convict Jean Valjean's lifelong flight from a _____ police inspector.

SYNONYMS: stern, merciless, persistent, unremitting
ANTONYMS: merciful, accommodating, indulgent

17. rivulet
(riv′ yü lət)

(n.) a small stream

While we could hear the running water, dense vegetation hid the _____ from view.

SYNONYMS: brook, creek, rill

18. squander
(skwän′ dər)

(v.) to spend foolishly, waste

I think that it is criminal to _____ our natural resources.

SYNONYMS: misspend, dissipate
ANTONYMS: save, economize, hoard, squirrel away

19. staccato
(stə kät′ ō)

(adj.) detached or disconnected in sound or style

We strained to listen, and we heard _____ hoofbeats striking the pavement.

SYNONYMS: abrupt, disjointed
ANTONYMS: continuous, flowing, unbroken

20. statute
(stach′ üt)

(n.) a law

The student body is governed by the _____ of the university.

SYNONYMS: rule, ordinance, enactment

Completing the Sentence

From the words for this unit, choose the one that best completes each of the following sentences. Write the word in the space provided.

1. The program featured a debate between _____ of gun control and critics of legislation restricting ownership of firearms.

2. "I'm not afraid of anyone!" the boy piped up bravely, but we noticed that his voice _____ as he said it.

3. Leaders are judged by how well they _____ themselves in times of crisis.

4. The assertive heroines portrayed in many TV programs are a far cry from the _____ young ladies depicted in nineteenth-century novels.

5. Economists will tell you that inflation results in an increase in the supply of money and a(n) _____ in its value.

6. The telltale _____ of gas reminded us that someone had left a burner open on the stove.

7. The witnesses have testified at great length, but how much really valuable information have they _____ to the investigating committee?

8. Now that the storm has damaged the crops, it's up to us to work twice as hard to _____ our losses.

9. Despite the creature comforts we now enjoy, I feel that the quality of life has somehow _____ in recent years.

10. How often have we heard candidates for public office promise that they will be tough and _____ in fighting organized crime!

11. A(n) _____ public opinion, said Jefferson, is essential to a democratic society.

12. In saying that "_____ is the soul of wit," Shakespeare was reminding comedians to keep their jokes short and snappy.

13. In a passage that a composer has marked _____, every note should sound like the quick thrust of a knife.

14. A President will often try to _____ the defeat of a legislative program by appealing for the public's support on TV.

15. Since you worked so long and hard for the money you earned, it's doubly foolish to _____ it on things you don't really want or need.

16. What we need is not a lot of new legislation, but tough enforcement of the _____ already on the books.

17. To the district attorney's dismay, the witness _____ all the facts and misled the jury.

18. The child _____ in fear and disgust as the harmless water snake slithered over the floor.

19. As it wound its way through the desert, the mighty river became a mere _____ that travelers could easily wade across.

20. Since you are charged for every word you use in a telegram, it pays to be as _____ as possible.

Synonyms

*Choose the word from this unit that is **the same** or **most nearly the same** in meaning as the **boldface** word or expression in the given phrase. Write the word on the line provided.*

1. the **devaluation** of currency _____

2. the **unremitting** persecution of Huguenots _____

3. a **small stream** of sweet water _____

4. an abrupt or **disjointed** style of speech _____

5. an **ordinance** passed by the legislature _____

6. an **informed** and intelligent electorate _____

7. clothes that **smell** of tobacco _____

8. **conduct** oneself with dignity _____

9. quake or **quiver** with emotion _____

10. **scramble** a radio message _____

11. value **conciseness** in a short story _____

12. **ward off** an attack _____

13. **flinch** at the sound of an explosion _____

14. present a **brief** summary _____

15. "**leak**" the secret to the public _____

Antonyms

*Choose the word from this unit that is **most nearly opposite** in meaning to the **boldface** word or expression in the given phrase. Write the word on the line provided.*

16. an ardent **critic** of states' rights _____

17. **squirrel away** a small fortune _____

18. **forfeit** money or property _____

19. accompanied by a **bold** glance _____

20. likely to **improve** with age _____

Choosing the Right Word

*Circle the **boldface** word that more satisfactorily completes each of the following sentences.*

1. The young woman's (**demure, staccato**) smile and flirtatious manner drew admiring glances.

2. (**Rivulets, Reeks**) of sweat ran down the faces of the men working in that terrible heat.

3. In an attempt to mislead the enemy, the crafty prisoner of war deliberately (**divulged, garbled**) his account of how the attack had been planned.

4. The speaker's (**enlightened, staccato**) delivery truly reminded us of a jackhammer breaking up concrete.

5. She tried to appear calm, but her voice (**quavered, squandered**), revealing her agitation.

6. A person accused of a crime is not obliged to (**divulge, deteriorate**) anything that might be incriminating.

7. Once a political leader has lost the confidence of voters, it is almost impossible to (**comport, recoup**) it.

8. I wish there were a (**rivulet, statute**) that would prevent people from revealing the ending of a detective story!

9. I'm not saying that you shouldn't watch TV, but why (**recoup, squander**) so much of your time on those inane programs?

10. In order to (**recoil, forestall**) criticism of my proposal, I prepared myself with relevant facts and figures before the meeting.

11. Seeing my childhood friend so gray and infirm, I became keenly aware of the (**relentless, demure**) passage of the years.

12. When I learned how the air and water were being polluted, I became a strong (**brevity, proponent**) of ecological reforms.

13. The charitable programs sponsored by this organization (**forestall, comport**) well with our conception of a just and compassionate society.

14. It's all very well to build new housing, but we should also rehabilitate neighborhoods that have (**deteriorated, garbled**) through neglect.

15. "Wear and tear" is the (**depreciation, proponent**) that results from ordinary use, not from misuse.

16. It's not surprising that the clothing of firefighters often (**quavers, reeks**) of smoke and sweat.

17. Early rifles had such a "kick" to them that inexperienced soldiers were often injured by their (**recoil, depreciation**).

18. In spite of the vast number of details in the United States Constitution, the document is remarkably (**relentless, concise**).

19. William Shakespeare expressed the tragic (**brevity, statute**) of life by comparing it to a candle that must soon go out.

20. An old Chinese proverb suggests: "Make a candle to get light; read a book to get (**enlightened, concise**)."

*Read the following passage, in which some of the words you have studied in this unit appear in **boldface** type. Then complete each statement given below the passage by circling the letter of the item that is **the same** or **almost the same** in meaning as the highlighted word.*

Florence Griffith-Joyner

(Line)

Delorez Florence Griffith, the seventh of eleven children, grew up in urban Los Angeles. Her parents insisted that all their children **comport** themselves properly at home and in public. They were taught to speak correctly, to help at home, and to excel in school. Delorez, nicknamed Dee Dee, had a special gift: speed. (5)

"Flo Jo" wins 100-meter dash and an Olympic gold medal.

The **demure** girl was quiet around others, but she had a blazing talent for running. One of her sisters **divulged** that Dee Dee used to chase jackrabbits for fun. At seven, Dee Dee joined a track club; by age fourteen, she had won the Jesse Owens National (10) Youth Games. She set her sights on the Olympics.

In 1984, Florence Griffith qualified for the Olympics, and won a silver medal in the 200-meter dash. But she was kept off the relay team because her nails were too long! The **brevity** of her first (15) Olympic experience did not deter her. She remained **relentless** in her training while pursuing other interests, such as writing, modeling, and fashion design. In 1987, she married Olympic athlete Al Joyner. For the 1988 Olympics, she was allowed to (20) participate in all events for which she qualified, flamboyant nails and all. She dazzled fans with her speed and flashy outfits. A journalist dubbed her Flo Jo—and the name stuck. Flo Jo became the first American woman to win four Olympic medals. (25)

A lifelong **proponent** of education, Flo Jo would tell young people who wished to be like her, "Be better than me." Flo Jo was the first woman to chair the President's Council on Physical Fitness and Sports, and was inducted into the U.S. Track & Field Hall of Fame in 1995. When she died suddenly in 1998, the world lost a unique hero. (30)

---

1. The meaning of **comport** (line 2) is
a. articulate
b. announce
c. distort
d. behave

2. Demure (line 6) is best defined as
a. shy
b. gangly
c. beautiful
d. persistent

3. Divulged (line 8) most nearly means
a. lied
b. promised
c. revealed
d. supported

4. The meaning of **brevity** (line 15) is
a. difficulty
b. shortness
c. disappointment
d. waste

5. Relentless (line 17) most nearly means
a. abrupt
b. succinct
c. persistent
d. diffident

6. Proponent (line 26) is best defined as
a. judge
b. advocate
c. critic
d. detractor

Definitions

Note carefully the spelling, pronunciation, part(s) of speech, and definition(s) of each of the following words. Then write the word in the blank space(s) in the illustrative sentence(s) following. Finally, study the lists of synonyms and antonyms given at the end of each entry.

1. appreciable
(ə prē′ shə bəl)

(*adj.*) sufficient to be noticed or measured

The injured woman lost an _____ amount of blood before the paramedics arrived.

SYNONYMS: perceptible, detectable, considerable
ANTONYMS: slight, trivial, inconsequential, negligible

2. autocratic
(ô tə krat′ ik)

(*adj.*) absolute in power or authority

For many years, the island was under the _____ control of a dictator.

SYNONYMS: domineering, dictatorial, tyrannical, bossy
ANTONYMS: democratic, egalitarian, lenient, permissive, indulgent

3. blanch
(blanch)

(*v.*) to remove the color from; to make or turn pale; to parboil

Even the veteran rescue worker _____ upon seeing the crash site.

SYNONYMS: bleach, drain, wash out, go white
ANTONYMS: color, dye, infuse, blush, flush

4. blasphemy
(blas′ fə mē)

(*n.*) an act, utterance, or writing showing contempt for something sacred

Galileo was accused of _____ for asserting that the sun, and not the earth, is the center of the universe.

SYNONYMS: curse, profanity, sacrilege, imprecation
ANTONYMS: reverence, veneration, devotion, respect

5. brawny
(brô′ nē)

(*adj.*) strong, muscular

In Arthurian legend, one _____ knight after another tries to pull the sword Excalibar from the stone, but none succeeds.

SYNONYMS: broad-shouldered, strapping, husky, burly
ANTONYMS: slight, frail, delicate, puny

6. concerted
(kən sər′ tid)

(*adj.*) planned or performed in cooperation with others

Teenagers and adults, northerners and southerners alike, participated in a _____ drive to register new voters.

SYNONYMS: joint, cooperative, combined, consolidated
ANTONYMS: unorganized, unilateral, diffused

7. contend
(kən tend')

v.) to fight, struggle; to compete; to argue

I enjoy watching the four major tennis tournaments in which brilliant players _____ for the "grand slam" titles.

SYNONYMS: battle, dispute, vie, maintain, assert
ANTONYMS: yield, acquiesce, submit, relinquish

8. humane
(hyü mān')

(*adj.*) kind, merciful

The _____ legal code of Hammurabi, king of Babylonia, was ahead of its time in seeking justice for the weak and the oppressed.

SYNONYMS: sympathetic, compassionate, kindhearted
ANTONYMS: cruel, merciless, unfeeling, brutal, heartless

9. illustrious
(i ləs' trē əs)

(*adj.*) very famous, distinguished

As a student of world politics, I would be thrilled to meet an _____ member of Parliament.

SYNONYMS: eminent, renowned, prominent, celebrated
ANTONYMS: unknown, obscure, nameless, anonymous

10. intolerable
(in täl' ər ə bəl)

(*adj.*) unbearable

To a perfectionist, mediocrity is more than unacceptable; it is simply _____ .

SYNONYMS: insufferable, unendurable, outrageous
ANTONYMS: enjoyable, pleasant, pleasing

11. irreverent
(i rev' ər ənt)

(*adj.*) disrespectful

The student's _____ comments show a lack of respect for people in authority.

SYNONYMS: profane, impious, sacrilegious, flippant
ANTONYMS: awed, respectful, devout, pious, deferential

12. laborious
(lə bôr' ē əs)

(*adj.*) not easy, requiring hard work; hardworking

After cleaning the gutters, we moved on to the _____ task of raking and bagging the leaves.

SYNONYMS: arduous, difficult, strenuous, wearisome
ANTONYMS: easy, effortless, facile

13. lithe
(līth)

(*adj.*) bending easily, limber

The burly linebacker was as _____ and agile as a ballet dancer.

SYNONYMS: supple, flexible, pliant, lissome
ANTONYMS: stiff, rigid, inflexible, taut

14. maltreat
(mal trēt′)

(*v.*) to abuse, use roughly or crudely

The candidate pledged to shut down any factory or manufacturing plant found to _____ workers.

SYNONYMS: misuse, mistreat, harm, aggrieve
ANTONYMS: coddle, pamper, indulge

15. ponder
(pän′ dər)

(*v.*) to consider carefully, reflect on

I need time to _____ all of my options before deciding how to spend the summer.

SYNONYMS: think over, ruminate, contemplate

16. subversive
(səb vər′ siv)

(*adj.*) intended to undermine or overthrow; (*n.*) one who advocates or attempts to undermine a political system

The underground movement circulated _____ pamphlets that criticized the government.

The Alien and Sedition Acts enacted in 1798 gave the U.S. president the power to deport any noncitizen deemed a

_____ .

SYNONYMS: (*adj.*) treasonous, traitorous; (*n.*) a revolutionary
ANTONYMS: (*adj.*) patriotic, loyal, true-blue

17. synthetic
(sin thet′ ik)

(*adj.*) made or put together by people; (*n.*) something artificial

Sometimes only a jeweler can detect the difference between an expensive _____ gem and a natural stone.

Nylon, rayon, and polyester are all _____ that have revolutionized the textile industry.

SYNONYMS: (*adj.*) artificial, ersatz
ANTONYMS: (*adj.*) natural, genuine

18. temperate
(tem′ pər ət)

(*adj.*) mild, moderate

It's impossible to have a _____ discussion with a hotheaded person.

SYNONYMS: composed, balanced, mellow, fair
ANTONYMS: immoderate, extreme, excessive, harsh

19. venomous
(ven′ ə məs)

(*adj.*) poisonous; spiteful, mean

It was only after we had rushed the child to the emergency room that we learned he'd been bitten by a _____ spider.

SYNONYMS: nasty, malicious, virulent, malevolent
ANTONYMS: harmless, innocuous, benign

20. wily
(wī′ lē)

(*adj.*) sly, shrewd, cunning

The fur trappers of colonial North America were known to be _____ traders.

SYNONYMS: clever, tricky, artful, foxy, cagey
ANTONYMS: dull-witted, dense, artless, straightforward

Completing the Sentence

From the words for this unit, choose the one that best completes each of the following sentences. Write the word in the space provided.

1. While a weight lifter generally has a muscular build, a gymnast typically is slim and _____.

2. The bite of the rattlesnake and the sarcastic words of a supposed friend can be equally _____.

3. Only when the new drug was administered did the patient begin to show _____ signs of improvement.

4. The years had _____ the auburn from her hair, which now resembled a crown of snowy white.

5. The _____ scout leader hoisted the canoe on his shoulders and carried it up the steep hill.

6. Our climb up the mountain was so _____ that we had to take a long rest before starting back down.

7. Some people were amused and others were outraged by the speaker's lighthearted, _____ attitude toward the institutions of government.

8. Some _____ fibers are actually better than natural materials for certain purposes.

9. We learned too late that the _____ fox had escaped our trap by doubling back on its own tracks.

10. Students joined with faculty in a(n) _____ effort to increase the school's involvement in community affairs.

11. The suspect was charged with writing and printing pamphlets that were considered _____ by the government.

12. In 1875 New York State instituted child protection laws that made it criminal to _____ children.

13. Mexico City is located deep in the tropics, but because of the altitude, its climate is _____.

14. The mountain climbers had to _____ with unfavorable weather and with the fatigue brought on by high altitude.

15. When I said that the famous rock star was singing off-key, his devoted fans seemed to think I was guilty of _____.

16. I resented the _____ manner in which he told us—without even asking for our opinion—what we should do to improve our situation.

17. I needed the job badly, but the working conditions in that company were so _____ that I finally had to quit.

18. Instead of trying to accomplish something worthwhile on her own, she spends her time boasting about her _____ ancestors.

19. Despite his image as a "hard-boiled businessman," he is notably _____ in his dealings with all of his employees.

20. "Once upon a midnight dreary, while I _____ weak and weary, Over many a quaint and curious volume of forgotten lore—"

Synonyms

*Choose the word from this unit that is **the same** or **most nearly the same** in meaning as the **boldface** word or expression in the given phrase. Write the word on the line provided.*

1. exiled for **treasonous** acts _____

2. a **joint** effort to find a solution _____

3. a **perceptible** increase in temperature _____

4. a comedian's **flippant** humor _____

5. take time to **think over** the offer _____

6. **maintain** that we are right _____

7. learn to accept **fair** criticism _____

8. prosecuted by the authorities for **sacrilege** _____

9. a **clever** and manipulative person _____

10. defamed by **malicious** slander _____

11. the **muscular** arms of the village blacksmith _____

12. institutions that **mistreat** laboratory animals _____

13. a toothache that is **unbearable** _____

14. a **supple** and graceful beech tree _____

15. **parboil** and freeze the vegetables _____

Antonyms

*Choose the word from this unit that is **most nearly opposite** in meaning to the **boldface** word or expression in the given phrase. Write the word on the line provided.*

16. made of **natural** rubber _____

17. set a precedent for **democratic** rule _____

18. **brutal** in their treatment of prisoners of war _____

19. writing that is **effortless** _____

20. a brilliant novel by an **obscure** writer _____

Choosing the Right Word

Circle the **boldface** word that more satisfactorily completes each of the following sentences.

1. Many novels about football players or boxers are written in a style as (**brawny, venomous**) as the athletes they portray.

2. Is it (**irreverent, appreciable**) of me to suggest that the "great man" may not be as great as he thinks he is?

3. We Americans believe that a government can be strong, resourceful, and efficient without being (**wily, autocratic**).

4. Computer-generated synthesizers that produce (**humane, synthetic**) speech enable individuals with Lou Gehrig's disease (ALS) to communicate.

5. As a public official, I have learned to expect criticism of my ideas, but not (**venomous, temperate**) attacks on my character.

6. It's unusual to have an election in which two siblings (**maltreat, contend**) for the same office.

7. All the nations of the world must join in a(n) (**concerted, irreverent**) attack on ignorance, poverty, and disease.

8. In a country as rich as ours, it is simply (**illustrious, intolerable**) that so many people live below the poverty level.

9. When the suspect (**pondered, blanched**) at the sudden accusation, her bloodless countenance as much as proclaimed her guilt.

10. He has the reputation of being a (**laborious, wily**) coach who can work with less experienced players and win.

11. Even those of us not philosophically inclined occasionally like to (**contend, ponder**) the meaning of life.

12. In days gone by, a dollar was a(n) (**concerted, appreciable**) sum, and was not to be spent lightly.

13. After months of counting calories, I learned to be (**temperate, lithe**) in eating.

14. Advocates of American independence were regarded by Great Britain not as patriots, but as dangerous (**subversives, blasphemy**).

15. Some people criticized the judge as being "too lenient," but I thought she was simply being (**autocratic, humane**).

16. After completing the textbook, the writer faced the (**laborious, brawny**) job of compiling the index.

17. To a skeptic, who doubts everything, the absolute belief in anything is (**blasphemy, synthetic**).

18. The official policy of the school is neither to pamper students nor to (**blanch, maltreat**) them.

19. Is there any other creature in the entire world that is as graceful and (**subversive, lithe**) as the common house cat?

20. Isn't it amazing how the Adams family of Massachusetts produced so many (**illustrious, intolerable**) men and women throughout the years?

Vocabulary in Context

Read the following passage, in which some of the words you have studied in this unit appear in **boldface** type. Then complete each statement given below the passage by circling the letter of the item that is **the same** or **almost the same** in meaning as the highlighted word.

Putting Animals First

(Line)

In the early 1860s, philanthropist and reformer Henry Bergh saw a New York City street merchant beating his horse. Spurred by the merchant's **intolerable** behavior, he organized a group of people to sponsor the American Society for the Prevention of Cruelty to Animals (ASPCA). Modeled after the **illustrious**
(5) Royal SPCA in England, the ASPCA was formed in 1866 to provide "effective means for the prevention of cruelty to animals throughout the United States." In its first year, the organization successfully lobbied the New York State
(10) legislature to pass the country's first animal anti-cruelty law.

More than a century later, the ASPCA is still driven by Bergh's mission. Now a modern organization with more than half
(15) a million members and donors, the ASPCA works to promote animal welfare in a variety of ways. For example, the **Humane** Education department holds classes, conducts workshops, and
(20) publishes materials for children and adults alike. The Government Affairs and

Heart-shaped paw on the ASPCA's Mobile Animal Clinic symbolizes Henry Bergh's mission.

Public Policy department advocates the passage of animal anti-cruelty laws at the local, regional, and national levels. The Animal Placement department makes a **concerted** effort to match homeless pets with loving families. The Humane Law
(25) Enforcement department investigates crimes committed against New York City's animal population, while ASPCA veterinarians at the Bergh Memorial Hospital provide expert animal care.

The ASPCA has had an **appreciable** effect on the quality of animals' lives nationwide. Thanks to Henry Bergh's vision, people are more likely to put
(30) animals first and less likely to **maltreat** dogs and cats in their homes—or horses in the street.

---

1. The meaning of **intolerable** (line 2) is
  a. pleasant   c. outrageous
  b. obscure   d. wearisome

2. Illustrious (line 4) most nearly means
  a. eminent   c. egalitarian
  b. sacrilegious   d. anonymous

3. Humane (line 18) is best defined as
  a. natural   c. compassionate
  b. harmless   d. unilateral

4. The meaning of **concerted** (line 24) is
  a. unorganized   c. slight
  b. cooperative   d. supple

5. Appreciable (line 28) most nearly means
  a. inconsequential   c. effortless
  b. sympathetic   d. considerable

6. Maltreat (line 30) is best defined as
  a. outfox   c. coddle
  b. trap   d. harm

Analogies *In each of the following, circle the item that best completes the comparison.*

1. voice is to **quaver** as
a. eye is to wink
b. nose is to sneeze
c. head is to turn
d. hand is to tremble

2. chore is to **laborious** as
a. feat is to cowardly
b. achievement is to obtrusive
c. deed is to commendable
d. exploit is to daring

3. wily is to **fox** as
a. energetic is to pig
b. slippery is to eel
c. docile is to mule
d. intelligent is to sheep

4. reek is to **unfavorable** as
a. stench is to favorable
b. fragrance is to unfavorable
c. aroma is to favorable
d. scent is to unfavorable

5. bleak is to **hospitality** as
a. wily is to cunning
b. concise is to brevity
c. slipshod is to care
d. humane is to mercy

6. staccato is to **music** as
a. choppy is to prose
b. extemporaneous is to oration
c. synthetic is to plastic
d. obtrusive is to art

7. obtrusive is to **unfavorable** as
a. enlightened is to favorable
b. temperate is to unfavorable
c. erroneous is to favorable
d. concerted is to unfavorable

8. rivulet is to **wet** as
a. mire is to dry
b. plateau is to wet
c. desert is to dry
d. fire is to wet

9. venomous is to **rattlesnake** as
a. lithe is to cheetah
b. diminutive is to elephant
c. rugged is to butterfly
d. brawny is to gnat

10. spendthrift is to **squander** as
a. beggar is to save
b. pickpocket is to invest
c. banker is to embezzle
d. miser is to hoard

11. forestall is to **prevent** as
a. blanch is to blush
b. chide is to scold
c. comport is to enjoy
d. aspire is to deny

12. blasphemy is to **irreverent** as
a. envy is to content
b. anger is to agreeable
c. doubt is to skeptical
d. pride is to humble

13. invincible is to **conquer** as
a. invisible is to hear
b. inaudible is to touch
c. inedible is to sell
d. intolerable is to bear

14. small is to **diminutive** as
a. big is to gigantic
b. tall is to appreciable
c. long is to concise
d. large is to petite

15. demure is to **sedate** as
a. illustrious is to obscure
b. languid is to listless
c. laborious is to agile
d. despicable is to remarkable

16. thinker is to **ponder** as
a. subversive is to recoup
b. proponent is to advocate
c. adept is to maltreat
d. critic is to contend

17. preamble is to **document** as
a. preface is to book
b. prelude is to statue
c. overture is to symphony
d. prologue is to painting

18. emancipate is to **enslave** as
a. impair is to consider
b. render is to contribute
c. garble is to confuse
d. divulge is to conceal

Word Associations

In each of the following groups, circle the word that is best defined or suggested by the given phrase.

1. valued speeches that were succinct and to the point
a. brevity
b. blasphemy
c. depreciation
d. wit

2. a law enacted by the government
a. rivulet
b. preamble
c. statute
d. depreciation

3. to carry oneself with dignity
a. squander
b. comport
c. blanch
d. chide

4. introduction to a formal statement
a. mire
b. preamble
c. brevity
d. statute

5. degenerate in quality, character, or value
a. deteriorate
b. aspire
c. contend
d. reek

6. dictatorial or despotic
a. humane
b. slipshod
c. autocratic
d. rugged

7. performed or carried out together
a. brawny
b. concise
c. concerted
d. irreverent

8. shrink from in fright
a. divulge
b. recoup
c. emancipate
d. recoil

9. turn as pale as a ghost
a. exploit
b. recoil
c. blanch
d. chide

10. think deeply
a. distort
b. ponder
c. maltreat
d. contend

11. having sensible ideas
a. despicable
b. demure
c. enlightened
d. illustrious

12. flexible and graceful
a. lithe
b. erroneous
c. invincible
d. wily

13. extremely small
a. diminutive
b. laborious
c. synthetic
d. intolerable

14. abuse cruelly
a. maltreat
b. forestall
c. squander
d. garble

15. of considerable size or quantity
a. slipshod
b. skeptical
c. appreciable
d. rugged

16. harm or damage the value or effectiveness of
a. recoup
b. impair
c. contend
d. comport

17. spiteful or poisonous
a. extemporaneous
b. temperate
c. languid
d. venomous

18. small stream
a. proponent
b. rivulet
c. depreciation
d. subversive

19. take advantage of
a. exploit
b. squander
c. ponder
d. aspire

20. showing disrespect for something sacred
a. brevity
b. reek
c. blasphemy
d. statute

Vocabulary in Context

*Read the following passage, in which some of the words you have studied in Units 10–12 appear in **boldface** type. Then complete each statement given below the passage by circling the item that is **the same** or **almost the same** in meaning as the highlighted word.*

Thru-Hikers on the A.T. Trail

(Line)

The A.T., as its admirers call it, is America's most **illustrious** long-distance hiking path, the Appalachian Trail. Conservationist Benton MacKaye

(5) first envisioned the trail in 1921. When its many sections were linked in 1948, the A.T. was an impressive 2,158 miles long, winding through green hills and **rugged** mountains in 14 states.

(10) Three kinds of hikers are found on the trail. Day hikers go on short, scenic jaunts. Section hikers tackle specific parts of the trail, on extended outings. Thru-hikers set out to hike the entire

(15) trail, starting from either the northern terminus (Mount Katahdin, Maine) or the southern terminus (Springer Mountain, Georgia).

Thru-hikers are women, men, and

(20) young adults from around the world. They differ widely from one another, but are united in their fierce desire to complete the A.T.—despite having to **contend** with hardship and danger.

(25) Before setting out they need to be well-equipped with packs, cooking gear, water bottles, and much more.

Durable boots that fit are essential, since nothing can **impair** a hiker's

(30) stride faster than badly blistered feet. Once on the A.T., a typical hiker can expect to travel at about one mile per hour. As he or she grows accustomed to the **laborious** nature

(35) of thru-hiking, two (or even three) miles per hour can be achieved.

But don't get the **erroneous** impression that life on the trail is dull. The Appalachian terrain is

(40) varied and beautiful, and hikers must be ever vigilant to avoid a host of ills; dehydration, hypothermia, leg injury, and bad water are just a few. It generally takes five or six

(45) months to complete the trail. Those who finish will tell you that the adventure, the friendships made, and the exultation at the end of the hike are worth every second of

(50) hardship.

---

1. Illustrious (line 2) most nearly means
a. noticeable   c. difficult
b. celebrated   d. discussed

2. Rugged (line 9) is best defined as
a. steep   c. well-traveled
b. tedious   d. rocky

3. The meaning of **contend** (line 24) is
a. battle   c. endure
b. coexist   d. yield

4. Impair (line 29) most nearly means
a. attack   c. disable
b. strengthen   d. exemplify

5. Laborious (line 34) is best defined as
a. tedious   c. repetitive
b. time-consuming   d. arduous

6. The meaning of **erroneous** (line 37) is
a. imaginary   c. doubtful
b. thoughtless   d. fallacious

Choosing the Right Meaning

Read each sentence carefully. Then circle the item that best completes the statement below the sentence.

Before its mass production in the 1800s, soap was commonly made at home by a process that involved rendering animal fat. (2)

1. The word **rendering** in line 2 is best defined as

a. delivering   b. adding   c. submitting   d. extracting

When Boss Tweed ruled New York City in the 1860s, government floundered in a mire of corruption and graft. (2)

2. In line 2 the word **mire** most nearly means

a. river   b. mud slide   c. assortment   d. swamp

In the arts, as in any field of endeavor, the laurels usually go to those who are as laborious as they are naturally gifted. (2)

3. In line 2 the word **laborious** is used to mean

a. difficult   b. wearisome   c. industrious   d. arduous

The naturalist produced an old wooden birdcall and with it expertly imitated the quaver of a meadowlark. (2)

4. The best definition for the word **quaver** in line 2 is

a. tremble   b. trill   c. shiver   d. cackle

Some scientists contend it is possible—even probable—that intelligent life not unlike our own exists elsewhere in the universe. (2)

5. The word **contend** in line 1 most nearly means

a. deny   b. struggle   c. vie   d. maintain

Antonyms

In each of the following groups, circle the word or expression that is most nearly the **opposite** of the word in **boldface** type.

1. staccato
a. low-pitched
b. shaking
c. musical
d. flowing

2. synthetic
a. scientific
b. natural
c. sincere
d. artificial

3. irreverent
a. droll
b. respectful
c. lowly
d. sneaky

4. relentless
a. empty
b. poor
c. merciful
d. noisy

5. impair
a. combine
b. disable
c. relate
d. improve

6. proponent
a. supporter
b. legislator
c. component
d. opponent

7. erroneous
a. correct
b. pleasant
c. slippery
d. mistaken

8. recoup
a. gain
b. avenge
c. lose
d. reveal

9. despicable
a. detestable
b. praiseworthy
c. cowardly
d. imaginary

11. bleak
a. sunny
b. pale
c. abrupt
d. huge

13. invincible
a. brave
b. vulnerable
c. peaceful
d. victorious

15. demure
a. cultured
b. strange
c. trite
d. bold

10. brawny
a. nasty
b. husky
c. puny
d. tricky

12. garble
a. clog
b. medicate
c. clarify
d. injure

14. laborious
a. easy
b. difficult
c. long
d. brief

16. forestall
a. win
b. lose
c. prevent
d. submit

Word Families

A. *On the line provided, write the word you have learned in Units 10–12 that is related to each of the following nouns.*
EXAMPLE: venom—**venomous**

1. irreverence

2. emancipation, emancipator

3. autocrat, autocracy

4. wiliness, wile(s)

5. deterioration

6. obtrusiveness, obtrusion, obtruder

7. invincibility, invincibleness

8. erroneousness, error

9. impairment, impairer

10. conciseness, concision

11. aspiration, aspirer

12. maltreatment

13. contender, contention, contest

14. skeptic, skepticism

15. languidness, languor

B. *On the line provided, write the word you have learned in Units 10–12 that is related to each of the following verbs.*
EXAMPLE: synthesize—**synthetic**

16. subvert

17. propound

18. appreciate

19. extemporize

20. revere

 **Two-Word Completions**

Circle the pair of words that best complete the meaning of each of the following passages.

1. The _____ statistics cited in the magazine article certainly _____ its effectiveness. If the author had made sure that his figures were correct, his argument might have been more convincing.
a. bleak . . . quavered
b. laborious . . . enlightened
c. slipshod . . . rendered
d. erroneous . . . impaired

2. I did everything I could to _____ his cunning attempts to undermine my authority in the company; unfortunately, he proved too _____ and persistent for me to anticipate all his moves all the time.
a. chide . . . impair
b. forestall . . . wily
c. divulge . . . slipshod
d. subvert . . . demure

3. A ballerina's _____ and graceful figure contrasts sharply with a weight lifter's massively _____ physique.
a. demure . . . languid
b. lithe . . . brawny
c. diminutive . . . concise
d. slipshod . . . rugged

4. Though a(n) _____ master might deal kindly and generously with his or her animals, a cruel one would _____ and abuse them.
a. autocratic . . . impair
b. enlightened . . . emancipate
c. humane . . . maltreat
d. relentless . . . exploit

5. When Shakespeare's Polonius says that _____ is the soul of wit, he extols the virtues of a _____ and succinct phrase.
a. brevity. . . concise
b. blasphemy . . . wily
c. depreciation . . . staccato
d. brawn . . . venomous

6. Her talents are just average, but she has _____ them to the fullest. On the other hand, he was given great natural abilities, but he has _____ them on trifles.
a. exploited . . . squandered
b. pondered . . . impaired
c. divulged . . . recouped
d. contended . . . forestalled

Building with Classical Roots

spec, spic—to look

This root appears in **despicable** (page 117), which means "that which is to be looked down at." Some other words based on this root are listed below.

aspect	**introspection**	**prospective**	**retrospect**
conspicuous	**perspicacious**	**respective**	**specter**

From the list of words above, choose the one that corresponds to each of the brief definitions below. Write the word in the blank space in the illustrative sentence below the definition.

1. a phantom, apparition; a fearful image or threatening possibility

The hooded figure was a frightening _____ that Haloween night.

2. looked forward to, expected

I plan to invite my _____ sister-in-law out to lunch next week.

3. an examination of one's own thoughts and feelings (*"looking within"*)

The recluse was given to long hours of _____ and meditation.

4. belonging to each; individual (*"looking back and forth"*)

Mother sent the children to their _____ rooms to cool off after the argument.

5. an appearance; a side or view; the direction something faces

It's important to consider all _____ of an issue before coming to a conclusion.

6. noticeable, drawing attention

We never expected to enjoy living in such a large and _____ building.

7. keen in observing and understanding (*"able to see through"*)

Nineteenth-century writer Alexis de Tocqueville was a _____ observer of American society, politics, and culture of the day.

8. with reference to the past; a survey of the past (*"a looking back"*)

"In _____," he mused, "my college years were probably some of the happiest times of my life, though I certainly didn't realize it at the time."

From the list of words on page 144, choose the one that best completes each of the following sentences. Write the word in the space provided.

1. Not in the habit of _____, she rarely considered her feelings about things, and instead believed solely in actions.

2. I can see now in _____ where I went wrong and created the conditions for our failure.

3. The best _____ of this situation is that we can work together for a worthwhile cause.

4. When the drought continued into a second year, government officials realized that the nation might soon face the terrible _____ of famine.

5. It's pretty hard not to be _____ in a crowd when you stand 6 feet 9 inches tall and have a thick head of flaming red hair!

6. After hearing the public debates, we will be better able to judge the _____ merits of the candidates.

7. It is dangerously unwise to base your future plans on _____ earnings.

8. We were quite confused until her _____ observation suddenly illuminated the crux of the problem.

---

*Circle the **boldface** word that more satisfactorily completes each of the following sentences.*

1. The President selected the most (**perspicacious, conspicuous**) colleague from among his inner circle to serve as National Security Advisor.

2. The early works of the inventive young painter at first seemed so promising and original, but in (**specter, retrospect**), they have not withstood the test of time.

3. Each Tuesday morning someone from the admissions office takes (**prospective, respective**) applicants on a tour of the facilities.

4. No matter how many times they tried to clean it, they simply could not remove that very (**perspicacious, conspicuous**) stain from the living room rug.

5. In the end it was the (**specter, aspect**) of summer school that eventually led the student to take responsibility for his learning.

6. Natural physical talent is but one (**introspection, aspect**) to consider when evaluating the promise of a young athlete.

7. After the bonfire went out, the campers retired to their (**respective, prospective**) tents to settle in for a good night's sleep.

8. The German poet and dramatist Goethe believed that it was by action rather than by (**retrospect, introspection**) that people could come to know their true selves.

Read the following sentences, paying special attention to the words and phrases underlined. From the words in the box below, find better choices for these underlined words and phrases. Then use these choices to rewrite the sentences.

WORD BANK

adept	chide	divulge	illustrious	slipshod
appreciable	comport	exploit	languid	squander
aspire	concise	forestall	ponder	temperate
brevity	despicable	garble	proponent	wily

One Writer's Legacy

1. From an early age Eudora Welty (1909–2001) <u>had ambitious hopes</u> to become a published writer of fiction.

_____

_____

2. But even she may not have anticipated winning the Pulitzer Prize in 1973, and the <u>highly distinguished and commendable</u> career that would span many decades.

_____

_____

3. Her first book, a collection of short stories set in rural Mississippi and titled *Curtain of Green*, was published in 1941. She was <u>thoroughly skilled</u> at creating memorable stories full of life's funny and unexpected moments, filtered through the lens of human relationships.

_____

_____

4. She has been both derided and extolled for her ability to sympathize with the characters she created, even those who commit <u>vile and unworthy</u> acts.

_____

_____

5. Because the subject of her fiction is often women in the rural south, critics have wondered whether her own experiences influenced Welty's works, but she steadfastly refused to <u>spill</u> the personal details of her life.

_____

_____

6. Her <u>short-winded</u> memoir, *One Writer's Beginnings* (1983), gives insights into this brilliant woman's methods, and explores the key ideas of listening, learning, and finding one's voice.

_____

_____

Analogies

In each of the following, circle the item that best completes the comparison.

1. languid is to **vigor** as
a. bleak is to timeliness
b. sparse is to direction
c. stagnant is to motion
d. brazen is to intention

2. emancipate is to **bondage** as
a. subjugate is to servitude
b. parole is to incarceration
c. liberate is to independence
d. adjourn is to convention

3. pensive is to **ponder** as
a. sardonic is to condone
b. incredulous is to believe
c. flippant is to suggest
d. skeptical is to doubt

4. chide is to **reprimand** as
a. squander is to salvage
b. abridge is to disentangle
c. recoil is to proliferate
d. compensate is to remunerate

5. incessant is to **relentless** as
a. laborious is to arduous
b. superfluous is to essential
c. despicable is to credible
d. rabid is to apathetic

6. illustrious is to **eminent** as
a. steadfast is to unflinching
b. cherubic is to devilish
c. ghastly is to humane
d. subversive is to obtrusive

7. diffuse is to **concise** as
a. momentous is to significant
b. lackadaisical is to diligent
c. odious is to repugnant
d. lucrative is to obese

8. brawny is to **strength** as
a. rugged is to genius
b. comely is to beauty
c. wily is to wisdom
d. lithe is to intelligence

9. irreverent is to **respect** as
a. irate is to anger
b. arbitrary is to sophistication
c. doleful is to joy
d. sterling is to wealth

10. words are to **garble** as
a. dreams are to succumb
b. hopes are to aspire
c. thoughts are to muddle
d. emotions are to forestall

Choosing the Right Meaning

Read each sentence carefully. Then circle the item that best completes the statement below the sentence.

"Love is a spirit all compact of fire.
Not gross to sink, but light, and will aspire." (Shakespeare)   (2)

1. The word **aspire** in line 2 is used to mean
a. soar   b. yearn   c. seek   d. desire

That fortune hunters catch scent of her so quickly may be due to the fact that the heiress fairly reeks of money.   (2)

2. The word **reeks** in line 2 most nearly means
a. spends huge amounts   c. gives the impression
b. smells unpleasantly   d. saves a great deal

Fresh spinach must be blanched before it is sautéed for dishes such as eggs Florentine.   (2)

3. In line 1 the word **blanched** is best defined as

a. whitened   b. discolored   c. seasoned   d. boiled briefly

Students have for generations memorized and recited the pensive lines of Walt Whitman's great elegy "O Captain! My Captain!"   (2)

4. In line 1 the word **pensive** most nearly means

a. formal   b. thoughtful   c. melancholy   d. reflective

Rugged weather had kept the fishing boats at their harbor moorings for the better part of a week.   (2)

5. The best definition for the word **Rugged** in line 1 is

a. Irregular   b. Rocky   c. Blunt   d. Stormy

Two-Word Completions

Circle the pair of words that best complete the meaning of each of the following sentences.

1. Though I'm perfectly willing to put up with the occasional hour or two of _____ that my job involves, the prospect of spending my entire day on menial or unpleasant tasks is _____.

a. larceny . . . daunting
b. fodder . . . repugnant
c. drudgery . . . intolerable
d. mire . . . despicable

2. Reporters who are willing to tell a jury what they have learned but refuse to _____ their sources are _____ to be brought up on charges of contempt of court.

a. sully . . . immune
b. maltreat . . . concerted
c. console . . . fated
d. divulge . . . liable

3. At the end of the grim novel, the spendthrift hero, who has recklessly _____ his entire fortune on riotous living, is buried in a _____ grave.

a. rejuvenated . . . vagrant's
b. impoverished . . . envoy's
c. relinquished . . . accomplice's
d. squandered . . . pauper's

4. Although the disastrous crash of 1929 did _____ many of those who had sunk money into the stock market, a few wily investors did eventually manage to _____ some or all of their losses.

a. impair . . . render
b. impoverish . . . recoup
c. reprieve . . . salvage
d. forestall . . . surmount

5. In verses that have resounded through the centuries, Homer recounts the daring _____ of the _____ heroes who fought so fearlessly beneath the walls of Troy.

a. exploits . . . intrepid
b. tirades . . . dissolute
c. statutes . . . subversive
d. hordes . . . militant

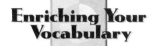

Enriching Your Vocabulary

Read the passage below. Then complete the exercise at the bottom of the page.

A Penny for Your Thoughts?

An old saying holds that "the love of money is the root of all evil." Whatever you think of this warning, you can agree that money is certainly the root of a rich vocabulary of money words and economic terms. Just think of all the money words we use in our daily lives: names of coins and bills; words such as *buy, sell, invest,* and *borrow*; and common banking terms such as *debit, credit, deposit,* and *withdrawal.* The field of *economics*—the social science that deals with the production, distribution, and consumption of goods and services—has given us a wealth of terminology. Are we in a *bear market* or a *bull market?* Do you have a balanced *stock portfolio?* Do you have any outstanding *liabilities* (Unit 8)—that is, debts?

N.Y. Stock Exchange, Oct. 28, 1997. A record one billion shares were sold.

Money lends itself to valuable expressions and quotations as well. Ben Franklin reminds us that "A penny saved is a penny earned." Shakespeare warns us that "All that glitters is not gold." Efficiency experts caution us that "Time is money." Do you worry that money "burns a hole in your pocket"? Are you a *spendthrift* or are you *parsimonious?* Spend some time acquainting yourself with a few of these priceless language resources.

In Column A below are 8 more words whose origins lie in the world of economics. With or without a dictionary, match each word with its meaning in Column B.

Column A

_____ **1.** depression
_____ **2.** recession
_____ **3.** inflation
_____ **4.** asset
_____ **5.** surplus
_____ **6.** deficit
_____ **7.** monopoly
_____ **8.** interest

Column B

a. any useful or valuable resource you own that has exchange value

b. the amount by which a sum of money falls below the required amount; shortfall; inadequacy, insufficiency

c. a charge made for the use of money, expressed as a percentage

d. a period of widespread decline in an economy, characterized by a serious decrease in business activity, falling wages and prices, and unemployment

e. an increase in consumer prices; a decline in the purchasing power of money

f. exclusive control of the means of producing or selling goods or services in a given market

g. a quantity or amount in excess of what is needed or used

h. a temporary decline in business activity

Definitions

Note carefully the spelling, pronunciation, part(s) of speech, and definition(s) of each of the following words. Then write the word in the blank space(s) in the illustrative sentence(s) following. Finally, study the lists of synonyms and antonyms given at the end of each entry.

1. ad infinitum
(ad in fə nī′ təm)

(*adv.*) endlessly

Children who hear a favorite story read over and over _____ are learning about language.

SYNONYMS: forever, unceasingly, incessantly, ceaselessly
ANTONYMS: succinctly, concisely, tersely, briefly

2. apportion
(ə pôr′ shən)

(*v.*) to divide and give out in shares

The aging king decided to _____ the lands of his vast kingdom among his three daughters.

SYNONYMS: distribute, allot, parcel out, allocate

3. bona fide
(bō′ nə fīd)

(*adj.*) genuine; sincere

The appraiser studied the old book and declared it to be a _____ first edition of *Moby Dick.*

SYNONYMS: authentic, indisputable, legitimate, certified
ANTONYMS: false, fake, bogus, spurious, counterfeit

4. buoyant
(boi′ ənt)

(*adj.*) able to float easily; able to hold things up; cheerful, hopeful

We were weary and anxious to get home, but our friend's _____ spirits kept us going.

SYNONYMS: blithe, jaunty, lighthearted, animated
ANTONYMS: downcast, depressed, gloomy, morose

5. clique
(klēk; klik)

(*n.*) a small, exclusive group of people

The queen was surrounded by a _____ of powerful nobles who actually ran the country.

SYNONYMS: inner circle, coterie

6. concede
(kən sēd′)

(*v.*) to admit as true; to yield, submit

Even though the votes were all in and counted, the losing candidate refused to _____ the election.

SYNONYMS: acknowledge, grant, allow, assent
ANTONYMS: contest, dispute, gainsay, challenge

7. congenial
(kən jēn′ yəl)

(*adj.*) getting on well with others; agreeable, pleasant

I was relieved when my bunkmate at summer camp turned out to be considerate and _____.

SYNONYMS: friendly, sociable, amiable, compatible
ANTONYMS: disagreeable, surly, cold, standoffish

8. lofty
(lôf′ tē)

(*adj.*) very high; noble

My mentor maintains _____ standards and works hard to adhere to them.

SYNONYMS: elevated, towering, exalted, grand
ANTONYMS: base, petty, low, sordid, despicable

9. migration
(mī grā′ shən)

(*n.*) a movement from one country or region to another

_____ from north to south has contributed to the political clout of the Sun Belt.

SYNONYMS: population shift, mass movement

10. perceive
(pər sēv′)

(*v.*) to be aware of through the senses, observe; to grasp mentally

I thought I _____ a flicker of guilt on my brother's face when I asked who ate my slice of pie.

SYNONYMS: notice, discern, understand
ANTONYMS: miss, overlook, be blind to

11. perverse
(pər vərs′)

(*adj.*) inclined to go against what is expected; stubborn; turned away from what is good and proper

Some teenagers get _____ pleasure from blasting music that their parents do not like.

SYNONYMS: obstinate, contrary, mulish, wayward
ANTONYMS: tractable, docile, amenable, yielding

12. prelude
(pre′ lüd)

(*n.*) an introduction; that which comes before or leads off

The orchestral _____ to the new opera seemed more interesting to me than the opera itself.

SYNONYMS: preface, overture, prologue, "curtain-raiser"
ANTONYMS: epilogue, postlude, aftermath

13. rancid
(ran′ sid)

(*adj.*) stale, spoiled

When he opened the door, there poured forth the unmistakably _____ odor of some ancient leftovers.

SYNONYMS: foul, rank, fetid, sour, rotten, putrid
ANTONYMS: wholesome, fresh

14. rustic
(rəs′ tik)

(*adj.*) country-like; simple, plain; awkward; (*n.*) one who lives in the country

We rented a _____ cabin, with no electricity or running water, twenty miles from the town.

On the trail we met an amiable old _____ carrying a fishing pole and a string of trout he'd caught.

SYNONYMS: (*adj.*) rough, unsophisticated, countrified
ANTONYMS: (*adj.*) citified, urban, sophisticated, suave

15. sever
(sev′ ər)

(*v.*) to separate, divide into parts

It was extreme of her to _____ ties with her former best friend, but that is what she did.

SYNONYMS: cut off, amputate, break off, dissolve
ANTONYMS: join, unite, weld together

16. sordid
(sôr′ did)

(*adj.*) wretchedly poor; run-down; mean or selfish

Nineteenth century reformers made people aware of just how _____ conditions were in city slums.

SYNONYMS: filthy, squalid, base, vile, seedy, sleazy
ANTONYMS: pure, noble, opulent, lavish

17. untenable
(ən ten′ ə bəl)

(*adj.*) not capable of being held or defended; impossible to maintain

Minutes into the debate she had a sinking feeling that her position was completely _____.

SYNONYMS: indefensible, insupportable, groundless
ANTONYMS: irrefutable, impregnable, incontestable

18. versatile
(vər′ sə təl)

(*adj.*) able to do many things well; capable of many uses

By moving from comedy to drama to musicals, he has shown himself to be a truly _____ actor.

SYNONYMS: adaptable, handy, all-around, many-sided
ANTONYMS: limited, specialized, restricted

19. vindicate
(vin′ də kāt)

(*v.*) to clear from hint or charge of wrongdoing; to defend successfully against opposition; to justify

Though the accused was _____ in the end, his career was all but ruined by the allegations.

SYNONYMS: acquit, absolve, exonerate, advocate
ANTONYMS: implicate, incriminate, condemn, convict

20. wane
(wān)

(*v.*) to lose size, strength, or power

As the moon _____, the nights grew darker; we could hardly see our way along the forest trails.

SYNONYMS: diminish, decline, subside, dwindle
ANTONYMS: grow, wax, amplify, balloon, increase

Completing the Sentence

From the words for this unit, choose the one that best completes each of the following sentences. Write the word in the space provided.

1. Although many of my friends seem to like him, I've never found him to be a particularly _____ companion.

2. The Declaration of Independence first set forth the _____ standards to which we as a nation have ever since aspired.

3. We found it easy to float in the lake because the high salt content makes the water extremely _____.

4. I am convinced that the Drama Club is run by a(n) _____ of students who reserve all the best roles for themselves.

5. New employees are assigned their duties by the office manager, who is responsible for _____ work among the staff.

6. Who would believe that this peaceful, _____ hideaway is only twenty-five miles from the city?

7. The accused clerk _____ himself by producing signed receipts for all the questioned items.

8. We began to _____ the impact of the tornado only after viewing the flattened neighborhood and interviewing residents.

9. The seasonal _____ of birds southward reminds us that we have come to the end of the summer vacation.

10. Since the theory is based on inaccurate and out-of-date information, it is clearly _____.

11. It is a regrettable fact of our history that several presidential administrations have been tainted by _____ scandals.

12. I realize that I made a bad mistake, but at least I possess the strength of character to _____ that I was wrong and apologize.

13. It takes a really _____ athlete to win varsity letters in three different sports.

14. Isn't it boring when people go on and on about *their* looks, *their* clothes, and *their* popularity _____?

15. In 1776 the Continental Congress moved to _____ all political connections between the colonies and Great Britain.

16. The oil, which had been inadvertently stored in a heated room, soon began to exude a rank odor that told us it had turned _____.

17. She's not really hungry; she's just being _____ in insisting on eating now.

18. Dismissing all his rivals as impostors, the undefeated heavyweight boxer pronounced himself the only _____ contender for the crown.

19. The early cold spell proved to be a fitting _____ to one of the most severe winters of modern times.

20. When the mayor failed to carry out his campaign promises, his popularity quickly _____, and he failed to win reelection.

Synonyms   *Choose the word from this unit that is **the same** or **most nearly the same** in meaning as the **boldface** word or expression in the given phrase. Write the word on the line provided.*

1. the **towering** mountain peaks   _____

2. a kind and **friendly** host   _____

3. tell jokes and giggle **incessantly**   _____

4. **discern** a change in attitude   _____

5. jaunty airs and **blithe** spirits   _____

6. ready to **acknowledge** an error   _____

7. **allocate** funds based on need   _____

8. **population shift** from north to south   _____

9. a **coterie** of influential donors   _____

10. shocked by their **wayward** behavior   _____

11. watched the initial enthusiasm **dwindle**   _____

12. ridiculously **indefensible** reasons   _____

13. a **handy** gadget with many uses   _____

14. an **unsophisticated**, charming scene   _____

15. new facts that **justified** her claim   _____

Antonyms   *Choose the word from this unit that is **most nearly opposite** in meaning to the **boldface** word or expression in the given phrase. Write the word on the line provided.*

16. made a **bogus** offer   _____

17. a shockingly **opulent** dwelling place   _____

18. wondered if the oil was **fresh**   _____

19. an intriguing **epilogue** to the story   _____

20. **weld together** sections of the sculpture   _____

 **Choosing the Right Word**

*Circle the **boldface** word that more satisfactorily completes each of the following sentences.*

1. I could tell from his animated expression and his sprightly step that he was in a (**buoyant, versatile**) mood.

2. They claimed to be unselfish patriots, but we knew that, in reality, they were acting from the most (**untenable, sordid**) motives.

3. There are more than 100 members in the state legislature, but the real power is held by a small (**clique, prelude**) of insiders.

4. A good politician must appear (**sordid, congenial**) even when he or she is feeling cross and unsociable.

5. Good citizens should not sit idly by while the vitality of their community (**wanes, concedes**).

6. Our problem now is not to (**sever, apportion**) blame for our failures, but to find a way to achieve success.

7. I appreciate her interest in me, but I am annoyed by her tendency to offer criticism and advice (**bona fide, ad infinitum**).

8. The successful invasion of France in June, 1944 was only a (**prelude, migration**) to the great Allied victories that ended the war in Europe.

9. You are at a stage of life when you should begin to (**wane, sever**) the apron strings that tie you to your mother.

10. Shakespeare's clowns are often simple (**cliques, rustics**) who are trying to behave like sophisticated men of the world.

11. Leonardo da Vinci was a (**versatile, buoyant**) genius who excelled in many different fields of art and science.

12. Because our tank forces had been destroyed, the position of the ground troops proved (**congenial, untenable**).

13. They will not be allowed to vote in the election because they are not considered (**ad infinitum, bona fide**) residents of the community.

14. American society in recent years has been deeply affected by the steady (**migration, clique**) from the inner city to the suburbs.

15. The atmosphere in the tiny, airless cell soon grew as (**buoyant, rancid**) as the foul-smelling soup the prisoner was fed every night.

16. One of the aims of education is to enable us to (**perceive, sever**) the difference between what is truly excellent and what is second-rate.

17. When he came home from college for Thanksgiving break, he treated us "high school kids" with (**sordid, lofty**) scorn.

18. The psychologist said that troubled young people often have a (**perverse, rancid**) impulse to do exactly what will be most injurious to them.

19. My faith in that seemingly ordinary young girl was entirely (**vindicated, perceived**).

20. He talks a great game of tennis, but I (**wane, concede**) nothing to him until he has shown that he can beat me on the court.

Vocabulary in Context

*Read the following passage, in which some of the words you have studied in this unit appear in **boldface** type. Then complete each statement given below the passage by circling the letter of the item that is **the same** or **almost the same** in meaning as the highlighted word.*

Watching the Whales

(Line)

See a 30-ton humpback whale hurl itself skyward and land with a mighty splash. Observe a gray whale and her **buoyant** calf float by. Look into the intelligent eye of a bottlenose dolphin and wonder what it **perceives** as it looks back at you. Listen to a pod of orcas in conversation. How? Go on a whale watch.

Over the past decade, whale watching has become one of the fastest (5) growing segments of the tourist industry worldwide. For the most part, this is good. Since a principal goal of whale watching is to educate the public about the importance of healthy whales and marine ecosystems, more (10) watching means greater public awareness and more effective conservation of whale populations. Unfortunately, more watching also means greater risk of whale/ship (15) collisions, and disruption of whale feeding grounds, breeding habits and

A humpback whale breaches the ocean's surface— a sight whale watchers love to see.

migration patterns.

Fortunately, excursion operators can do a lot to ensure that whale watching does not bother the whales. Operators (20) should adhere to a **lofty** code of ethics and follow guidelines such as these:
- Do not charge towards whales or dolphins.
- Approach slowly from behind and to the side.
- Approach one boat at a time.
- Do not approach closer than 100 meters. (25)
- Leave before the whales show signs of distress.

Customers should always follow the rules and choose a tour with a **bona fide** biologist or nature guide on board.

Whale watching is a privilege. We should act as guests in the whales' home and watch with open eyes, minds, and hearts. (30)

---

1. The meaning of **buoyant** (line 2) is
a. adaptable   c. animated
b. authentic   d. amiable

2. Perceives (line 3) most nearly means
a. acknowledges   c. distributes
b. submits   d. observes

3. Migration (line 18) is best defined as
a. mass movement   c. preface
b. coterie   d. exclusive group

4. The meaning of **lofty** (line 21) is
a. base   c. authentic
b. animated   d. very high

5. Bona fide (line 27) most nearly means
a. obstinate   c. grand
b. certified   d. fetid

Definitions

Note carefully the spelling, pronunciation, part(s) of speech, and definition(s) of each of the following words. Then write the word in the blank space(s) in the illustrative sentence(s) following. Finally, study the lists of synonyms and antonyms given at the end of each entry.

1. annex
(*v.* ə neks′;
n. an′ eks)

(*v.*) to add to, attach; to incorporate; (*n.*) an attachment or addition

The two nations protested when their militant neighbor _____ the disputed territory.

All back issues of magazines are kept next door on the second floor of the new library _____.

SYNONYMS: (*v.*) join, acquire, appropriate, procure

2. cleave
(klēv)

(*v.*) To cut or split open; to cling to

It is possible to _____ a ripe coconut neatly in two with just one swing of a machete.

SYNONYMS: sever, halve, sunder, adhere, clasp

3. cordial
(kôr′ jəl)

(*adj.*) in a friendly manner, hearty; cheery; (*n.*) a liqueur

Our aunt's _____ welcome made us all feel right at home in her huge, drafty, Victorian house.

Grasshopper pie is made not with grasshoppers but with crème de menthe, a _____.

SYNONYMS: (*adj.*) hospitable, affable, warm, convivial
ANTONYMS: (*adj.*) gruff, unfriendly, unsociable

4. cornerstone
(kôr′ nər stōn)

(*n.*) the starting point of a building; a fundamental principle or element

The _____ of the American judicial system is the presumption of innocence.

SYNONYMS: foundation, base, underpinning, support

5. debacle
(di bäk′ əl)

(*n.*) an overwhelming defeat, rout; a complete collapse or failure

After the _____ of their crushing loss in the World Series, the team vowed to return next year.

SYNONYMS: disaster, fiasco, calamity
ANTONYMS: success, triumph, victory, coup

6. devitalize
(dē vīt′ ə līz)

(*v.*) to make weak or lifeless

The long, dark winter, with its cold rain and gloomy skies, _____ her usually buoyant spirit.

SYNONYMS: enfeeble, sap, enervate
ANTONYMS: enliven, stimulate, energize, excite

7. embroil
(em broil')

(*v.*) to involve in a conflict or difficulty; to throw into confusion

The last thing I want is to _____ myself in a dispute between two of my best friends.

SYNONYMS: entangle, ensnarl
ANTONYMS: disentangle, separate, disconnect

8. exonerate
(eg zän' ə rāt)

(*v.*) to clear from a charge or accusation

The prisoner was set free after ten years, thanks to new evidence that _____ him of all charges.

SYNONYMS: absolve, acquit, vindicate, exculpate
ANTONYMS: implicate, incriminate, inculpate

9. glib
(glib)

(*adj.*) ready and fluent in speech; thoughtless, insincere

The salesman had such _____ answers to every objection that I grew extremely skeptical of his claims.

SYNONYMS: superficial, pat, oily, unctuous, facile,
ANTONYMS: halting, tongue-tied, speechless, awkward

10. haphazard
(hap haz' ərd)

(*adj.*) by chance, not planned; lacking order

The _____ arrangement of facts in his presentation left his listeners completely confused.

SYNONYMS: random, accidental, slapdash
ANTONYMS: deliberate, purposeful, orderly, meticulous

11. improvise
(im' prə vīz)

(*v.*) to compose or perform without preparation; to construct from available materials

After the earthquake, stunned villagers were forced to _____ shelters from the debris.

SYNONYMS: ad-lib, play it by ear, wing it, extemporize
ANTONYMS: plan, rehearse, practice, prepare

12. incite
(in sīt')

(*v.*) to rouse, stir up, urge on

Company agents were hired to _____ a riot at the steelworkers' protest demonstration.

SYNONYMS: spur, kindle, provoke, instigate, prompt
ANTONYMS: check, curb, impede, restrain, smother

13. influx
(in' fləks)

(*n.*) a coming in, inflow

An _____ of arctic air has brought unseasonably cold weather to half the country.

SYNONYMS: inpouring, inrush, invasion
ANTONYMS: outpouring, exodus, departure

14. pallor
(pal′ ər)

(*n.*) an extreme or unnatural paleness

"A ghost!" the girl gasped, her ＿＿＿＿＿＿＿＿＿＿＿＿
making her look much like a ghost herself as she ran away.

SYNONYMS: wanness, lividness, bloodlessness
ANTONYMS: flush, blush, rosiness, bloom

15. pedigree
(ped′ ə grē)

(*n.*) a list of ancestors, family tree; the history or origins of something

Despite his impressive ＿＿＿＿＿＿＿＿＿＿＿＿＿＿,
the colt showed little enthusiasm for racing.

SYNONYMS: lineage, ancestry, genealogy

16. precipitous
(pri sip′ ət əs)

(*adj.*) very steep

The novice hikers were very nervous as they carefully
negotiated the ＿＿＿＿＿＿＿＿＿＿＿＿ mountain trail.

SYNONYMS: sheer, abrupt, sharp
ANTONYMS: gradual, shallow, graded, incremental

17. profuse
(prō fyüs′)

(*adj.*) very abundant; given or flowing freely

How can I stay upset with someone when they are so sincere
and ＿＿＿＿＿＿＿＿＿＿＿＿ with their apologies?

SYNONYMS: extravagant, lavish, bounteous, plenteous
ANTONYMS: sparse, scanty, meager, insufficient

18. reconcile
(rek′ ən sīl)

(*v.*) to restore to friendship; to settle; to resign (oneself)

After so many years of feuding, it will be difficult for the
brothers to ＿＿＿＿＿＿＿＿＿＿＿＿ and begin anew.

SYNONYMS: unite, conciliate, mend fences
ANTONYMS: antagonize, alienate, drive a wedge between

19. shackle
(shak′ əl)

(*v.*) to put into chains; (*n., usually pl.*) a chain, fetter

The guards attempted to ＿＿＿＿＿＿＿＿＿＿＿＿
the prisoner before allowing him to board the waiting airplane.

His wicked plot discovered, the prince was bound in

＿＿＿＿＿＿＿＿＿＿＿＿, and taken to the dank dungeon.

SYNONYMS: (*v.*) manacle, enslave; (*n.*) handcuffs, bonds, irons
ANTONYMS: (*v.*) free, unfetter, emancipate, liberate

20. threadbare
(thred′ bâr)

(*adj.*) shabby, old and worn

My brother has carefully collected a closetful of faded,

＿＿＿＿＿＿＿＿＿＿＿＿ jeans, sweatshirts, and sneakers.

SYNONYMS: frayed, seedy, ragged, shopworn, trite
ANTONYMS: luxurious, plush, costly, sumptuous

Completing the Sentence

From the words for this unit, choose the one that best completes each of the following sentences. Write the word in the space provided.

1. As we grow older and perhaps wiser, we _____ ourselves to the fact that we will never achieve all that we had hoped in life.

2. Three customers fought noisily over the last sale-priced sweater until they finally _____ the store manager in their dispute.

3. His books are scattered around in such a(n) _____ manner that it is a mystery to me how he can find the ones he wants.

4. The illness so _____ her that it was several weeks before she could return to her job.

5. He is certainly a(n) _____ talker, but does he have a firm grasp of the subject he is discussing?

6. The Roman numeral MCMXCVI is inscribed on the commemorative plaque that adorns the _____ of the building.

7. My dog Rover may look like a mutt at first glance, but in fact he has a distinguished

   _____ .

8. His old-fashioned clothes were patched and _____, but we could see that he had made every effort to keep them spotlessly clean.

9. By proving that his 18th birthday came one day before the election, the student was _____ of the charge of unlawful voting.

10. The entertainer cleverly _____ limericks and other comic rhymes on subjects suggested by the audience.

11. Our dress rehearsal was a disaster: actors blew their lines, doors on the set got stuck shut; it was a complete _____!

12. The heavy rains of June brought a(n) _____ of mosquitoes into the neighborhoods bordering the marshland.

13. With one flashing stroke of his mighty axe, the skilled woodsman was able to _____ the heavy branch from the tree trunk.

14. In the untended garden the weeds were so _____ that they all but smothered the few flowers that managed to blossom.

15. We certainly did not expect to receive such a(n) _____ greeting from someone who had been described to us as cold and unsociable.

16. Of the millions of immigrants who came to America from all over the world, only the Africans arrived here in _____ .

17. Her deathly _____ and distraught expression told us she had already received the tragic news.

18. Rebels would find it difficult to _____ people who are reasonably well satisfied with their government to rise up against it.

19. With the Louisiana Purchase of 1803, Jefferson _____ a vast territory that doubled the size of the nation.

20. I saw nothing but peril in the prospect of trying to scale a cliff so sheer and _____ that even expert climbers shied away from it.

Synonyms

*Choose the word from this unit that is **the same** or **most nearly the same** in meaning as the **boldface** word or expression in the given phrase. Write the word on the line provided.*

1. became **entangled** in a furious debate _____

2. a **sheer** drop of 300 feet into the old quarry _____

3. an **invasion** of deer stripping the foliage _____

4. may **appropriate** the land along the border _____

5. able to **sunder** a knight's shield with one blow _____

6. six principles as the club's **foundation** _____

7. conversation that revealed a **facile** wit _____

8. tried to **unite** the warring factions _____

9. bored by the driver's **trite** jokes _____

10. a **lineage** traced back to early Scottish kings _____

11. the embarrassing **fiasco** of her mother's party _____

12. an ability to **extemporize** when solving problems _____

13. a **wanness** betraying her sufferering _____

14. loosened the **manacles** so the prisoner could eat _____

15. took the chance to **instigate** a little mischief _____

Antonyms

*Choose the word from this unit that is **most nearly opposite** in meaning to the **boldface** word or expression in the given phrase. Write the word on the line provided.*

16. a team **energized** by the news _____

17. the same crops that were so **sparse** a decade ago _____

18. key medical evidence that **incriminated** the suspect _____

19. a **deliberate** approach to solving the problem _____

20. puzzled by his unusually **gruff** reply _____

Choosing the Right Word

*Circle the **boldface** word that more satisfactorily completes each of the following sentences.*

1. Although I had never even met her, the letters she wrote me were so (**cordial, threadbare**) that I felt we were old friends.

2. Runaway inflation can cause a (**glib, precipitous**) decline in the value of a nation's currency.

3. Modern processing methods (**devitalize, annex**) many foodstuffs sold today, resulting in a loss of both taste and nutritional value.

4. The famous actor applied a layer of ashen makeup to simulate the ghastly (**pallor, pedigree**) of a ghost.

5. The story of his unhappy childhood aroused our sympathy but did not (**exonerate, improvise**) him from the charge of criminal assault.

6. Separation of powers is one of the (**cornerstones, shackles**) upon which the American form of government is built.

7. We learned from the TV film that Spartacus was a Roman gladiator who (**reconciled, incited**) his fellow slaves to armed rebellion.

8. He is the kind of speaker who is more effective when he (**improvises, exonerates**) his remarks than when he reads from a prepared script.

9. The disaster was so great that the overcrowded hospital was forced to house some patients in a makeshift (**annex, debacle**).

10. To seaside resorts, the annual (**influx, pallor**) of tourists marks the true beginning of the summer season.

11. In spite of all the progress made in recent years, we are still not entirely free from the (**shackles, debacles**) of prejudice and superstition.

12. In a time of unrest and bewildering change, it is more important than ever to (**incite, cleave**) to the basic principles that give meaning to our lives.

13. The president said in his inaugural address that he firmly believes that we must not (**embroil, devitalize**) ourselves in the quarrels of other nations.

14. My campaign for the class presidency ended in an utter (**influx, debacle**) when I forgot my speech as I was about to address the assembly.

15. We are tired of listening to those (**cordial, threadbare**) old excuses for your failure to keep your promises.

16. The elderly couple thanked me so (**profusely, haphazardly**) for the small favor I had done them that I was almost embarrassed.

17. What we need is not *talkers* with (**glib, cordial**) solutions for all our problems, but *doers* who are prepared to pitch in and help.

18. With such a (**precipitous, haphazard**) way of keeping accounts, is it any wonder that your budget is a disaster area?

19. True, he comes from an aristocratic family, but he won that promotion on the basis of merit, not because of his (**pedigree, cornerstone**).

20. How can he (**cleave, reconcile**) his claim that he is a "good citizen" with the fact that he doesn't even bother to vote?

Vocabulary in Context

*Read the following passage, in which some of the words you have studied in this unit appear in **boldface** type. Then complete each statement given below the passage by circling the letter of the item that is **the same** or **almost the same** in meaning as the highlighted word.*

Ah Yes, the Gadsden Purchase

(Line)

We've all heard of the Louisiana Purchase. With one stroke of the pen, Thomas Jefferson doubled the size of the United States. Then there was the Alaska Purchase, or Seward's Folly. What a bargain! And that little one, out West somewhere. What was the name of that one

(5) again? Ah yes, the Gadsden Purchase. That was more than the mere purchase of a dry parcel of land in the 1850s. It involved the Mexican War, Manifest Destiny, and the dream of a coast-to-coast railway.

(10) When the United States proposed admitting Texas to the Union in 1845, the Mexican government was infuriated. Granting Texas statehood would be equivalent to **inciting** war. But many Americans wanted to fulfill

(15) Manifest Destiny, a **cornerstone** of American policy that meant occupying the continent "from sea to shining sea." Finally, after a clash in Texas in 1846, the United States declared war on Mexico. Two years later, the war ended

(20) in a **debacle** for Mexico.

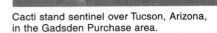
Cacti stand sentinel over Tucson, Arizona, in the Gadsden Purchase area.

The United States *did* admit Texas to the Union and **annex** the vast New Mexico and California territories. A huge **influx** of settlers arrived, many to seek their fortunes in the 1849 California Gold Rush. The need grew for a transcontinental railway. Blustery railroad baron James Gadsden

(25) argued that the best route passed right through Mexican territory. President Franklin Pierce sent him to acquire the land.

Mexican General Antonio Santa Anna agreed to sell the land, perhaps because he did not want to **embroil** Mexico in another war, and in 1854 the Gadsden Purchase was completed. The United States paid $10 million for a parcel of about 30,000 square

(30) miles. Years later, the Southern Pacific Railroad was built through the region—a narrow band of today's southern New Mexico and roughly the southern quarter of Arizona.

---

1. The meaning of **inciting** (line 13) is
a. provoking c. debating
b. eliminating d. committing

2. cornerstone (line 15) most nearly means
a. basement c. foundation
b. aspect d. symbol

3. Debacle (line 20) is best defined as
a. disappointment c. mistake
b. triumph d. overwhelming defeat

4. The meaning of **annex** (line 22) is
a. sever c. overrun
b. appropriate d. reject

5. Influx (line 22) most nearly means
a. mob c. demonstration
b. departure d. inpouring

6. Embroil (line 28) is best defined as
a. embarrass c. defeat
b. involve d. trick into

Definitions

Note carefully the spelling, pronunciation, part(s) of speech, and definition(s) of each of the following words. Then write the word in the blank space(s) in the illustrative sentence(s) following. Finally, study the lists of synonyms and antonyms given at the end of each entry.

1. abase
(ə bās′)

(*v.*) to lower in esteem, degrade; to humble

My friend refused to _____ herself by admitting to something she had not done.
SYNONYMS: lower, humiliate, prostrate, demean
ANTONYMS: elevate, ennoble, exalt

2. actuate
(ak′ chü āt)

(*v.*) to move to action; to impel

A third bad accident at the notorious intersection finally

_____ an angry community protest.
SYNONYMS: trigger, incite, instigate

3. avert
(ə vərt′)

(*v.*) to turn aside, turn away; to prevent, avoid

Rigorous training of the new lifeguards will quite probably

_____ several tragedies each summer.
SYNONYMS: stop, deflect, ward off, preclude
ANTONYMS: invite, induce, provoke, cause

4. boorish
(bür′ ish)

(*adj.*) rude, unrefined; clumsy

Her musical genius was rivaled only by her legendary

_____ behavior in public.
SYNONYMS: vulgar, crude, uncouth, ill-mannered, gauche
ANTONYMS: suave, urbane, polished, courtly, well-bred

5. brunt
(brənt)

(*n.*) the main impact, force, or burden

Fortunately, a sparsely populated area bore the

_____ of the hurricane.
SYNONYMS: blow, shock
ANTONYMS: aftershock, aftermath, repercussion

6. combatant
(kəm bat′ ənt)

(*n.*) a fighter; (*adj.*) engaged in fighting

Several times the referee had to step in and separate the

two _____ after the bell rang.

The _____ forces from France and England met on the fields near Agincourt.
SYNONYMS: (*n.*) soldier, disputant, warrior; (*adj.*) hostile, battling
ANTONYMS: (*n.*) civilian; (*adj.*) peaceful, neutral

7. dormant
(dôr' mənt)

(*adj.*) inactive; in a state of suspension; sleeping

The warm spring sun stirred the _____
daffodil bulbs we planted in the park last fall.

SYNONYMS: resting, still, quiescent
ANTONYMS: awake, active, lively, productive

8. dubious
(dü' bē əs)

(*adj.*) causing uncertainty or suspicion; in a doubtful or uncertain state of mind, hesitant

Experts have said that the manuscript first attributed to
Mark Twain was of _____ authenticity.

SYNONYMS: questionable, suspect, unsettled, undecided
ANTONYMS: certain, positive, indubitable, reliable

9. harangue
(hə raŋ')

(*v.*) to deliver a loud, ranting speech; (*n.*) a loud speech

From the moment we walked in, our math teacher began to

_____ us about our midterm exam scores.

The speaker was supposed to discuss the criminal justice

system, but delivered a _____ against lawyers.

SYNONYMS: (*v.*) rant, lecture; (*n.*) tirade, diatribe
ANTONYMS: (*n.*) whisper, murmur, undertone

10. harry
(har' ē)

(*v.*) to make a destructive raid on; to torment, harass

My parents are forever _____ me
about cleaning up my room and playing music too loudly.

SYNONYMS: badger, pester, hound, pillage, ravage

11. impenitent
(im pen' ə tənt)

(*adj.*) not feeling remorse or sorrow for errors or offenses

His _____ demeanor during the trial
probably encouraged the judge to impose a harsh sentence.

SYNONYMS: remorseless, unrepentant, incorrigible
ANTONYMS: ashamed, remorseful, contrite, apologetic

12. knave
(nāv)

(*n.*) a tricky, unprincipled, or deceitful fellow

Her friends always knew that _____
of a first husband was only after her inheritance.

SYNONYMS: rascal, rogue, scoundrel, miscreant

13. legion
(lē' jən)

(*n.*) a large military force; any large group or number; (*adj.*) many, numerous

It would undoubtedly take a _____
of skilled mechanics to repair an old rattletrap like my car.

Her reasons for not attending the Community Gourmet Club's

"Cooking with Beets Night" were _____.

SYNONYMS: (*n.*) multitude, host, throng, division, regiment
ANTONYMS: (*n.*) squad, platoon; (*adj.*) few, sparse

14. liberality
(lib ə ral' ə tē)

(*n.*) generosity, generous act; breadth of mind or outlook

The dean's well-known _____ allowed an atmosphere of spirited debate to flourish at the college.

SYNONYMS: largesse, magnanimity, broad-mindedness
ANTONYMS: stinginess, miserliness, narrow-mindedness

15. plaintiff
(plān' tif)

(*n.*) one who begins a lawsuit

His lawyers objected that the _____ rather than the defendant was being put on trial.

SYNONYMS: complainant, accuser
ANTONYMS: defendant, accused

16. probe
(prōb)

(*v.*) to examine, investigate thoroughly; (*n.*) an investigation; a device used to explore or examine

An auditor was brought in to _____ the company's financial irregularities.

An unmanned _____ was sent to examine the geology of the Martian surface.

SYNONYMS: (*v.*) explore, scrutinize; (*n.*) inquiry, detector
ANTONYMS: (*v.*) conceal, hide; (*n.*) cover-up, whitewash

17. protract
(prō trakt')

(*v.*) to draw out or lengthen in space or time

Militants opposed to the peace treaty attempted to _____ the negotiations.

SYNONYMS: prolong, extend, elongate, spin out
ANTONYMS: contract, compress, concentrate

18. quarry
(kwär' ē)

(*v.*) to cut or take from (or as if from) a quarry; (*n.*) a place from which stone is taken; something that is hunted or pursued

The Internet makes it easier to _____ information from the world's vast supply.

Bargain hunters armed with sale ads raced through the store, urgently seeking their _____ .

SYNONYMS: (*n.*) prey, game, victim, excavation, pit, mine
ANTONYMS: (*n.*) hunter, predator, pursuer

19. spurn
(spərn)

(*v.*) to refuse with scorn, disdain

He _____ a full scholarship offered by a small college to go to a big state university instead.

SYNONYMS: turn down, reject, decline, snub, repudiate
ANTONYMS: accept, welcome, greet

20. subterfuge
(səb' tər fyüj)

(*n.*) an excuse or trick for escaping or hiding something

The accused embezzler's "heart attack" could be a clever _____ to avoid his upcoming trial.

SYNONYMS: dodge, blind, ruse, deception, artifice

Completing the Sentence

From the words for this unit, choose the one that best completes each of the following sentences. Write the word in the space provided.

1. The soldiers of the mighty Roman _____ were organized in battle units called cohorts and maniples.

2. The two _____ fought it out with words rather than with fists.

3. The "Speakers' Corner" in London's Hyde Park is home to soapbox orators who _____ idlers and passersby.

4. Isn't friendship with a person who mistrusts you of _____ value?

5. The Mississippi riverboats were home to crooks and _____ of every description, from cardsharps to confidence men.

6. His sudden fainting spell was a(n) _____ to get out of taking me to the Spring Dance!

7. Our planned stopover in Denver was unexpectedly _____ when a blizzard prevented us from leaving the city for days.

8. In A.D. 79, the sudden and violent eruption of a volcano that had been _____ for many years destroyed Pompeii in two days.

9. We learned that the bizarre sequence of events was _____ by an accidental tug on the switching device.

10. Divers from the salvage ship will try to _____ the ocean floor where the Confederate warship sank in 1863.

11. Why should you _____ yourself by begging to be admitted to a club made up of snobs and phonies?

12. The entire boardwalk at the beach was smashed to bits when the full _____ of the hurricane struck it.

13. Because his feelings were hurt, he _____ any attempts on my part to provide help.

14. As a lawyer for the _____, you will have full opportunity to cross-examine the witnesses for the defendant.

15. On the surface she seemed stubbornly _____, but secretly she regretted the damage her thoughtlessness had caused.

16. Bands of guerillas _____ the straggling soldiers as they retreated in disarray.

17. The police were quickly ordered to the scene as a precautionary measure to _____ a threatened riot.

18. His many donations of large sums of money to organizations dedicated to relieving world hunger are evidence of his _____ .

19. The bloodhounds pursued their human _____ through the swamps.

20. Fortunately, the loud and generally _____ behavior of a few of the guests did not spoil the party for the rest of us.

Synonyms

*Choose the word from this unit that is **the same** or **most nearly the same** in meaning as the **boldface** word or expression in the given phrase. Write the word on the line provided.*

1. the **shock** of the collision _____

2. conflict **extended** by cease-fire violations _____

3. escape by means of a **ruse** involving false noses _____

4. a **tirade** prompted by a messy room _____

5. an attempt to **trigger** impeachment proceedings _____

6. an arts foundation famous for its **largesse** _____

7. marble **excavated** from deep underground _____

8. did much to earn his reputation as a **scoundrel** _____

9. a new contract which **precluded** a labor dispute _____

10. besieged by a **multitude** of ravenous black flies _____

11. investigators who will **scrutinize** their files _____

12. reported Elvis sightings of a **suspect** nature _____

13. no wish to **demean** the excellence of the works _____

14. tried to **badger** her mother into changing her mind _____

15. **disputants** for whom a mediator was needed _____

Antonyms

*Choose the word from this unit that is **most nearly opposite** in meaning to the **boldface** word or expression in the given phrase. Write the word on the line provided.*

16. guerrillas who **welcomed** the offer of amnesty _____

17. the **contrite** face of the little cake thief _____

18. a classroom inhabited by **lively** minds _____

19. a **suave** manner that surprised her parents _____

20. interviewed the **defendant** after the verdict _____

Choosing the Right Word

*Circle the **boldface** word that more satisfactorily completes each of the following sentences.*

1. He pretended to be speechless with anger, but we recognized this as a (**subterfuge, harangue**) to avoid answering the charges against him.

2. I think that we can settle this dispute in a friendly way, without either of us becoming a defendant or a (**quarry, plaintiff**).

3. It is written in the Bible that "whosoever shall humble himself shall be exalted, and he that shall exalt himself shall be (**dormant, abased**)."

4. For many years after the Civil War, thousands of (**combatants, legions**) in the great battle of Gettysburg met in annual reunions.

5. The detective story was so cleverly constructed that the character whom we took to be the pursuer turned out to be the (**quarry, brunt**).

6. We demand that the committee be made up of legislators who will (**actuate, probe**) fearlessly into the causes of the energy crisis.

7. A pack of reporters (**averted, harried**) the Senator with pointed and persistent questions even as he was being whisked into his limousine.

8. A new popular singing idol will often (**actuate, abase**) changes in clothing fashions.

9. How can that heartless beauty (**combat, spurn**) my offers of devotion!

10. Since the prisoner remained defiantly (**impenitent, boorish**), the review panel saw no reason for granting him parole.

11. Since his absurd scheme was never really intended to harm us, we regard him as more of a fool than a (**quarry, knave**).

12. When the referee called back a touchdown by the home team, he had to bear the (**probe, brunt**) of the crowd's anger.

13. After World War II, the United States and the Soviet Union became locked in a(n) (**protracted, actuated**) struggle known as the Cold War.

14. Your (**liberality, subterfuge**) is to be admired, but it must be controlled so that it is not out of proportion to your means.

15. Let us not (**spurn, avert**) our attention from the sufferings of the people living in the slums of our community.

16. We began with confidence in his success in the election, but as he made one mistake after another, we grew more and more (**dubious, abased**).

17. During the great Depression millions of Americans were out of work as much of the nation's productive capacity lay (**dormant, impenitent**).

18. People who think only of themselves, with no concern for the feelings of others, are bound to be (**brunt, boorish**).

19. At a time when we need good will and cooperation, nothing will be gained by an emotional (**quarry, harangue**) about old abuses and mistakes.

20. The dinner to celebrate the 50th anniversary of Mrs. Roth's teaching career was attended by a (**legion, probe**) of her former students.

Read the following passage, in which some of the words you have studied in this unit appear in **boldface** type. Then complete each statement given below the passage by circling the letter of the item that is **the same** or **almost the same** in meaning as the highlighted word.

Remembering Mount St. Helens

(Line)

Mount St. Helens, in the Cascade Range of Washington, was, in early 1980, considered a **dormant** volcano, having been silent for the previous 123 years. On March 20, 1980, the mountain was awakened by an earthquake that measured 4.1 on the Richter scale. Scientists said magma, or molten rock, was moving beneath the mountain. A week later, a series of steam explosions prompted the closing of (5) nearby recreational areas. Earthquakes and minor eruptions followed, but **legions** of tourists eager to see a volcano in action kept coming.

By mid-April, a bulge appeared on the north side of the mountain. Some (10) geologists thought the protrusion foreshadowed a lateral eruption; others did not. The public received conflicting media reports, which they deemed of **dubious** value. The bulge grew (15) ominously larger, sometimes by as much as five feet per day.

On May 18, Mount St. Helens erupted with a violence that shocked everyone. First, the bulge collapsed on (20) itself, triggering an enormous landslide. Then, the north side of the mountain exploded, blasting 203 square miles of forest into a desolate, ash-covered wasteland of flattened trees. Fifty-seven people died, among them (25) spectators who had **spurned** warnings and evaded roadblocks.

Mt. St. Helens erupts, sending a plume of smoke and ash 60,000 feet into the air.

Mount St. Helens is quiet now, and we are much wiser. We can only hope that new, advanced monitoring instruments, better communication, and well-planned evacuation procedures will **avert** needless deaths should the sleeping giant awaken once more.

(30)

---

1. The meaning of **dormant** (line 2) is
a. thoughtful   c. quiescent
b. fidgety   d. extinct

2. Legions (line 6) most nearly means
a. hordes   c. caravans
b. units   d. platoons

3. Dubious (line 15) is best defined as
a. bogus   c. certain
b. annoyed   d. doubtful

4. The meaning of **spurned** (line 26) is
a. ignited   c. doused
b. rejected   d. evaded

5. Avert (line 29) most nearly means
a. miss   c. prevent
b. restrain   d. cover

Analogies   *In each of the following, circle the item that best completes the comparison.*

1. threadbare is to **suit** as
a. obsolete is to model
b. bald is to tire
c. scratched is to surface
d. latent is to talent

2. pallor is to **ghost** as
a. red is to knave
b. tan is to sunbather
c. blue is to plaintiff
d. green is to recluse

3. legion is to **many** as
a. migration is to few
b. brunt is to many
c. clique is to few
d. probe is to many

4. protract is to **duration** as
a. enlarge is to scale
b. reduce is to diet
c. concede is to size
d. cleave is to length

5. sordid is to **unfavorable** as
a. perverse is to favorable
b. congenial is to unfavorable
c. versatile is to favorable
d. buoyant is to unfavorable

6. boor is to **rude** as
a. skinflint is to profuse
b. miser is to cordial
c. knave is to wicked
d. plaintiff is to impenitent

7. dormant is to **volcano** as
a. fertile is to valley
b. lukewarm is to bath
c. rundown is to building
d. fallow is to field

8. untenable is to **hold** as
a. inedible is to cook
b. inflammable is to hear
c. indomitable is to wound
d. immobile is to move

9. skyscraper is to **lofty** as
a. mansion is to sordid
b. log cabin is to rustic
c. car wash is to glib
d. quarry is to dubious

10. war is to **combatant** as
a. game show is to contestant
b. debate is to mediator
c. boxing match is to spectator
d. footrace is to panelist

11. rancid is to **butter** as
a. tepid is to tea
b. pasteurized is to milk
c. aromatic is to coffee
d. tainted is to water

12. sever is to **apart** as
a. apportion is to together
b. improvise is to apart
c. reconcile is to together
d. actuate is to apart

13. shackle is to **slave** as
a. helmet is to quarterback
b. crown is to king
c. beret is to fool
d. tiara is to artist

14. moon is to **wane** as
a. sun is to shine
b. volcano is to erupt
c. planet is to revolve
d. tide is to ebb

15. liberal is to **open hand** as
a. taciturn is to green thumb
b. dour is to glad hand
c. stingy is to tight fist
d. talkative is to closed mouth

16. vindicate is to **exonerate** as
a. incite is to arouse
b. perceive is to ignore
c. spurn is to accept
d. embroil is to roast

17. prelude is to **opera** as
a. overture is to novel
b. preface is to sculpture
c. footnote is to report
d. prologue is to play

18. annex is to **more** as
a. influx is to less
b. cornerstone is to more
c. eclipse is to less
d. debacle is to more

Word Associations

In each of the following groups, circle the word that is best defined or suggested by the given phrase.

1. impel to action
a. actuate　　　b. concede　　　c. exonerate　　　d. improvise

2. question the witness at length
a. spurn　　　b. probe　　　c. vindicate　　　d. sever

3. cling to
a. exonerate　　　b. embroil　　　c. concede　　　d. cleave

4. the object of a hunt
a. annex　　　b. reconcile　　　c. abase　　　d. quarry

5. shabby or overused
a. lofty　　　b. ad infinitum　　　c. dubious　　　d. threadbare

6. cut off completely
a. devitalize　　　b. improvise　　　c. sever　　　d. wane

7. an utter failure
a. subterfuge　　　b. shackle　　　c. cornerstone　　　d. debacle

8. involve in difficulties
a. spurn　　　b. protract　　　c. avert　　　d. embroil

9. unable to be defended
a. versatile　　　b. dormant　　　c. haphazard　　　d. untenable

10. reject with contempt
a. harangue　　　b. harry　　　c. apportion　　　d. spurn

11. pester relentlessly
a. harangue　　　b. embroil　　　c. harry　　　d. incite

12. a rush of children entering a park after school
a. influx　　　b. brunt　　　c. clique　　　d. annex

13. lacking depth and forethought
a. untenable　　　b. versatile　　　c. glib　　　d. rancid

14. hiding a true motive behind deceptions
a. pallor　　　b. harangue　　　c. prelude　　　d. subterfuge

15. one who settles problems in court
a. knave　　　b. plaintiff　　　c. rustic　　　d. quarry

16. the main impact
a. annex　　　b. influx　　　c. pedigree　　　d. brunt

17. anything that prevents free action
a. cornerstone　　　b. shackle　　　c. subterfuge　　　d. debacle

18. unrepentant
a. impenitent　　　b. cordial　　　c. versatile　　　d. bona fide

19. discover through the senses
a. concede　　　b. perceive　　　c. spurn　　　d. avert

20. steeply sloping
a. sordid　　　b. congenial　　　c. precipitous　　　d. buoyant

Vocabulary in Context

*Read the following passage, in which some of the words you have studied in Units 13–15 appear in **boldface** type. Then complete each statement given below the passage by circling the item that is **the same** or **almost the same** in meaning as the highlighted word.*

The Glory of Bad Art

(Line)

One of New York's many superb art museums is the Museum of Modern Art (MOMA). MOMA showcases art and design from the twentieth and
(5) twenty-first centuries—work of notable originality and excellence.

Meanwhile, to the north, in Boston, lurks a lesser-known, yet formidable institution. This rising star vying for
(10) admission to the small **clique** of the world's finest museums goes, not by MOMA, but by MOBA. It is the Museum of Bad Art.

According to its statement of
(15) purpose, the mission of MOBA is to "bring the worst art to the widest of audiences" by being dedicated to "the collection, preservation, exhibition, and celebration of bad art in all its
(20) glory." And what, you might ask, constitutes bad art? What **perverse** criteria do MOBA staffers apply when judging a submitted work?

For MOBA, museum quality bad
(25) art must be compelling. It must be so bad that the viewer can't stop looking at it, yet somehow **congenial** at the same time. In the words of administrators, works must have "a

(30) special quality that sets them apart from the merely incompetent." Highly prized qualities include: no artistic control; courage and enthusiasm; and an inappropriate frame.
(35) The MOBA permanent collection (housed in the basement of a community theatre) exemplifies these standards. Many of the works have an unrivaled **pedigree**, having been
(40) rescued from Boston-area dumpsters. "Lucy in the Field with Flowers" (a scene of **rustic** strangeness), "Peter the Kitty," and "Two Trees in Love" are just a few of MOBA's worst.
(45) In addition, the Museum has mounted many superb exhibitions since its 1993 founding, including "Awash in Bad Art: the world's first drive-through art exhibition and car
(50) wash." And recent acquisitions are described as "the worst yet in the museum's long, proud tradition of ever-dropping standards."

The Museum of Bad Art offers a
(55) refreshing, funny alternative to the world's **profuse** collections of ordinary masterpieces.

---

1. The meaning of **clique** (line 10) is
a. number   c. coterie
b. organization   d. notary

2. Perverse (line 21) is best defined as
a. contrary   c. rude
b. strange   d. imaginative

3. The meaning of **congenial** (line 27) is
a. laughable   c. understandable
b. ridiculous   d. pleasant

4. Pedigree (line 39) most nearly means
a. education   c. history
b. appearance   d. title

5. The meaning of **rustic** (line 42) is
a. corroded   c. natural
b. autumnal   d. countrified

6. Profuse (line 56) most nearly means
a. abundant   c. serious
b. redundant   d. profound

Choosing the Right Meaning

Read each sentence carefully. Then circle the item that best completes the statement below the sentence.

Of as much interest as the exquisite workmanship of the ancient silver goblet was its notorious pedigree. (2)

1. The best definition of the word **pedigree** in line 2 is

a. breeding   b. family   c. price   d. history

Though the two politicians claimed to be reconciled, there were strong hints that some hard feelings remained. (2)

2. The word **reconciled** in line 1 is best defined as

a. resigned
b. allied
c. restored to friendship
d. victorious

In my opinion the auctioneer's assistant was far too boorish to be entrusted with objects so fragile and costly as those. (2)

3. In line 1 the word **boorish** most nearly means

a. rude   b. clumsy   c. young   d. snobbish

The peace commission invited representatives of the combatant parties to talks aimed at bringing the bloodshed to an end. (2)

4. The word **combatant** in line 1 most nearly means

a. warring   b. neutral   c. diplomatic   d. wounded

Only a fool would regard as bona fide the declarations of friendship offered by so shameless a double-dealer as he. (2)

5. In line 1 the phrase **bona fide** is best defined as

a. proven   b. sincere   c. certified   d. bogus

Antonyms

*In each of the following groups, circle the word or expression that is most nearly the **opposite** of the word in **boldface** type.*

1. pallor
a. chill
b. warmth
c. blush
d. paleness

2. abase
a. strike out
b. cover
c. elevate
d. stall

3. buoyant
a. swimming
b. dry
c. depressed
d. expensive

4. rustic
a. urban
b. crude
c. wrong
d. isolated

5. dormant
a. quiescent
b. active
c. willing
d. present

6. concede
a. dispute
b. permit
c. review
d. follow

7. incite
a. rebel
b. befriend
c. alarm
d. restrain

8. spurn
a. accept
b. reject
c. encourage
d. discourage

9. profuse
a. expensive
b. sparse
c. active
d. gruff

11. cordial
a. urban
b. mellow
c. ruddy
d. gruff

13. haphazard
a. risky
b. deliberate
c. random
d. delightful

15. lofty
a. heavy
b. lowly
c. level
d. uneven

10. liberality
a. friendliness
b. stinginess
c. conservatism
d. reactionary

12. sever
a. slice
b. finish
c. polish
d. join

14. quarry
a. marble
b. hunter
c. deer
d. mine

16. ad infinitum
a. slowly
b. sharply
c. briefly
d. exceptionally

Word Families

A. On the line provided, write the word you have learned in Units 13–15 that is related to each of the following nouns.

EXAMPLE: annexation—**annex**

1. rancidness, rancidity _____

2. exoneration, exonerator _____

3. concession _____

4. severance _____

5. vindication, vindicator _____

6. devitalization _____

7. perception, perceptiveness _____

8. boor, boorishness _____

9. reconciliation, reconcilement, reconciler _____

10. dormancy _____

11. buoyancy _____

12. improvisation, improviser, improvisator _____

13. profusion, profuseness _____

14. congeniality _____

15. apportionment, apportioner _____

B. On the line provided, write the word you have learned in Units 13–15 that is related to each of the following verbs.

EXAMPLE: combat—**combatant**

16. doubt _____

17. migrate _____

18. buoy _____

19. pervert _____

20. rusticate _____

Two-Word Completions

Circle the pair of words that best complete the meaning of each of the following passages.

1. Over the years, the _____ of our patrons and sponsors has kept the wolf from our door more than once. Without their generous support, I honestly don't know how our little theater company would have _____ disaster.
a. clique . . . reconciled
b. versatility . . . spurned
c. liberality . . . averted
d. migration . . . shackled

2. "You'll usually win a debate if your arguments are valid and convincing," I observed. "But if your position is _____, you'll eventually be forced to _____ defeat."
a. untenable . . . concede
b. dubious . . . spurn
c. bona fide . . . avert
d. glib . . . improvise

3. We can go ahead with this project just as soon as we know we have the money to finance it in the bank. Unfortunately, the plan must remain _____ as long as the necessary financial resources are _____.
a. untenable . . . profuse
b. dormant . . . dubious
c. sordid . . . haphazard
d. bona fide . . . perverse

4. Though urban life may suit some people to a tee, I have always found a _____ environment more _____.
a. lofty . . . protracted
b. sordid . . . perverse
c. cordial . . . haphazard
d. rustic . . . congenial

5. Before the curtain goes up on the first act, the orchestra plays a short _____ depicting in musical terms the _____ ideals of the high-minded knight who is the hero of the opera.
a. debacle . . . buoyant
b. prelude . . . lofty
c. brunt . . . glib
d. pedigree . . . threadbare

6. Most dictators don't just address their audiences; they _____ them. Their words are not meant to soothe or enlighten; they are designed to _____ the listener to violence and hatred.
a. harangue . . . incite
b. probe . . . harry
c. apportion . . . reconcile
d. improvise . . . embroil

7. As Great Britain's power and prestige began to _____ and lose its luster, subjects all over the empire rose up to demand release from the onerous _____ that bound them so firmly to the motherland.
a. cleave . . . subterfuges
b. pall . . . cornerstones
c. wane . . . shackles
d. concede . . . cliques

Building with Classical Roots

vert, vers—to turn

This root appears in **versatile** (page 152). The literal meaning of this word is "able to be turned." In modern usage it now refers to the ability to turn from one task to another with ease. Some other words based on the same root are listed below.

adversity	conversion	divert	reversion
aversion	diversion	invert	version

From the list of words above, choose the one that corresponds to each of the brief definitions below. Write the word in the blank space in the illustrative sentence below the definition.

1. to turn aside; to entertain, amuse

A magician's most important task is to _____ the attention of an audience from the sleight of hand that makes the trick work.

2. a return to a former state, belief, or condition; a reversal

After some false starts, the coach made a _____ to a more traditional practice routine.

3. a particular form of something; an account of an incident

After much gossip and speculation, we were eager to hear the official _____ of the story.

4. to turn upside down; to change direction

The trick required them to _____ a glass of water without spilling any of its contents.

5. a strong dislike; a thing disliked (*"turning against"*)

I'm not really sure why I've developed such a strong _____ to country music.

6. distress, misfortune, hardship

It is said that _____ can make victory sweeter.

7. a change in condition or belief (*"turning toward"*)

The physical _____ of solid ice into liquid water is known as melting.

8. a turning aside; any distraction of attention; amusement, entertainment; pastime

Many students find athletics to be an excellent _____ from the academic pressures of school.

From the list of words above, choose the one that best completes each of the following sentences. Write the word in the blank space provided.

1. The drainage ditch will _____ water from the pond and into the nearby fields.

2. Rising energy and labor costs have led to a _____ of some domestic production to foreign countries where those expenses are considerably lower.

3. To prevent a _____ to his former depressed state, we redoubled our efforts to keep him in good spirits.

4. Her _____ toward cats is so strong that she refuses to visit friends who own them.

5. A person's true character becomes evident in the face of _____ .

6. The factory owners decided that the _____ of the old machinery would cost more than replacing it with new equipment.

7. As reflected in the lake, the row of trees along the bank appears to be

_____ .

8. Sally's _____ of the song is so different from the one I'm used to that it hardly seems like the same tune.

---

*Circle the **boldface** word that more satisfactorily completes each of the following sentences.*

1. The corrupt banker was trying to work out a scheme to (**invert, divert**) money from corporate funds into his own personal accounts.

2. Anyone who has lived through the horrors of battle knows the real meaning of courage in the face of (**adversity, aversion**).

3. After moving to a new house, the toddler experienced a temporary (**reversion, diversion**) in her ability to sleep through the night.

4. Do you know the mathematical formula to use to make the (**adversity, conversion**) from degrees Fahrenheit to degrees Celsius?

5. The maritime invaders created a noisy (**reversion, diversion**) at the harbor, which drew attention from the foot soldiers advancing on the town from the surrounding hills.

6. The one-way valve on a child's covered drinking cup allows it to be (**inverted, diverted**) without making a messy spill.

7. The Broadway show *West Side Story* is a modern musical (**version, conversion**) of Shakespeare's *Romeo and Juliet.*

8. She has such a fanatical (**version, aversion**) to red meat that she will not eat at a table where it is served.

Read the following sentences, paying special attention to the words and phrases underlined. From the words in the box below, find better choices for these underlined words and phrases. Then use these choices to rewrite the sentences.

WORD BANK				
annex	concede	haphazard	knave	subterfuge
avert	cordial	harangue	legion	versatile
buoyant	cornerstone	impertinent	lofty	vindicate
combatant	exonerate	improvise	pallor	wane

Human Powered Boats

1. Few would not <u>admit as true</u> that early boats were propelled by human power—probably with paddles, oars, or long poles.

_____

_____

2. Looking for easier ways to travel, boat makers undoubtedly experimented with many varieties of local trees in order to find the most <u>able to float easily</u> kind of wood.

_____

_____

3. Now, despite modern engines that make boat travel fast and efficient, <u>plenty</u> of environmentally astute water enthusiasts are returning to HPBs—human powered boats.

_____

_____

4. The <u>main building block</u> of the HPB movement is based on the idea that human-powered boats will make the beaches cleaner, and the water more tranquil.

_____

_____

5. Many HPB supporters are craftsmen who tinker and <u>construct from available materials</u> to make one-of-a-kind boats that are practical to build, repair, store, and move.

_____

_____

6. Depending on design and method of operation, some HPBs are <u>all-around</u> enough to be used by tandem teams, solo sailors, and even the physically challenged.

_____

_____

7. HPB sailing is no <u>unplanned</u> or casual endeavor. People have crossed the Atlantic and Pacific Oceans in HPBs, setting unique records for endurance and innovation.

_____

_____

Analogies *In each of the following, circle the item that best completes the comparison.*

1. impenitent is to **atone** as
a. invincible is to conquer
b. sardonic is to jeer
c. pugnacious is to fight
d. irreverent is to honor

2. extemporaneous is to **improvise** as
a. erroneous is to rectify
b. heterogeneous is to exploit
c. synthetic is to fabricate
d. versatile is to protract

3. miserly is to **liberality** as
a. timid is to pugnacity
b. persistent is to tenacity
c. brazen is to temerity
d. genial is to cordiality

4. bona fide is to **bogus** as
a. biased is to prejudiced
b. cunning is to wily
c. perilous is to dangerous
d. authentic is to spurious

5. goods are to **shoddy** as
a. possessions are to subversive
b. methods are to slipshod
c. finances are to sordid
d. clothes are to haphazard

6. tenacious is to **relinquish** as
a. diligent is to toil
b. unflinching is to recoil
c. incredulous is to doubt
d. relentless is to perceive

7. skeptic is to **dubious** as
a. customer is to irate
b. coward is to intrepid
c. host is to boorish
d. crybaby is to doleful

8. intolerable is to **endure** as
a. untenable is to maintain
b. unbridled is to grasp
c. invincible is to hoard
d. unflagging is to enjoy

9. quarry is to **hunter** as
a. loot is to marauder
b. message is to envoy
c. protest is to militant
d. larceny is to brigand

10. tirade is to **harangue** as
a. anarchy is to order
b. business is to drudgery
c. quandary is to dilemma
d. epilogue is to preamble

11. buoyant is to **float** as
a. autocratic is to warp
b. plastic is to bounce
c. erratic is to spring
d. elastic is to recoil

12. influx is to **exodus** as
a. breach is to rift
b. statute is to law
c. realm is to metropolis
d. advent is to departure

13. heterogeneous is to **uniformity** as
a. sardonic is to bite
b. terse is to edge
c. diffuse is to focus
d. paramount is to clout

14. sparse is to **profuse** as
a. intricate is to superfluous
b. garbled is to lucid
c. grievous is to sordid
d. preposterous is to exorbitant

15. militant is to **act** as
a. circumspect is to hurry
b. surly is to behave
c. sprightly is to loiter
d. pensive is to think

16. brawny is to **build** as
a. comely is to age
b. diminutive is to size
c. prim is to weight
d. pensive is to shape

17. wane is to **dwindle** as
a. estrange is to reconcile
b. garble is to muddle
c. incinerate is to inundate
d. hamper is to facilitate

18. dormant is to **activity** as
a. diffuse is to vigor
b. obtrusive is to focus
c. stagnant is to movement
d. concise is to punch

19. vagrant is to **migrate** as
a. combatant is to contend
b. pauper is to dissent
c. accomplice is to prattle
d. knave is to meander

20. surmount is to **triumph** as
a. usurp is to defeat
b. abridge is to triumph
c. succumb is to defeat
d. deadlock is to triumph

21. course is to **erratic** as
a. claim is to spurious
b. handwriting is to illegible
c. publication is to posthumous
d. pitch is to wild

22. shackle is to **unfetter** as
a. subjugate is to emancipate
b. vindicate is to exonerate
c. compensate is to remunerate
d. assimilate is to escalate

Choosing the Right Meaning

Read each sentence carefully. Then circle the item that best completes the statement below the sentence.

Engineers used robotic probes equipped with radiation meters to check the interior of the stricken reactor. (2)

1. The word **probes** in line 1 most nearly means
a. private investigators
b. cross-examinations
c. detectors
d. trial balloons

Language students soon discover that in every tongue there are expressions impossible to render satisfactorily in another. (2)

2. In line 2 the word **render** most nearly means
a. reproduce   b. extract   c. memorize   d. submit

The lot that saw the most spirited bidding of the evening was a set of hand-cut eighteenth-century cordial glasses. (2)

3. In line 2 the word **cordial** is best defined as
a. hospitality   b. liqueur   c. friendship   d. ceremony

The scullery maid used a scuttle to carry coal from the bin in the cellar to the kitchen stove. (2)

4. In line 1 the word **scuttle** is used to mean
a. scurry   b. sink   c. wagon   d. pail

"It is my burning hope," quoth he, "that never come the day
When from my face thou shouldst avert thy noble azure gaze." (2)
(A. E. Glug, *The Clodyssey* IV, 471–472)

5. The word **avert** in line 2 is best defined as
a. avoid   b. turn away   c. preclude   d. detour

The question paramount in everyone's mind was: How will the new mayor handle the city's unexpected financial crisis? (2)

6. The word **paramount** in line 1 is used to mean
a. of least importance
b. forgotten
c. above all others
d. lingering

Two-Word Completions *Circle the pair of words that best complete the meaning of each of the following sentences.*

1. When the refrigerator began to _____ like overripe cheese, I checked its contents for a rotten egg or some _____ butter.
   a. blanch . . . pliant
   b. feign . . . bleak
   c. reek . . . rancid
   d. defray . . . mediocre

2. Every Friday afternoon of summer, millions of urban Americans join the _____ to our beaches and shorelines in a determined and sometimes wholly unsuccessful attempt to replace an unbecoming winter _____ with a healthy tan.
   a. expulsion . . . prognosis
   b. advent . . . pedigree
   c. venture . . . cubicle
   d. exodus . . . pallor

3. The _____ in the case were seeking _____ for damage they claimed the defendants had done to the lawn and garden in the course of putting a new wing on the house.
   a. plaintiffs . . . compensation
   b. brigands . . . maltreatment
   c. catalysts . . . depreciation
   d. incorrigibles . . . remuneration

4. Although I had tried my best to _____ the tasks involved in the project as evenly as possible, I found to my horror that those who were most capable had, as usual, been forced to bear the _____ of the workload.
   a. reconcile . . . influx
   b. exonerate . . . pallor
   c. improvise . . . cornerstone
   d. apportion . . . brunt

5. The play ends happily, however, when one of the gods descends from heaven in a fiery chariot to _____ the knotted threads of the plot and _____ the lovers from the horrible death to which they have been condemned.
   a. incinerate . . . supplant
   b. rectify . . . hew
   c. defray . . . succumb
   d. disentangle . . . reprieve

6. In 1980, a violent volcanic eruption transformed the _____ alpine terrain around Mount St. Helens into a barren wasteland as _____ and uninviting as any lunar landscape.
   a. relentless . . . obtrusive
   b. laborious . . . slipshod
   c. staccato . . . subversive
   d. rugged . . . bleak

7. During the _____, people throughout Europe strove to _____ their minds from the bonds of obsolete ideas and attitudes that often harked back to the Dark Ages, hundreds of years before.
   a. Age of the Autocrats . . . render
   b. Skeptical Era . . . divulge
   c. Enlightenment . . . emancipate
   d. Great Depreciation . . . mire

8. There are some people who might not be so moved by the sight, but I still
_____ in horror and disgust when I see old film clips of Adolf
Hitler _____ his followers at the Nuremberg rallies of the 1930s.
a. dilate . . . inciting
b. recoil . . . haranguing
c. succumb . . . maligning
d. feint . . . impelling

9. Dense woods intersected by small streams and _____ give the
area in which I live a decidedly _____ appearance.
a. precipices . . . perennial
b. mire . . . impoverished
c. rivulets . . . rustic
d. interims . . . repugnant

10. If the Kaiser and his saber-rattling cronies had been less _____ in
their attitudes, the First World War and the horrible waste of human life it entailed
might both have been _____ .
a. pugnacious . . . averted
b. boorish . . . actuated
c. circumspect . . . forestalled
d. opinionated . . . facilitated

11. Once a(n) _____ without a penny to his name, the boy grew up to
be the founder of a global company and, subsequently, the government's special
_____ to a United Nations conference on global warming.
a. knave . . . proponent
b. pauper . . . envoy
c. marauder . . . preamble
d. exploit . . . interim

12. To impress the critics on opening night, the actress brought a large _____
of friends who applauded after every scene; but the critics were not
_____—they all panned her dreadful performance.
a. clique . . . hoodwinked
b. metropolis . . . subjugated
c. debacle . . . deadlocked
d. subterfuge . . . perverse

13. As we _____ along the main thoroughfare of the village, the
_____ aroma of fresh-baked bread made us hurry toward the
bakery across the street.
a. dwindled . . . congenial
b. harried . . . latent
c. meandered . . . tantalizing
d. prattled . . . repellent

14. "This is the most _____ story I have ever heard," said the
prosecuting attorney as he listened to the defendant attempt to explain why he was
innocent of the charge of passing _____ checks.
a. brazen . . . erratic
b. garbled . . . extemporaneous
c. circumspect . . . metaphorical
d. preposterous . . . bogus

Enriching Your Vocabulary

Read the passage below. Then complete the exercise at the bottom of the page.

Fused Phrases

If you drew a cartoon of someone shouting "Good-bye!" you'd probably write the farewell as two words separated by a hyphen, spelled with an *e* or without, as "good-by." This common send-off can be spelled either way. But did you know that *good-bye* actually began as four separate words? In fact, *good-bye* is the fusion of the phrase "God be with ye." Eventually, the four words were compressed, letters were cut, and English ended up with *good-bye* (or *good-by*).

Fused phrases have entered English from a variety of languages, including Old English. The word *pedigree* (Unit 14), or "list of ancestors," is a word based on a fused phrase. Its origin lies in the Middle French phrase *pié de grue*, meaning "crane's foot." This is a reference to a three-line symbol used on family trees to indicate lines of descent. Evidently, genealogists thought that this symbol looked like the crane's bony footprint. Over time, its spelling evolved into

Red-crowned cranes march smartly along behind their leader.

pied de grue, then *peé de grew, petigrew,* and *peti degree,* among others, before finally fusing into *pedigree.*

In Column A below are 8 more words that derive from fused phrases. With or without a dictionary, match each word with its meaning in Column B.

Column A

_____ **1.** akimbo
_____ **2.** checkmate
_____ **3.** debonair
_____ **4.** jeopardy
_____ **5.** legerdemain
_____ **6.** orotund
_____ **7.** pedestal
_____ **8.** puny

Column B

a. of inferior size, strength, or significance; weak (from Middle French *puis* + *né* = born afterward)

b. jaunty, genial; urbane, suave (from Old French *de bon aire* = of good disposition)

c. with hands on hips, elbows out (from Middle English *in kenebowe* = bent bow)

d. architectural support or base, as of a column or pillar (from Old Italian *pie di stallo* = foot of a stall)

e. in chess, the move that wins the game by leaving the opponent's king unprotected (from Arabic *shā māt* = the king is unable to escape)

f. sleight of hand; trickery, deceit (from Middle French *leger de main* = light of hand)

g. clear, strong, full in sound, sonorous (from Latin *ore rotundo* = with a round mouth)

h. danger or peril; risk of loss or injury (from Old French *jeu parti* = an evenly divided game)

Selecting Word Meanings

*In each of the following groups, circle the word or expression that is **most nearly the same** in meaning as the word in **boldface** type in the given phrase.*

1. **brazen** conduct
   a. shameless   b. modest   c. deadly   d. acceptable

2. a brief **altercation**
   a. shower   b. argument   c. relief   d. statement

3. a **lucid** explanation
   a. clear   b. inadequate   c. learned   d. foolish

4. **jeer at** our efforts
   a. examine   b. reject   c. criticize   d. ridicule

5. a major **exodus**
   a. entrance   b. discussion   c. departure   d. battle

6. **dissolute** behavior
   a. unsuccessful   b. stylish   c. immoral   d. modest

7. made a **trite** remark
   a. stale   b. witty   c. original   d. in bad taste

8. **daunted** by their threats
   a. encouraged   b. ridiculed   c. destroyed   d. intimidated

9. **subjugate** the enemy
   a. torture   b. release   c. kill   d. defeat

10. **efface** a wrong
    a. discover   b. wipe out   c. hide   d. apologize for

11. **revile** the umpire
    a. adore   b. train   c. pay   d. abuse

12. a **semblance** of order
    a. appearance   b. lack   c. result   d. opposite

13. **rectify** an impression
    a. explain   b. make   c. correct   d. confirm

14. a child's **prattle**
    a. clothing   b. outlook   c. play   d. talk

15. an **intrepid** camper
    a. tireless   b. strong   c. fearless   d. skilled

16. an **irate** guest
    a. sociable   b. welcome   c. talkative   d. angry

17. a firm **adherent**
    a. enemy   b. outsider   c. supporter   d. student

18. an **impoverished** neighbor
    a. learned   b. poor   c. beloved   d. unfriendly

19. **admonish** the child
    a. dress   b. teach   c. praise   d. warn

20. a **perennial** favorite
    a. old-fashioned b. recent   c. temporary   d. enduring

Synonyms

*In each of the following groups, circle the **two** words or expressions that are **most nearly the same** in meaning.*

21. a. scream   b. draw back   c. avert   d. recoil

22. a. rugged   b. rustic   c. rough   d. pliant

23. a. profuse   b. scarce   c. sincere   d. plentiful

24. a. increase   b. escalate   c. venture   d. sever

25. a. protest   b. quaver   c. waste   d. squander

26. a. skeptical   b. relentless   c. well-educated   d. doubting

27. a. expulsion   b. advent   c. arrival   d. opposition

28. a. supporter   b. proponent   c. opponent   d. plaintiff

29. a. institute   b. end   c. improve   d. begin

30. a. liability   b. conciseness   c. brevity   d. prelude

31. a. rancid   b. garbled   c. confused   d. latent

32. a. introduction   b. tirade   c. catalyst   d. preamble

33. a. sweet   b. candid   c. outspoken   d. alert

34. a. awkward   b. skilled   c. concerted   d. adept

35. a. destroy   b. build up   c. annihilate   d. torture

Antonyms

*In each of the following groups, circle the **two** words that are **most nearly opposite** in meaning.*

36. a. languid   b. illustrious   c. haphazard   d. circumspect

37. a. emancipate   b. fortify   c. shackle   d. taunt

38. a. versatile   b. bona fide   c. bogus   d. biased

39. a. apportion   b. rejuvenate   c. incite   d. devitalize

40. a. lucid   b. opaque   c. lithe   d. rabid

41. a. tenacious   b. repugnant   c. comely   d. cumbersome

42. a. annex   b. reek   c. surmount   d. succumb

43. a. commandeer   b. actuate   c. hoodwink   d. terminate

44. a. glib   b. lofty   c. abased   d. alien

45. a. embroil   b. disentangle   c. defray   d. abscond

Supplying Words in Context

In each of the following sentences, write on the line provided the most appropriate word chosen from the given list.

Group A

abridge	wily	untenable	terse
recoup	immunity	shoddy	dilemma
pilfer	malign	stagnant	impair
taunt	depreciation	exorcise	relentless

46. Then they began the _____ pursuit of the escaped criminal that was to last for many weeks.

47. A piece of furniture that costs so little must be _____ in its construction.

48. All that we heard from him was the _____ message, "I have arrived."

49. As he presented his explanation of the causes of inflation, his position seemed to me weak and _____ .

50. His job was to _____ the two-volume biography into a single, medium-sized book.

51. Lack of practice will certainly _____ your tennis game.

52. The suspect agreed to testify against the other conspirators in exchange for _____ from prosecution.

53. Not until later did I realize how his _____ strategy had saved us from defeat.

54. So there was my _____: either to keep working at a job I hated, or to quit and find myself unemployed and all but penniless.

55. He who begins by _____ pennies may end by stealing millions.

Group B

interim	bleak	incessant	impel
despicable	access	realm	exorbitant
relinquish	wane	apex	debris
spasmodic	intricate	flippant	predispose

56. The _____ chatter of the birds kept us awake for many hours.

57. Their charge for preparing a tax return is so _____ that I am going to do the work myself.

58. The President stands at the very _____ of power in our national government.

59. We felt rather gloomy as we looked out at the _____ winter scene.

60. In the _____ between the two semesters, we will enjoy a brief vacation.

61. Although I am no public speaker, I feel _____ to say a few words in his defense.

62. His _____ wisecracks were clever but in bad taste.

63. As night came on and it became much colder, the courage of the runaways _____ .

64. Scattered all over the beach was _____ from the wrecked ship.

65. Do you realize how _____ a job it is to reschedule the programs of hundreds of students?

Words That Describe People

Some words that describe people are listed below. Write the appropriate word on the line next to each of the following descriptions.

brawny	sterling	unflinching	vagrant
autocratic	alien	opinionated	accomplice
despicable	arbitrary	buoyant	irreverent
knave	momentous	impenitent	enlightened

66. The pioneers faced many hardships without thought of turning back. _____

67. Since he was convinced that he had done no wrong, Rod felt no pangs of conscience. _____

68. She is well informed on social problems, and takes a humane, forward-looking attitude toward them. _____

69. Tom is a big, strong fellow with muscles that he hasn't used yet. _____

70. She is set in her ideas and refuses even to consider that she may be wrong. _____

71. George III of England believed that it was his right to rule the American colonists with an iron hand. _____

72. The poor homeless man trudged through the city streets, hoping to find a night's lodging. _____

73. Laura always looks on the bright side of things and refuses to be gloomy, even when the situation is discouraging. _____

74. In my opinion, Tom fails to show the proper respect for things that many people consider sacred. _____

75. The police arrested the man who had assisted the bank robber by acting as a lookout. _____

Words Connected with Occupations

*The words in Column A may be applied to occupations and professions. In the space before each word, write the **letter** of the item in Column B that best identifies it.*

Column A	Column B
_____ **76.** statute	a. law passed by the state legislature
_____ **77.** prognosis	b. oil painting
_____ **78.** salvage	c. used by a farmer to feed livestock
_____ **79.** rebuttal	d. job of Senate investigating committee
_____ **80.** fabricate	e. head of a school
_____ **81.** fodder	f. a defense attorney's forte
_____ **82.** consolation	g. put together parts, as in a factory
_____ **83.** envoy	h. representative of our government abroad
_____ **84.** probe	i. often done by jazz musicians
_____ **85.** improvise	j. a physician's forecast
	k. offered by a clergyman
	l. material in a junkyard

Word Associations

*In each of the following, circle the word or expression that best completes the meaning of the sentence or answers the question, with particular reference to the meaning of the word in **boldface** type.*

86. An argument that is **opaque** is lacking in
- a. facts
- b. sincerity
- c. lucidity
- d. strong language

87. Which of the following would specifically not apply to a typical **metropolis**?
- a. bustling
- b. crowded
- c. perilous
- d. rustic

88. Which nickname would a **doleful** person be most likely to have?
- a. Sad Sam
- b. Big John
- c. Little Mo
- d. Broadway Joe

89. We may apply the word **dormant** to
- a. a poem and a song
- b. a talent and a volcano
- c. the moon and the stars
- d. shackles and freedom

90. An **invincible** team is one that has never known
- a. the joy of victory
- b. the agony of defeat
- c. the fear of flying
- d. injury or illness

91. A person who seeks **asylum** is looking
- a. an orphan to adopt
- b. an easy job
- c. public office
- d. protection

92. The word **horde** might be used to describe
- a. an efficient group of workers
- b. an individual working alone
- c. an invading army
- d. a symphony orchestra

93. We can apply the word **meander** to
a. rivers and arguments
b. victories and defeats
c. sellers and buyers
d. plaintiffs and defendants

94. A country in a state of **anarchy** lacks
a. arts and sciences
b. law and order
c. fun and games
d. food and drink

95. Which of the following events cannot occur **posthumously**?
a. signing one's will
b. an increase in one's fame
c. being awarded a medal
d. the sale of one's house

96. Which of the following might apply to a person who is **mediocre**?
a. illustrious
b. immortal
c. undistinguished
d. sterling

97. A word closely associated with **pauper** is
a. incorrigible
b. inquisitive
c. invariable
d. impoverished

98. A story that goes on **ad infinitum** is
a. short and snappy
b. pointless
c. too long
d. worth repeating

99. You might say **adieu**
a. when someone sneezes
b. when you arrive
c. when you leave
d. when you step on someone's toes

100. If you say that your vocabulary program has been **arduous**, you mean that it has been
a. demanding
b. too easy
c. worthwhile
d. a lot of fun

The following tabulation lists all the basic words taught in the various units of this book, as well as those introduced in the *Vocabulary of Vocabulary, Working with Analogies, Building with Classical Roots,* and *Enriching Your Vocabulary* sections. Words taught in the units are printed in **boldface** type. The number following each entry indicates the page on which the word is first introduced. Exercises and review materials in which the word also appears are not cited.